The Yellow Court Scripture

Volume One

Text and Main Commentaries

by

Livia Kohn

Three Pines Press
St. Petersburg, FL 33713
www.threepinespress.com

© 2023 by Livia Kohn

All rights reserved. No part of this book may be reproduced in any form or by any means, electronic or mechanical, including photocopying, recording, or by any information storage and retrieval system, without permission in writing from the publisher.

9 8 7 6 5 4 3 2 1

Printed in the United States of America

First Edition, 2023

⊗ This edition is printed on acid-free paper that meets the American National Standard Institute Z39.48 Standard. Distributed in the United States by Three Pines Press.

Cover Art: Design by Brent Christopher Wulf. Selection from Qing imperial painting, "Along the River during the Qingming Festival." National Palace Museum, Taipei, Taiwan. Open data. https://digitalarchive.npm.gov.tw/Painting/Content?pid=3782&Dept=P

Library of Congress Cataloging-in-Publication Data

Names: Kohn, Livia, 1956- translator, writer of added commentary.
Title: The Yellow court scripture : text and main commentaries / by Livia Kohn.
Other titles: Huang ting jing. Chinese.
Description: First edition. | St. Petersburg, FL : Three Pines Press, 2023. | Includes bibliographical references and index.
Identifiers: LCCN 2023007581 | ISBN 9781931483735
Classification: LCC BL1900.H862 E5 2023 | DDC 299.5/1482--dc23/eng/20230523
LC record available at https://lccn.loc.gov/2023007581

Contents

Acknowledgments	iv
Abbreviations	v
Introduction	1
The Outer Scripture	
Part One	25
Part Two	47
Part Three	56
The Inner Scripture	
Prefaces	85
Verses 1-6	95
Verses 7-12	115
Verses 13-18	141
Verses 19-24	150
Verses 25-30	172
Verses 31-36	196
Recitation Ritual	217
Appendix: Texts Cited in *Neijing* Commentaries	223
Bibliography	227
Index	239

Acknowledgments

This book grew over the past several years, initiated first by a translation of the *Huangting neijing wuzang liufu buxietu* 黃庭內景五臟六腑補瀉圖 (Illustrated Outline of the Tonification and Dispersal [of the Qi] of the Five Organs and Six Viscera According to the *Inner Lights of the Yellow Court*) by the Tang woman Daoist Hu Yin 胡愔 (dat. 848).

This came about in 2016, when Anne Harley, professor of musicology at Scripps College, asked me to translate a portion of this text for her project, Voices of the Pearl. This project commissions, performs, records, and tours new contemporary classical music setting of texts by and about female esoteric practitioners from all world cultures. The resulting piece was performed at the 13th International Conference on Daoist Studies, held at Loyola Marymount University in Los Angeles in June 2019.

My translation of the *Buxietu* in due course became the subject of a one-day intensive seminar on Daoist Body Cosmology, held at the annual meeting of the German Physicians Association for Acupucture (Deutsche Ärztegesellschaft für Akupunktur) in Bad Nauheim near Frankfurt, Germany, in May 2017. Following this, I continued to be interested in the *Huangting jing* and its various manifestations, commentaries, and supplementary works, leading eventually to the commencement of a larger project, of which this book is the first result.

I am indebted to Mehdi Arronis and Jiang Sheng who greatly helped with the procurement of Chinese secondary studies; to Robin Wang for providing helpful resources; to Catherine Despeux for her careful and detailed reading as well as insightful comments; and to Thomas E. Smith for numerous corrections, invaluable suggestions, and pertinent additional information.

Abbreviations

DZ *Daozang* 道藏 (Daoist Canon), printed in 1445, numbers based on the catalog in Schipper and Verellen 2004

SV Schipper and Verellen 2004

YQ *Yunji qiqian* 雲笈七籤 (Seven Tablets in a Cloudy Satchel, DZ 1032), dat. 1125.

Introduction

The *Huangting jing* 黃庭經(Yellow Court Scripture) comes in two major versions, an "outer" and an "inner" text, formally called the *Huangting wai/neijing jing* 黃庭外/內景經(The Outer/Inner Lights Scripture of the Yellow Court, hereafter called *Waijing* and *Neijing*, respectively).[1] Both are written in lines of seven characters: the *Waijing* consists of 1358 words in 194 lines, divided alternatively into three parts—either of equal length or with a shorter second section—or 24 divisions; the *Neijing* has 3312 words in 473 lines, presented in 36 verses of uneven length.[2]

Both are revealed works, the *Waijing* claiming its source as Lord Lao 老君, the divinized Laozi, while the *Neijing* associates itself with the Lord of Jade Morning Light (Yuchen jun 玉晨君), an early deity of the school of Highest Clarity (Shangqing 上清). They are rather mysterious and poetic in content, describing the human body in terms of energies and spirits, chambers and palaces. Without giving specific instructions, they suggest visualization and energy circulation to maintain these internal powers intact to enhance life, increase longevity, and reach for immortality.[3] Both texts, moreover, carry celestial power in themselves and have been chanted since they first appeared.

While both were present in the 4th century CE, early documents referred to either one only as *Huangting jing*, without specifying "inner" or "outer." Once the division arose, as scholars generally agree, the appellation "inner" came to indicate to a more esoteric and intricate work, while "outer" signaled a more generally accessible and exoteric variant (Robinet 1993, 56).

The relative date and mutual relationship between the two versions have been the subject of extended debates, going back several centuries.[4] To-

---

[1] The texts appear in DZ 332 and 331 (SV 96-97, 184-85). A comprehensive edition with concordance is found in Schipper 1975. Previous renditions include Saso 1995; Olson 2017 for the *Waijing*; Archangelis and Lanying 2010; Hwang 2015 for the *Neijing*. There are also translations in German (Homann 1975) and French (Carré 1999).
[2] Yang 1995, 68; Yu 2001, 212; Arronis in Lai 2021, 485, 489.
[3] Maspero 1971, 531; Needham et al. 1983, 85; Schipper 1994, 136; Strickmann 1996, 121; Robinet 1993, 84-85; Baldrian-Hussein 2004, 193.
[4] The earliest discussion is by the Song scholar Ouyang Xiu 歐陽修 (1007-1072), who places the *Waijing* first. He is later followed by the Qing exegetes Yang Renfang 楊任芳 and Yejun Mizhai zhuren 鄴郡牧齋主人 (19th c). The position that the *Neijing* is

day, some scholars see the *Neijing* as the original and more profound text and the *Waijing* as a generalized summary for non-initiates.[5] Others take the *Waijing* to be the more ancient and primary work and understand the *Neijing* as a later expansion, a more subtle and detailed presentation.[6] Yet others remain neutral and just note that the issue has yet to be resolved.[7]

Recent research suggests that the second position covers the more likely scenario. An extensive and meticulous analysis of the rhyme structure of both texts shows clearly that the language of the *Waijing* ranges from the Western Han to the Three Kingdoms, with the 2nd century of the Eastern Han as its most likely date of origin. The *Neijing*, in contrast, is about a hundred years later, most appropriately dated to the Wei-Jin or the 3rd to 4th centuries (Yu 2001, 230; Schipper in SV 96).

The *Waijing*

The earliest appearance of the term "Yellow Court" as part of Daoist body cosmology is in the *Laozi ming* 老子銘 (Inscription for Laozi) by Bian Shao 邊邵.[8] Dated to 24 September 165, it contains a record of the imperial sacrifices to the divinized Laozi undertaken by Emperor Huan at the sage's birthplace in Bozhou 亳州 and begins with a summary of the facts known about the ancient philosopher, then praises Laozi as the central deity of the cosmos. He was born from primordial energy, came down to earth to establish culture and save humanity, to eventually ascend back into the heavenly realm as an immortal. It says:

---

earlier and takes priority was first proposed by the Qing scholars Dong Dening 董德寧 and Jiang Guozuo 蔣國祚 (18th c). (Li 1988, 39; Xu 1998, 98; Yang 1995, 68-69).

[5] Wang 1984 [1948], 332; Yoshioka 1955, 212, 228; Kaltenmark 1967, 118; Homann 1971, 23; Chen 1980; Qing 1988, 352; 1994, 60-63; Xu 1990, 21; Xu 1998, 99.

[6] Maspero 1971 [1937], 489; 1981, 372; Schipper 1975, 11; in SV 96, 185; Chen 1980, 25; Li 1988, 40; Yang 1995, 70; Gong 1997, 1:72; 1998, 89; Bokenkamp 1997, 164n32; Li 1988, 15; 1989, 344; 1995, 105; Yang 1999, 289; Yu 2001, 238; Li 2010b, 111; Zheng 2018, 27.

[7] Robinet 1984, 2:255; 1993, 56, 59, 237n20; in Pregadio 2008, 511-13; Zhu 1996, 296; Kim 1999, 250; Baldrian-Hussein 2004, 191; Cai 2006, 134; Cao 2009, 184; Yang 2010, 165-66; Arronis in Lai 2021, 48.

[8] Yang 1995, 75; Yu 2001, 230. For more on the inscription, see Yoshioka 1959, 21-31; Seidel 1969a, 37, 121-28; Kusuyama 1979, 303-15; Maspero 1981, 394; Neswald 2009, 29.

> Laozi joins the movements of the sun and the moon, is at one with the five planets. He freely comes and goes from the Elixir Field; easily travels up and down the Yellow Court. He rejects ordinary customs, conceals his light, and hides himself. Embracing the prime, he transforms like a spirit and breathes the essence of perfection. (Kohn 1998a, 41)

This places the notion of internal cultivation, the presence of the Yellow Court among the energy centers of the human body, as well as a close link to Lord Lao clearly into the mid-2nd century CE.

Probably from the same period is a passage in the *Liexian zhuan* 列仙傳 (Immortals' Biographies, DZ 294, SV 114), a text that is officially associated with the Han erudite Liu Xiang 劉向 (77-6 BCE), but was compiled later. Here, the biography of Zhu Huang 朱璜 notes his recitation of Lord Lao's *Huangting jing* as a key practice of immortality (2.21a; Kaltenmark 1988, 177), indicating the presence of the work in a culture of textual veneration and spiritual self-cultivation.[9]

Another early mention of the term and also of the practice of recitation occurs in the *Laozi bianhua jing* 老子變化經 (Scripture of the Transformations of Laozi), a Dunhuang manuscript (S. 2295) dated to around 185.[10] It gives expression to the beliefs of a popular messianic cult, located in southwest China, where the Celestial Masters were also active at the same time. Besides expressing Laozi's identity with Dao and his powers before and during creation, it contains a description of his repeated descents as the teacher of dynasties. It transforms his birth under the Zhou into a supernatural event, involving a pregnancy of seventy-two years and numerous marvelous signs of sagely physiognomy, and elevates the *Daode jing* to the status of revealed scripture (Kohn 1998a, 12). Laozi says,

> I go through death and come back to life, circulate freely through the four seas, time and again emerge from the Yellow Court, pass through history and go beyond [ ], step on the Three Sovereigns, and support the Three Terraces [constellation]. I wear clothes but am essentially formless; ignorant, I rest in unknowing. (Lines 72-73)

---

[9] Li 1988, 39; Yang 1995, 70; Yu 2001, 230; Baldrian-Hussein 2004, 192; Schipper 1975, 11; in SV, 96; Wang 2010, 166; Campany 2023, 220n156.

[10] The text is dated on the basis of internal evidence (Laozi's last appearance happens in 155), but its current edition goes back to the year 612. The manuscript is reprinted in Seidel 1969a, 131-36 and can also be found online at https://www.newton.com.tw/wiki-老子變化經. A French translation appears in Seidel 1969a, 60-73. See also Robinet 1997, 51-52; Gao 1920.

Here the Yellow Court is a more cosmic entity, related to the center. A later passage outlines the three core energies of the cosmos, linking the color yellow with the center: "Life *qi* is on the left, source *qi* is on the right, and the center contains yellow *qi*" (Line 87).

In addition, the *Bianhua jing* has Laozi admonish his followers to chant the *Daode jing* ten thousand times continuously, after which they can know him personally. Combined with good relations between fathers and sons, abstention from alcohol, and assiduous self-cultivation, the practice will ensure good fortune and freedom from disease as well as control over the spirits (Lines 79-83). It is essential to rest in calm and stillness, remain in nonaction and free from desires—all values strongly emphasized in the *Waijing* (Xu 1990, 24) and also essential to Celestial Masters practice.

Another 2nd-century document that echoes the *Waijing* even more closely is the *Laozi zhongjing* 老子中經 (Central Scripture of Laozi, DZ 1168, SV 92-94; YQ 18-19), also known as *Zhugong yuli* 珠宮玉曆 (Jade Calendar of the Pearly Palace) and in the *Huanting jing* commentary by Liangqiuzi cited as *Yuli jing* 玉曆經 (Jade Calendar Scripture).[11] The text consists of fifty-five sections in two scrolls that provide instructions on visualization, breathing techniques, healing exercises, as well as sexual and other methods. Spoken by Lord Lao, who refers to himself in the first person, it is called "central" because it claims to form part of the *Daode jing*, which divides into upper and lower sections (Schipper 1995, 118; Puett 2010a, 239).

Predicting a coming apocalypse, the text outlines the various gods of the universe, who all emanate from the Great One (Taiyi 太一), and places them both in the world and in the human body. In outlook, it presents a Han cosmological vision that is also expressed in the diviners' compass (*shi* 式) and sacrificial structure of the dynasty.[12] In practice, it continues the tradition of self-divinization, present since the 4th century BCE, that works through exerting control over the spirits and keeping them in the body by concentrating energy and refining essence, the central method at the core of the *Huangting jing* (Puett 2010a, 226; see also Puett 2002; 2005; 2010b).

The Yellow Court in this text is the residence of Laozi who appears under the title Yellow Lord Lao of Central Ultimate (Huanglao zhongji jun 黃老中極君) and is identified as the core deity among all the stars and the Dipper.

---

[11] On the text, see Schipper 1979; 1995; Kohn in Pregadio 2008, 624-25; Neswald 2009, 30-32; Huang 2010, 62-63; 2012, 28-29.

[12] Schipper 1995, 117; Lagerwey 2004, 165; Robinet in Pregadio 2008, 83; Puett 2010a, 242. On the compass, see Harper 1978; Kalinowski 1983. For more on early visualizations, see Pregadio 2006; Raz 2007.

His female aspect, or queen, is the Jade Maiden of Mysterious Radiance of Great Yin (Taiyin xuanguang yunü 太陰玄光玉女). Wearing robes of yellow cloudy energy, they join to give birth to the immortal embryo.

To activate the pair, adepts visualize a sun and moon in their chests underneath their nipples, from which a yellow essence and a red energy radiate. These vapors then rise up to enter the Scarlet Palace in the heart and sink down to the Yellow Court in the abdomen. Filling these internal halls, the energies mingle and coagulate to form the immortal embryo, which grows gradually and becomes visible as an infant facing south, in the position of the ruler. As he is nurtured on the yellow essence and red energy still oozing from the adept's internal sun and moon, all illnesses are driven out and the myriad disasters are allayed (ch. 1, sect. 11; YQ 18.7ab).

Other passages, too, mention the Yellow Court in conjunction with the Scarlet Palace and the Purple Chamber, indicating the spiritual dimensions of the spleen, heart, and kidneys that manifest in yellow, red, and black, respectively (1.3, 2.36, 2.37). In addition, it states that as "the Great One enters the Yellow Court, he fills the Great Storehouse [stomach] and nourishes the Infant" (1.17), the practitioner's immortal alter ego (see Pregadio 2006). Beyond that, the text acknowledges a Perfected and a Jade Maiden of the Yellow Court, placing them in the center of the body (1.27, 2.30). While wider in overall scope (Robinet in Pregadio 2008, 78-79), the cosmology here matches that presented in the *Waijing*, where the Yellow Court is also in the center, connected to the heart and kidneys, then called the Dark Towers, and which equally relies on the system of the five phases as it became dominant in the Han dynasty.

Also at the core of practices described in the third chapter of the *Lingbao wufuxu* 靈寶五符序 (Explanation of the Five Talismans of Numinous Treasure, DZ 388, SV 232-33) (Lagerwey 2004, 141),[13] which incidentally cites the *Laozi zhongjing* several times (Schipper 1995, 118), this thinking finds further expression in the *Taiping jing* 太平經 (Scripture of Great Peace, DZ 1101, SV 277-80; ed. Wang 1979). Another work of the Eastern Han, this too outlines the positions and movements of the spirits in the body in conjunction with five-phases cosmology.[14] All this places the *Waijing* in a late Han context.

---

[13] The materials outlined in the *Lingbao wufuxu* go back to the 2nd century and match the cosmology of the apocrypha (Kaltenmark 1982, 10; Schipper 1995, 118-19; Yamada 1989). For more on the text and the dietary practices outlined in the second chapter, see Arthur 2013.

[14] The *Taiping jing* was revealed to Gan Ji 干吉 by the Yellow Lord Lao 黃老君 around the year 140 CE. It was presented to Emperor Xun (r. 125-144) and memorial-

The Celestial Masters

The Celestial Masters (Tianshi 天師), officially known as the school of Orthodox Unity (Zhengyi 正一), were founded in 142 CE by the spiritual seeker Zhang Daoling 張道凌, who encountered Lord Lao in a personal revelation in Sichuan, variously placed to Mounts Heming 鶴鳴山 or Qingcheng 青城山. In a time of great upheaval and uncertainty, he created "a new covenant that bound the demons and faithful into an alliance through a mutual oath to adhere to sets of rules and prohibitions" (Lai 2002, 270) as well as community rituals and regular incantations. The group's members were "minor functionaries on the margins of the vast bureaucratic pantheon of the otherworld" (Nickerson 1994, 49), thus forming a "guild of ordained religious specialists" (1994, 64) who exerted control over the spirits both in the world and the body (Kleeman 1998, 72; 2016, 189).

Each community member occupied a particular rank in the overall hierarchy. The so-called libationers (*jijiu* 祭酒), administrators of the twenty-four districts or parishes (*zhi* 治), ranked at the top. Beneath them were "register disciples" (*lusheng* 錄生), devotees in ritual training who represented smaller units in the organization (Kleeman 1998, 69-70; 2016, 5; Lai 2002, 253). Their alternate appellation, "demon troopers" (*guizu* 鬼卒), indicated their semi-military status, including the fact that "they controlled a host of otherworldly warriors to protect themselves against the attack of unsubjugated demons" (2002, 271; Kleeman 2016, 52-53). In contrast to mainstream Chinese society, the community allowed men and women, Han Chinese and ethnic minorities to fill leadership positions (Kleeman 1998, 74-75; 2016, 312).

At the bottom were the common followers, organized and counted according to households. Each household, in accordance with the number of working members, had to pay a tax of five pecks of rice or its equivalent in silk, paper, brushes, ceramics, or handicrafts (Hendrischke 2000, 156-58; Kleeman 2016, 57-58). Everyone, from children on up, underwent formal initiations at regular intervals to receive registers (*lu* 錄) that contained a list of spirit generals and specified its bearer's identity, rank, and home district. He or she had to wear the written list in a piece of silk at the waist constantly,

---

ized to Emperor Huan in 166. Lost after the defeat of the Yellow Turban rebellion, it was reconstituted under Highest Clarity auspices by Zhou Zhixiang 周志享 and presented to Emperor Xuan of the Chen (r. 568-582). For a study and translation, see Hendrischke 2006. Its relation to the *Huangting jing* is noted in Robinet 1993, 64-66; in Pregadio 2008, 81; Cao 2009, 185; Zheng 2018, 26.

making sure these protective entities as well as inherent vitalizing spirits remained within the body.[15]

Various other organizations of a similar kind had also sprung up in other parts of the country, some of which—in 184, the first year of a new sexagenary cycle—rose in rebellion to replace the failing Han administration with a new dispensation of religiously inspired rulership. The most important among these was the Way of Great Peace (Taiping dao 太平道), whose leaders instigated the Yellow Turban rebellion.[16] A lesser uprising also occurred in Sichuan under the leadership of Zhang Xiu 張秀, who may have been a parish leader of the Celestial Masters (Bokenkamp 1997, 34).

The Celestial Masters stayed clear of the revolts since they saw themselves as advisers to rather than rulers of the new dispensation (Seidel 1969b). To escape the upheaval, in 191, Zhang Lu 張魯, the founder's grandson, moved his followers to Hanzhong 漢中, an isolated valley north of Xi'an, where his community remained intact and largely independent for over thirty years (1997, 35). In 215, he surrendered to Cao Cao 曹操, the local warlord and founder of the Wei dynasty. While he gave Zhang Lu and his sons fiefdoms and official titles, he split up the followers and relocated them in the tens of thousands to various other locations under his rule to prevent them from establishing a state within the state (1997, 149). As a result, the tightly knit millenarian community morphed into a more open religious organization and formed part of a variegated religious landscape, laying the foundation of new schools and teachings. At the same time, the loss of central leadership caused their internal structures to disintegrate and practices to fall into decline (1997, 154-55).

Two texts remain from this period that relate to the *Huangting jing*. The first is the *Xiang'er zhu* 想爾注 (Thinking of You Commentary) to the *Daode jing*, possibly written by Zhang Lu himself.[17] The Celestial Masters considered the *Daode jing* primary among revealed texts, bestowed it formally upon new initiates, chanted it regularly, and used it as the basis for their core ethical rules (1997, 30). The *Xiang'er zhu* explains just how they understood the role of the sacred text and its concepts in their project of creating an integrated society based on an inherently moral cosmos. Its overall vision

---

[15] Kleeman 2016, 276-81, 303. See also Bumbacher 2012, 107; Kleeman 1998, 72; Kohn 1998a, 37; Lai 2002, 262; Schipper 1985; 1994, 60-71.

[16] See Levy 1956; Kaltenmark 1979; Peterson 1989-90; 1990; Hendrischke 2000

[17] The text survives in the Dunhuang manuscript S. 6825, ed. Rao 1992 [1956]. It is translated in Bokenkamp 1997, 78-148. For studies, see also Boltz 1982; Bokenkamp 1993; Littlejohn 2020; Puett 2010b.

and the practices that it recommends closely echo those of the *Waijing* (Puett 2010a, 230).

In both the *Xiang'er zhu* and the *Waijing*, Dao—personified in Lord Lao—is a conscious and intentional entity, with likes and dislikes, that acts in all things through vital energy (*qi* 氣). In its purest and most condensed form, this energy appears as pure spirit as well as in spirit entities (*shen* 神) who inhabit both world and body and have to be placated, preserved, and enhanced to ensure the smooth functioning of life. Energy and spirits, moreover, function in patterns of yin and yang and the five phases, centered in the five organs and six viscera and moving in alignment with the seasons—matching Han cosmology and the core theory of Chinese medicine. Strong emotions and sensual desires are detrimental, while meditative calmness and relaxed serenity are supportive.[18]

Both texts further encourage the development of clarity and stillness as well as being weak and soft like water or a small child. To control and nourish the spirits, they suggest that practitioners focus on them incessantly with great concentration while guiding pure *qi* with the help of breathing practices.[19] The ultimate goal is to gain not only health, harmony, and longevity, but also a state of no-death. Rather than the bypassing of death, to the Celestial Masters this meant entering Grand Darkness, an otherwordly realm for perfecting the body and attaining rebirth rather than being confined to the subterranean earth-prisons, the standard fate of the deceased (Bokenkamp 1997, 47).

The other relevant text is the *Da daojia lingjie* 大道家令戒 (Commands and Admonitions for the Families of the Great Dao), one of five early documents collected in the *Zhengyi fawen tianshi jiao jieke jing* 正一法文天師教戒科經 (Scripture of the Commandments and Observances of the Celestial Masters, in the Ritual Writings of Orthodox Unity, DZ 789, SV 120-22; trl. Bokenkamp 1997, 149-85).[20] Dated to the 1st day of the 7th month in 255, the day of the general assembly of the community, and formulated in the first person, it presents cosmological principles, administrative commandments, and practical admonitions for the followers that cohere with the teachings expressed in the *Xiang'er zhu*. Probably read to the community at the time, it was quite possibly received from the spirit of Zhang Lu after his death—

---

[18] Puett 2010a, 228-31; Bokenkamp 1997, 39-40; Zheng 2018, 30-31
[19] Bokenkamp 1997, 41-42, 156; Puett 2010a, 232-34. See also Kim 1999, 256; Cai 2006, 132.
[20] The *Da daojia lingjie* is the second work (12a-19b). The other texts include two ritual hymns or verses, a general treatise on the moral cosmos, and a more technical work on administration. See Zhang 1994; Li 2017; Ma 2005.

maybe in 231, the date when, according to the text, parish leaders started to be self-appointed (Bokenkamp 1997, 151-52).

The text is the first to actually mention the *Huangting jing*. It notes that the work is "true and correct" (14b) and states that "Laozi revealed it through me" (16b). This clearly indicates the *Waijing*, the version revealed by Laozi, and places it not only in the mid-3rd century but also within the community of the Celestial Masters, possibly revealed to Zhang Lu himself (1997, 172, 175, 164n32). It seems the work was a supplementary text to the sacred scripture and commentary of the *Daode jing*, offering the revealing deity's meditation instructions and encouraging personal refinement and regular recitation.

The Fourth Century

Over the following decades, the Celestial Masters continued to serve the local rulers—now of the Jin dynasty—and engage in their ritual and cultivation practices. The *Huangting jing* remained a mainstay of their recitation and visualization but, as they continued to intermingle with wider segments of the population, it also spread further into other religious communities.

Evidence for this appears in the *Baopuzi neipian* 抱朴子內篇 (Book of the Master Who Embraces Simplicity, Inner Chapters, DZ 1185, SV 70-71; trl. Ware 1966). Dated to about 317, the text was compiled by the retired official and would-be alchemist Ge Hong 葛洪 (283-363), who claims to have received teachings and texts that go back to the alchemist Zheng Yin 鄭隱 (ca. 200). He not only lists the *Huangting jing* as a work in his library (19.5a),[21] but also tells the story of a certain Cai Dan 蔡誕 from Wuyuan who dedicated his life to the pursuit of immortality.

> Completely neglecting the livelihood of his family, he spent days and nights reciting such classics as the *Huangting, Taiqing* 太清 (Great Clarity), and *Zhonghuang* 中黃 (Central Yellow) . . . . He was totally ignorant of anything practical; he merely deluded others by lauding the vague, flowery language of these texts and teaching that one's heart's desire could be had merely by reciting them a thousand times. (20.4b-5a; Ware 1966, 244)

---

[21] Li 1988, 39; Xu 1990, 21; Yu 1991, 333; Robinet 1993, 55; Yang 1995, 69; Schipper in SV 97; Chan 2000, 2; Baldrian-Hussein 2004, 192; Wang 2010, 169.

Cai Dan engaged in recitation at his house over several years, then became a hermit but was not successful and returned home, "black and emaciated, a standing skeleton." To explain his status, he claimed to have attained a position in the celestial hierarchy, "shepherding several head of dragons for Lao Dan [Laozi]." Having neglected his duties, he was punished by being stationed at the "foot of Mount Kunlun to weed thirty or forty acres of herbs growing there." He did ten years of this, then was pardoned and, with the support of several senior immortals, returned to his hold home to complete his quest. "Whereupon he died of old age" (20.5ab; Ware 1966, 245; see also Yang 1995, 69; Zheng 2018, 27).

The text mentioned as *Huangting* in this tale must refer to the *Waijing* since it connects to Laozi as the presumed divine employer of the hapless seeker. The passage documents the established presence of the text and its spread into the wider populace, a feature also indicated by the warning in the text itself against distributing it recklessly (Yang 1995, 70). It also shows that chanting of sacred texts in general was a popular practice, accessible even to non-initiates of any specific religious organization. Ge Hong may well have included this tale to document its inefficiency, himself being much in favor of alchemical transformation with methods that were transmitted under strict secrecy, requiring blood covenants and serious pledges.

As part of more esoteric cultivation, Ge Hong yet also supports visualization, focusing particularly on Lord Lao as the deity of the center and using imagery and descriptions that closely echo the *Huangting jing*. In addition, the effects of the practice are quite similar, leading to longevity, clarity, and enhanced knowledge.

To being, adepts gaze at themselves in a bright mirror. They do so continuously over several days, after which a divine figure will appear, eventually giving rise to a vision of Lord Lao.

> When you see his true likeness, bear in mind that his family name is Li, his personal name Dan, his courtesy name Boyang. His body is nine feet tall and of yellow color; his face is bird-mouthed and has an arched nose. His bushy eyebrows are five inches long, his ears measure seven inches. There are three vertical lines on his forehead, his feet are marked with the eight trigrams, and his back shows the golden turtle.
>
> He lives in a multi-storied abode of gold, where the rooms are lined with jade and steps are of silver. His clothing is a cloud of many colors; his hat consists of multiple layers and his sword is a pointed lance.
>
> He is attended by 120 yellow divine lads. To his left are twelve green dragons, to his right thirty-six white tigers; before him go twenty-four

vermilion birds, to his rear follow seventy-two dark warriors. His vanguard consists of twelve heavenly beasts; his rear guard, of thirty-six evil-dispellers. Above him hover thunder and lightning in brilliant flashes.

If you see Lord Lao, your years will be extended, your heart and mind will become as clear as the sun and the moon, and there will be nothing you do not know. (15.9ab)[22]

A classic example of basic Daoist visualization practice and also an early case of Three Sovereigns ecstatic divination (Andersen 1994, 12), the passage names and describes the god and his abode with precision, also listing the numinous beasts of his entourage, all starry constellations of demon-dispelling nature. The deity thus visualized—as much as the various body spirits in the *Huangting jing*—protects the practitioner, granting longevity, clear insight, omniscience, and eternal life.

A similar presentation further appears in the *Mingjian jing* 明鑑經 (Scripture of Magical Mirrors, DZ 1207, SV 97-98), also listed in Ge Hong's library chapter (Kaltenmark 1974).[23] Divided into twenty sections, each beginning with "Laozi said," it is like the *Huangting jing* in that it claims to be revealed by the god as a set of instructions for immortality practitioners. It describes the wondrous powers to be gained:

Anyone mastering this method can multiply himself and spread out his body, take one and turn it into ten thousand, set up the six armies, or place himself a million miles away. By simply inhaling and exhaling, he can come and go to distant places, ride on the clouds and walk on water, merge in and out of the spaceless, and render visible the divinities of heaven, gods of earth, evil demons, ancient sprites, and all sorts of hid-

---

[22] See Ware 1966, 256-57; Yamada 1995a, 23; Kohn 1998, 70. The green dragon, white tiger, vermilion bird, and dark warrior (turtle and snake) are the heraldic animals of the four directions. See Major 1986, 65; Staal 1984; Robinet 1993, 74; Pankenier 2013, 196. The heavenly beast (*qiongqi* 窮奇), an ox-like creature covered with bristles, and the evil-dispeller (*bixie* 避邪), a one-horned furry deer with a long tail, are baleful constellations associated with demonic powers.

[23] A forerunner of the practice using mirrors is also found in a Han dynasty text, the *Xijing zaji* 西京雜記 (Miscellanea from the Western Capital), which describes a magical mirror that would show a person's intestines and indicate both diseases and bad humors within. For example, "If a woman had an evil heart the mirror would reflect her gall bladder elongated and her heart in movement" (ch. 3). For the use of mirrors in Highest Clarity practice, see Robinet 1993, 163-64.

den dead. By mere concentration he can see ahead and predict the future—mastering this, anyone can become a king among immortals. (1a; Kohn 1998a, 69)

The text next outlines various methods involving mirrors, beginning with the basic requirements of purification and the establishment of a secluded chamber where "you won't hear the rumblings of carriages, the clanging of bells, or even the chirping of birds" (1ab). Then a set of clear mirrors must be obtained, ideally with few ornaments and no bumps or scratches (2a). As adepts gaze into them, a plethora of gods will appear in the four directions, not the least of whom is the divine Laozi in his nine transformations.

There is a personage six feet five inches tall, wearing an angled cap and a white robe with a red collar, embroidered with tiger script and phoenix seals. His surname is Li, first name Er, also called Boyang. You will see him at the break of day. (3b)

In each transformation, the god appears in a different size and garb, is called by a different name, and manifests at a different time of day, all the way to the ninth, when he is "nine feet five inches tall, wears a spontaneity cap and a green and purple robe, is called Li Yuan, aka Bowen, and appears at dusk" (4b). Through the figure of the god, adepts participate in the rhythm of the day, creating a tangible image of the energies of yin and yang as they transform in regular cycles and approach the wholeness of Dao (Kohn 1998a, 70). A simpler and more accessible presentation of essential visualization techniques, the *Mingjian jing* as much as the *Baopuzi neipian* show the spread of this self-cultivation methodology in close association with Lord Lao in the early 4th century, a time when the *Huangting jing* was increasingly honored and appreciated.

This appreciation is also manifest in the fact that the earliest transmitted copy of the *Waijing* dates from this period, written in the hand of the famous calligrapher Wang Xizhi 王羲之 (303-361), whose family followed the Celestial Masters.[24] The character *zhi* in his name indicates that he was a fourth-generation follower, with about thirty other people known on same level. His biography in the *Jinshu* 晉書 (History of the Jin Dynasty) mentions that

---

[24] Dated to 337 or 340, it is edited in Nakata 1970, 83-142. For discussions, see Chen 1980, 25; Ledderose 1984, 261; Li 1988, 39; Xu 1990, 21; Robinet 1993, 56; Yang 1995, 69; Zhan 2000, 3; Schipper in SV 96; Baldrian-Hussein 2004, 192. A total of twenty-one texts in Wang's calligraphy survive in Tang copies on steles (Yu 1991, 331).

he copied the *Daode jing*, a text he most likely also recited as part of Celestial Masters practice. It further notes that Wang greatly enjoyed raising geese and once copied the text for a Daoist recluse in exchange for a flock of particularly nice specimens.

This story was later associated with the *Huangting jing*, as mentioned in the poem *Song He binke gui Yue* 送賀賓客歸越 (Sending off Guest He on His Return to Yue) by the famous Tang poet Li Bai 李白 (701-762), He says, "You have appeared like a Daoist mountain hermit, compelling us to copy the *Huangting* in exchange for white geese" (Wang 2010, 169). Following this, the tale is noted in the preface by the commentator Wuchengzi, found in the *Yunji qiqian* edition (Yu 1991, 331).

To sum up the status of the *Waijing* by the fourth century: "Zheng Yin possessed it, Ge Hong saw it, Cai Dan chanted it, and Wang Xizhi copied it" (Yang 1995, 70).

The *Neijing*

The *Neijing* essentially came out of this overall milieu to flourish in an environment of intense spiritual cultivation, ecstatic visions, and sectarian organization. Like the *Waijing*, which it contains almost in its entirety, it is neither an explanation nor a manual or a hymn, but more a prompt book to provide a reminder of key ideas and techniques already known (Robinet 1993, 56, 58). Consisting of thirty-six sections, it can be divided thematically into three parts after the introductory first chapter. Chapters 2 to 18 present a vision of the body in relation to the greater universe; 19 through 28 focus on specific organs with their deities; and 29 to 36 discuss ways of immortality and methods of activating the text (Kim 1999, 250).

The work goes back to a dedicated adept and senior leader of the Celestial Masters, who most likely recited the *Waijing* on a regular basis: Wei Huacun 魏華存 (351-334), aka Xian'an 賢安, by all accounts its original compiler.[25] According to her biography,[26] she was the daughter of Wei Yangyuan 魏陽元, a Jin-dynasty official and Celestial Masters follower. Receiving a good education, she dedicated herself to spiritual cultivation from an early

---

[25] Chen 1980, 25; Wang 1984, 332; Yu 1984, 386; Xu 1990, 21; Robinet 1993, 55; Yu 2001, 209; Zhan 2000, 3; Li 2010b, 815; Zheng 2018, 27.
[26] Her biography is the *Nanyue furen zhuan* 南岳夫人傳, recorded in the Song encyclopedias *Taiping guangji* 太平廣記 (Expansive Record of the Tai-ping Era, 57.256-59) and *Taiping yulan* 太平御覽 (Imperial Encyclopedia of the Taiping Era, 678.7a), as well as in the *Maoshan zhi* 茅山志 (Gazetteer of Mount Mao; see Schafer 1980; ch. 10). The transmission is also recorded in YQ 4.6b-7a.

age. When she was 24, giving in to social and parental pressure, she married the official Liu Yan 劉彥 or Youyan 又[幼]彥, and gave birth to two sons, Liu Pu 劉璞 and Liu Xia 劉瑕. In due course she rose to the rank of libationer among the Celestial Masters, however, once her children reached their teens, she again withdrew into seclusion (Li 1988, 38; Xu 1998, 98).

At age 37, in 288, in a series of deep trance experiences, she connected with various immortal figures. One of them was Wang Bao 王褒, aka Zideng 子登, also known as the Perfected of Clear Emptiness (Qingxu zhenren 清虛真人). According to his biography,[27] he came from Fanyang 范陽 in modern Hebei and lived under the rule of the Han emperor Yuandi (ca. 36 CE). Secluding himself on Mounts Hua 華山 and Yangluo 陽洛山, he connected to various immortals and received thirty-one scrolls of scriptures, which he in due course bestowed upon Wei Huacun (Xu 1998, 98; Li 1988, 38).

Another personage that appeared to her was the Perfected of the Forest of Lights (Jinglin zhenren 景林真人), also known as the Divine King of the Valley of the Rising Sun (Yanggu shenwang 暘谷神王),[28] from whom she received the *Neijing* (Yang 1995, 70). Reciting it continuously, she attained an even higher spiritual status. In 317, she moved south with the Jin court. While her sons served as government officials, she retreated to Mount Heng 衡山, the Southern Peak (Nanyue 南岳), from where she ascended into heaven in 334. Her posthumous title is Lady of the Southern Peak (Nanyue furen 南岳夫人), and her main sanctuary is still located on the mountain (Robson 2009, ch. 6).

As regards the *Neijing*, Wei Huacun passed it on to her eldest son who in turn transmitted it to the medium Yang Xi 楊羲 (330-ca. 386) around the year 350 together together with a copy of the *Lingbao wufuxu* (Espesset in Pregadio 2008, 1147), a text Wei had also received (Lagerwey 2004, 140). A fragment of the *Huangting jing* was later handed down in Yang Xi's autograph (Schipper in SV 185). He moved on to become the key recipient of the Highest Clarity revelations in the mid-360s, working closely with the Xu brothers, Xu Mai 許邁 (b. 301) and Xu Mi 許謐 (303-376) (see Smith 2017). As reported in the school's constituting record, the *Zhen'gao* 真誥 (Declarations of the Perfected, DZ 1016, SV 198-200; ch. 9) by Tao Hongjing 陶弘景

---

[27] YQ 106; *Lishi zhenxian tidao tongjian* 歷史真仙體道通鑑 (Comprehensive Mirror through the Ages of Perfected Immortals and Those Who Embody the Dao, DZ 296, SV 887-92), by Zhao Daoyi 趙道一 of the early Yuan (dat. 1294), 14.8b.

[28] Yanggu is a location in the east where an official under the sage-king Yao was stationed to observe the rising of the sun and maintain the accuracy of the calendar.

(456-536),[29] Wei Huacun was one of the major revealing spirits, presenting numerous texts that eventually made up the Highest Clarity corpus.

The *Neijing*, too, became part of the Highest Clarity system. However, while it was listed variously in relevant catalogs,[30] it never had quite the same status as the main corpus, reflecting its origin in a different religious environment, its earlier revelation to Wei Huacun, and its separate transmission to Yang Xi (Robinet 1993, 56). It was also significantly different in outlook and cosmological system from the central work of the school, the *Dadong jing* 大洞經 (Scripture of Great Pervasion, DZ 6, SV1043-45; see Robinet 1983). It provided a different nomenclature and numbering system for the deities, and thus came to occupy a separate position in the corpus (Robinet in Pregadio 2008, 512-23). Still, like all other Highest Clarity scriptures, it was passed on to Xu Mi's son, Xu Huangmin 許黃民 (361-429), who compiled and distributed the works among his friends and family to be later were collected and codified by Tao Hongjing (*Zhen'gao* 19; Strickmann 1978, 42; 1981; Yang 1995, 71).

As he notes in the *Zhen'gao*, the key practice associated with the *Neijing* was recitation.[31] Thus Xu Mi himself chanted it regularly (18.4ab; Schipper in SV 195; Strickmann 1981, 201); Master Meng recited it every evening to appease his internal agents and ensure a good night's sleep (9.23b; Zhan 2000, 3);[32] and Lady Jiang of the Northern Peak used it to eliminate disease (15.10a; Robinet 1993, 59). Overall, the text in this activation was geared toward health and longevity, providing a first step toward perfection, rather outlining advanced ecstatic endeavors and immortality pursuits.

In his *Dengzhen yinjue* 登真隱訣 (Secret Instructions on the Ascent to the Perfected, DZ 421, SV 201-05), Tao Hongjing further notes that the proper practice of visualization rendered recitation superfluous: "Activate the spirits in the physical form from morning to night: remember them constantly without ever forgetting, and you won't even have to recite the *Huangting* [*jing*]" (3.5a). Still, he took the trouble to outline the specific techniques of

---

[29] For studies and translations of the *Zhen'gao,* see Bokenkamp 2020; Smith 2013; 2020; Strickmann 1981.
[30] They include the *Shangqing dadong zhenjing mu* 上清大洞真經目 (Catalog of Perfect Scriptures of Great Pervasion of Highest Clarity), where it appears as no. 34 (Schipper in SV 185), and the early Tang manual *Fengdao kejie* 奉道科戒 (Rules and Precepts for Worshiping the Dao, DZ 1125, SV 451-53; trl. Kohn 2004), 5.2.
[31] Robinet 1993, 58; in Pregadio 2008, 256; Baldrian-Hussein 2004, 192.
[32] This usage is also recorded in ch. 10 of the early Tang collection *Sandong zhunang* 三洞珠囊 (A Bag of Pearls from the Three Caverns, DZ 1139, SV 440-41; see Reiter 1990) in a section on clicking the teeth (Li 2010a, 114; 2010b, 816).

chanting the text properly (3.1a-5a).³³ Adepts should first undergo purification, then visualize a purple cloud of energy as they enter the quiet chamber or oratory. Here they burn incense, swallow the saliva, and click the teeth in preparation. Once ready, they first face north and pay homage to the Highest Lord of the Dao, presenting a petition for his support, then repeat the procedure to the east, addressing the Great Emperor of Fusang and Divine King of the Valley of the Rising Sun. Chanting should be continuous, ten repetitions making up one round, after which four bows are offered to the deities. The ultimate goal is to reach ten thousand repetitions, after which immortality and divine connection would be open.

This pattern is quite similar to the recitation of the *Daode jing*. Here, too, ten thousand repetitions would grant perfection in Dao, so that, for example, Laozi required the guardian of the pass, Yin Xi 尹喜, to complete this number before he allowed him on his western travels.³⁴ The *Zhen'gao* similarly tells the story of a certain Old Lord who instructed three brothers of the Zhou 周 family to recite the text. The older brother succeeded in completing the chore and duly ascended to the immortals. The others, however, were interrupted by a fire in the cave and only managed to complete 9,733 recitations and accordingly had to remain on earth (5.6a; Smith 2020, 50; Yoshioka 1959, 123).

Procedures, too, were quite similar. As documented in the fifth-century preface to the *Daode jing,* the *Xujue* 序訣 (Introductory Explanations, S. 75, P. 2370; trl. Kohn 1993, 173-74), adepts purified themselves and entered an oratory where they would light incense and bow to the deities, then kneel formally and close their eyes. They then offered a prayer to the guardian deities for protection and visualized the Northern Dipper to hover over their space to create the right level of sacred ambiance (Kohn 1998b, 150).

Next, in preparation of recitation proper, they bowed to the ten directions and visualized Laozi and his major assistants, Yin Xi and Heshang gong 河上公, the Master on the River. Once these divine figures were present, adepts called upon the Lord of the Niwan Palace in the head. As this divinity approached, the room would undergo mysterious changes: a radiance as of seven jewels spread, doors and windows opened spontaneously. A link of

---

³³ See Robinet 1993, 58; in Pregadio 2008, 513; Li 2010a, 110; 2010b, 815. The latter part of the text, 3.2b-5a, is recouped at the end of YQ 12 and translated below under the heading "Recitation Ritual." Other passages on chanting include the last section of Wuchengzi's preface to the *Neijing* and parts of section 36 of the *Neijing*.
³⁴ This is documented in Yin Xi's official biography, the *Wenshi neizhuan* 文始內傳 (Esoteric Biography of the Master at the Beginning of the Scripture), contained in the *Sandong zhunang* (9.10b). See Kohn 1998b, 148; 2023.

light to the higher spheres thus established, practitioners could float up and away into the purple empyrean, entering the heavens. Finding themselves among the stars, with sun and moon at their sides, they would approach the gods and in a formal chant ask for immortality for themselves and their ancestors of seven generations. From here, they would click their teeth and swallow the saliva to establish a direct bodily connection to the divine, then move on to an even more powerful visualization, which alone would afford the optimal benefits of recitation practice (Kohn 1998b, 151; 2023).

In addition, the procedures prescribed for the *Huangting jing* and the *Daode jing* echo those used when reciting the key Highest Clarity scripture *Dadong jing*. Here, too, adepts begin by envisioning a purple cloud and entering the oratory. They summon protective deities and offer a petition for support, announcing their intention to recite the text. Turning first north, then east, they connect to the divine, seeing themselves decked out with all the insignia of a deity and surrounded by the four heraldic animals. "His head covered by a flowery canopy, he is seated on lions while immortal youths burn incense and jade maidens scatter blossoms. Around him everything is luminous with purple or five-colored clouds." The adept then recites stanzas from the scripture while performing various body movements to connect to different divine dimensions and spirits (Robinet 1993, 99).

Commentaries

The main commentary to both *Huangting* texts is by Liangqiuzi 梁丘子, in ordinary life known as Bai Lüzhong 白履忠.[35] His biography in the *Tangshu* 唐書 (History of the Tang Dynasty, 192.5124) states that he came from Chunyi 浚儀 village near Kaifeng in modern Henan. Widely erudite, he embraced seclusion and made his home at the old site of Daliang 大梁, northwest of the city. People in due course came to call him the Master of Liang Hill (Liangqiuzi).

Around the year 711, he was summoned to serve as a secretary in the imperial administration, but soon left office. In 722, Wang Zhiyin 王誌愔, a secretary in the Ministry of Justice, recommended him to replace the cabinet members Zhu Wuliang 褚無量 and Ma Huaisu 馬懷素, but he declined and did not leave seclusion. In 729, the prince and libationer Yang Changlu 楊瑒

---

[35] His commentary to the *Neijing* is found in DZ 402, SV 347 to both texts, in *Xiuzhen shishu* 修真十書 (Ten Books on the Cultivation of Perfection, DZ 263, SV 348, 58-60) as well as in *Jiyao* 077-078 (Arronis in Lai 2021, 483-88 and 489-91). His preface appears in YQ 11.1ab.

篆 ordered him back to the capital. This time, Bai went but soon pleaded old age and ill health and returned to his hermitage.[36] Supported by a small stipend, he was able to spend most of his life as a scholar-recluse, not only producing a commentary to the *Daode jing* and the *Huangting neijing jing*, but also a work of his own, entitled *Sanxuan jingbian lun* 三玄精辯論 (Essential and Analytical Discussion of the Three Mysteries), which is no longer extant.

In his commentary to the *Neijing*, Liangqiuzi cites various other sources, including another early commentary—by the legendary immortal Yuanyangzi 元陽子.[37] As the *Yunji qiqian* describes him:

> Yuanyangzi is an immortal. He was born at the tip of the North Culmen and raised in the midst of emptiness and nonbeing. He floats along with heaven and earth and follows the orbits of the sun and the moon. He is garbed in pure naturalness, contains the hard and embraces the soft. He wanders beyond the great desert and steps beyond the central peak....
>
> Once he encountered Lord Lao who took pity on him and transmitted one scroll of scripture to him. It was called *Huangting* [*jing*]. The text represents the primordial beginning of the Great Immaculate, the utmost Dao of yin and yang, the perfect core of share and principle, as well as key instructions on nourishing spirit.
>
> People in high antiquity practiced pure Dao and attained perfection, but since middle antiquity, they have not been able to get it right. Ever since, and for a very long time, the transmission has been faulty. Thus, the Yellow [Lord] Lao created this scripture to make sure all adepts would attain spirit immortality.
>
> Following this, various erudite scholars compiled commentaries and explanations to the scripture without yet getting its original point, losing its core ideas. Yuanyangzi, sad at this state of affairs, retreated into seclusion and extricated the Yellow [Lord] Lao's most wondrous hints. He duly compiled them into a basic commentary, yet quite unable to reach the full depth of their Dao-based intention. Still, he reached deep and far, so that disciples studying hard could subtly awaken to it.
>
> The original creator of the *Huangting jing* is Laozi. The *Shiji* notes, "Yellow, that is the Yellow Emperor; Lao, that is Laozi." Thus, it is also

---

[36] Both the invitation and Bai's response are reprinted in the *Tangshu* biography.
[37] He appears in the *Neijing* commentary to sections 6.7, 9.3, 12.7, 15.1, 18.1, 28.5, 34.2, and 35.6.

proper to call the text the *Taishang jing* 太上經 (Scripture of the Most High). (YQ 104)

Yuanyangzi's work is not known otherwise, but referring to his exegesis not only reminds readers of the mythical origins of the text but also elevates Liangqiuzi's own reading to a more divine and cosmic level.

In addition, Liangqiuzi cites statements from about fifty sources, including classics such as the *Daode jing*, *Zhuangzi*, and *Yijing*; early Daoist works such as the *Taiping jing* and *Baopuzi*; generic texts such as the *Xianjing*, *Dongshen jing*, and *Lingbao jing*; as well as works from the Highest Clarity, Numinous Treasure, and other Daoist schools, including also materials supplementing the Highest Clarity corpus in the Tang (see the Appendix below). Overall, this establishes Liangqiuzi as an erudite and sophisticated thinker whose explanations and interpretations add greatly to the understanding of the rather cryptic original.

The second major commentator is Wuchengzi 務成子, about whom nothing is known.[38] The *Chuxue ji* 初學記 (Record of Initial Learning, ch. 8) by Xu Jian 徐堅 (659-729) cites a *Huangting jing* commentary, however it speaks about a grotto heaven underneath Mount Huo 霍 in a passage that does not appear in either of the main commentaries. If that in fact referred to Wuchengzi's work, it would date him to the early Tang. On the other hand, his preface to the *Waijing* mentions Wang Xizhi's copying of the text in exchange for a flock of geese, a story otherwise only known from the mid-8th century, which would place him after Liangqiuzi.

Wuchengzi's work focuses strongly on the *Waijing* and only presents a separate reading to the *Neijing* for the first three verses plus isolated later passages. He too cites various sources, but only in seven passages, in three of which he uses the *Daode jing*, *Xianjing*, and *Dadong jing*. In the other four, he cites works not used by Liangqiuzi, but similarly of Highest Clarity provenance.

---

[38] His commentary appears in YQ 11-12 The name adopts the title of an ancient immortal who, as mentioned in the *Xunzi* 荀子 (Book of Master Xun, ch. 27), supposedly taught the sage-king Yao 堯 in prehistory. The Mawangdui medical manuscript *Shiwen* 十問 (Ten Questions) mentions him by the name Wucheng 巫成 and notes that he had cosmic powers. A book associated with him, in 36 scrolls, is listed in the literary chapter of the *Hanshu* 漢書 (History of the Han Dynasty), and Ge Hong in his *Baopuzi* associates an alchemical method with him.

Not relying on Yuanyangzi, in his preface he twice refers to yet another early figure, the legendary immortal Juanzi 涓子. According to the *Liexian zhuan*,[39]

> Juanzi was a person of the state of Qi. He loved to ingest atractylis [*shu* 术] and eventually just ate its essence. When he got to be 300 years old, he was seen in Qi. He wrote the *Tiandiren jing* 天地人經 (Book of Heaven, Earth, and Humanity) in 48 *juan*.
>
> Later, he fished in Lake Ge [in Qi] and caught a carp that had a talisman in its belly, then went to live in seclusion on Mount Tang. He was able to rouse wind and rain.
>
> He had received Boyang's [Laozi] [text on the] nine methods of immortality. The Prince of Huainan, An, got hold of it in his youth but could not comprehend its depth. His work *Qinxin* 琴心 (Strumming the Heart) in 3 *juan* is well structured. (Kaltenmark 1988, 68)

Wuchengzi in his preface claims that *Qinxin* is an alternative title of the *Huangting jing*, formally called *Taishang qinxin wen* 太上琴心文 (Text of the Most High on Strumming the Heart), which would make Juanzi another major recipient of the text. In addition, he is linked with Highest Clarity in his biography in the *Sandong qunxian lu* 三洞群仙錄 (Record of the Host of Immortals of the Three Caverns, DZ 1248, SV 886-87), by Chen Baoguang 陳葆光 (dat. 1154; see Boltz 1987, 59). This cites the Highest Clarity work *Su Lin zhuan* 蘇林傳 (Biography of Su Lin) to the effect that once, when Juanzi was fishing in the river, he encountered the Lesser Lad, Lord of the Eastern Sea who told him to make sure to cut open any carp he might catch.

> Juanzi in due course indeed caught a carp and, when he cut it open, found a pure jade casket in its belly. When he opened it to see what was inside, he found it contained the methods of the Three Primes and perfect oneness transmitted by Imperial Lord Goldtower [Jinque dijun 金闕帝君]. Juanzi followed them in his cultivation practice and soon was able to summon clouds and rouse rain. In due course he climbed on emptiness and rose into the empyrean. (5.19b)

This places Juanzi more strongly into the tradition of Highest Clarity and may indicate that Wuchengzi, too, was a member of this school.

---

[39] The text is reprinted in YQ 108; it also appears in *Lishi zhenxian tidao tongjian*

INTRODUCTION / 21

Another, distinctly human, commentary, dated to the late Tang or early Song, is by the official Jiang Shenxiu 蔣慎修 who is otherwise unknown. Listed in the literary section of the Song encyclopedia *Tongzhi* 通志 (Comprehensive Records) by Zheng Qiao 鄭樵 (dat. 1161), it originally consisted of ten scrolls, but only one survives in the Daoist Canon (DZ 403, SV 348). It covers verses 28 to 30 of the *Neijing*, waxing philosophical and presenting a rather intricate and subtle vision that engages with the text on a deeper, more psychological level (Schipper in SV 348).

In the wake of these major early commentaries, the *Huangting jing* was adopted into internal alchemy, and numerous further exegeses were compiled, including also one that channels Lü Dongbin 呂洞濱 and other immortals.[40] In addition, during the Tang, a series of supplementary works appeared, offering related presentations of deities and methods (Robinet 1993, 239n44).

Contents

In contents, the *Huangting jing* presents ways of activating, maintaining, and controlling the spirits in the body, understood as agents of light and brightness and considered essential for health, well-being, and longevity.[41]

The *Waijing*, narrated in the first person and repeatedly using the direct pronoun, starts by setting out a framework of cosmic features within the person: above is the Yellow Court, a central gateway to the heavenly realm. Usually placed in the abdomen, near the spleen, here it might possibly be at the acupuncture point Spirit Court (*shenting* 神庭) on the Governing Vessel (*dumai* 督脈) (GV-24), located at the third eye, which is also the entrance to the palaces in the head. Below is the Pass Primordial (*guanyuan* 關元), a passageway to the earth and underworld (Robinet 1993, 81). Called Gate of Origin in acupuncture, it is located three inches below the navel on the Con-

---

[40] The latter is edited in *Jiyao* 074; Katō Chie 加藤千惠 in Lai 2021, 472-76. For a comprehensive collection of editions, commentaries, and supplementary works, see Zhou and Sheng 2015. A list appears in Gong 1997, 1:66-68.

[41] The term often used is *shenming* 神明, "gods as light" or "spirits in their brightness." In early longevity literature, it refers to the mental state of "spirit-like illumination" as the result of a sexual encounter (Pfister 2006, 185; Small 2018, 6). In early ritual texts, it designates two kinds of gods, atmospheric (*shen*) and stellar (*ming*). In more philosophical writings, it expresses the mysterious function of Dao (Small 2018, 2). More widely, the term may refer to gods in general (Knoblock 1988, 253), from where its Daoist and Buddhist usage derives (Machle 1992, 160). See also Robinet 1993, 60; Zheng 2018, 28.

ception Vessel (renmai 任脈) (CV-4) and associated with primary vital energy (Kaptchuk 2000).

Behind are the Dark Towers (*youque* 幽闕), twin guardian fortresses that in the commentaries and later literature are associated with the kidneys (Robinet 1993, 78). They might possibly relate to the acupuncture point Spirit Tower (*shenque* 神闕, CV-8), right at the navel, where humans receive nourishment from their mothers during gestation. In front, finally, is the Gate of Destiny (*mingmen* 命門), usually placed between the kidneys or identified with the right kidney and in acupuncture located on the Governing Vessel (GV-4).[42] More specifically, the Yellow Court, also called Central Pond and associated with the Hall of Light, houses a personage dressed in red, called the Infant or Child Cinnabar. The Pass Primordial is tightly locked, and the Dark Towers rise up tall and lofty in support.

Practitioners activate energy flow between these by breathing deeply and steadily through the nose (Spirit Hut) and gathering saliva in the mouth (Jade Pond), then guiding them downward. They are advised to eat *qi* rather than food and abstain from sexual engagements, keeping the essence steady, the three passes (mouth, hands, feet) closed, and the body fluids—*qi*, essence (semen), saliva (Robinet 1993, 89-94)—energized within. In this manner, they enhance the Elixir Field in the lower abdomen and stabilize the Numinous Root, in the commentaries identified as the tongue, but quite possibly a more sexual center or a central line of potent *qi*.

In the course of practice, adepts further activate the five organs and six viscera, following the system of medical cosmology, dominant since the Han dynasty (Robinet 1993, 66-72). The *Waijing* describes them rather sketchily, mentioning that the spleen is horizontal, the liver is like a ring, the lungs are the Flowery Canopy, the kidneys bring forth essence, and the heart—also called Numinous Terrace, Red City, and Scarlet Palace—is the chief of the organs, working like the ruler of a country. In addition, the text speaks of engaging the Great Storehouse (stomach), the Great Wall (intestines), and the Multi-storied Tower or Mysterious Sphincter, ways of referring to the esophagus. Overall, the emphasis is on dynamic exchange and energy flow through the organs rather than maintaining certain features or figures within them, allowing the deities to appear of their own accord while also exerting control over their functions.

The energy circulation throughout is closely associated with the heavenly bodies, encouraging adepts to "rise with the sun and set with the moon"

---

[42] On the Gate of Destiny, see Robinet 1993, 79-80; Gong 1997, 3:58-59; Neswald 2009, 39; Wang and He 2012.

(2.13), "absorb heaven and follow earth" (2.19), "revolve through Qian and Kun" (3.3) (Robinet 1993, 72). In addition, the *Waijing* strongly emphasizes the optimal mental state to be attained, relying heavily on terms and concepts of the *Daode jing*. Adepts are to remain free from affairs and rest in great peace, engage in clarity and stillness, reside in solitude and nonaction, embrace emptiness and nonbeing, remain clod-like and free from desires, live in quietude and blandness, harbor purity and chastity, and closely match naturalness or so-being, the most fundamental inherent quality of Dao.

The ultimate goal is to be free from disease and recover vigor so one can grow old but not weak. Beyond strong health, the text stresses longevity, using the *Daode jing* expression, "long life and eternal vision" (2.5), and lightness in body and being, as well as the state of no-death (*busi* 不死), that is, the attainment of postmortem transformation.

Overall, in terms of content, the *Waijing* inherits the *Daode jing* and Han body cosmology, while utilizing meditative terminology also found in the *Taiping jing* and the *Laozi zhongjing*. There is nothing revolutionary about its worldview or practices,[43] but its cryptic language and poetic expression render it rather mysterious, and the commentators—writing from a perspective 600 years later—imbue it with a high level of intricacy and complexity.

The *Neijing* essentially follows the same overall pattern but raises the scope to a higher level. It begins by introducing the text as revealed by a potent deity of Highest Clarity, lists its alternative titles, emphasizes its potency, and encourages its recitation. Next, it matches the *Waijing's* framework of cosmic features, but in addition to above, below, back, and front it also places powers to the right and left, creating a six-directional set-up. Above, rather than the Yellow Court, there is now the "numinous force of the cloud spirit agent" (*hunling* 魂靈), clearly identified as representing heaven in the commentaries, while the Pass Primordial—just as in the *Waijing*—is below and matches earth. Behind, rather than the Dark Towers, the text here places the Secret Doors (*mihu* 密戶), linked with the kidneys and the direction of the north; in front, it has the Gate of Life (*shengmen* 生門), matching the south and identified as the Gate of Destiny, just as in the *Waijing*. To complete the framework, lesser yang is on the left and greater yin on the right—in later sections associated with the sun and the moon.

---

[43] Many other texts provide similar instructions and cosmological outlines. For studies, see Bumbacher 2001; Despeux, 2005; 2019; Kohn1991; 2013; Pregadio 2004; 2021.

From here, the text similarly emphasizes the containment and circulation of internal energies and fluids, but then moves on to explain the inner organs and functions in much more detail, outlining a total of thirteen deities who represent the five organs plus the gall bladder as well as specific features of the head: hair, brain, eyes, ears, nose, tongue, and teeth. In each case, it provides specific names and styles of these spirits as well as information on their looks and garb, parlors and palaces, functions and cosmic correspondences (Robinet 1993, 66-67; 75-79). Beyond that, the text introduces a variety of other divine entities such as the Graceful Woman associated with the ears, the Eight Daunters for external protection, as well as the jade lads and jade maidens associated with the structure of time and known as the Six Jia and Six Ding (the latter also mentioned in the *Waijing*). In many cases, it lists their specific accessories, such as talismans, bells, pendants, flags, and banners.

Like the *Waijing,* the text links the activation and circulation of energies with the celestial bodies, but it presents a much wider range of methods with regard to stars and constellations. The sun and the moon—here also called by their immortal names Yuyi and Jielin—are not only present within the body as the eyes and the functions of yin and yang but also serve as the destination of ecstatic excursions, opening an expansion of the person into the greater cosmos. Similarly, adepts invoke and connect to the Northern Dipper, and in one passage even work with a set of five dippers. In addition, the text makes allusion to several other Highest Clarity methods: the absorption of solar and lunar essences, the nine methods of hiding oneself in the earth, ways of eliminating the three deathbringers, procedures of having one's name inscribed in the registers of life, as well as techniques of mastering their cloud and white spirit agents, *hun* 魂 and *po* 魄 (Robinet 1993, 59).

All this contributes to the greater scope of the *Neijing*, where the overall goal of cultivation goes beyond health, longevity, and the bypassing of the underworld. While the text still emphasizes meditative *Daode jing* values, it yet postulates that adepts ultimately enter Highest Clarity and have their names registered in the ledgers of the immortals. On earth not only free from sickness but from all calamities and misfortunes, they extend their years forever, ascend into the heavens, take up positions of high rank in the otherworld, attend divine audiences, and command not only the spirits within their own bodies but the gods, spirits, ghosts, and demons of the world at large.

The Outer Scripture[1]

Preface by Wuchengzi

The *Huangting jing* 黃庭經 (Yellow Court Scripture) was created by Lord Lao. Its pointers are far-reaching, its words are subtle, and its subject matter is enormous and esoteric. Indeed, it can be considered a key classic. Strongly acknowledging its essence, it is concerned with the very root of life. Now, yellow is the right color of the two forces, while court indicates the central space within the four directions. Applying this nearby to the human body, this means that the spleen is its ruler; applying it far-off to the stars, this means that the heavenly patterns assemble naturally. Accordingly, "the valley spirit does not die: it is called the mysterious female."[2] For this reason, we must treasure our life.

Later, during the Jin dynasty [265-420], Daoists who greatly valued the arts of the Yellow Court set their intention on writing and copying the text, always hoping to help people. In this context, I have heard that Wang Youjun 王右軍 [Wang Xizhi 王羲之, 303-361] excelled at writing grass script and in his disposition was very fond of white geese. When several birds were offered to him, he agreed to produce a wondrous copy [of the text] in return.[3] Yet despite his great calligraphic ability and the fact that he copied the text, he was often dissolute, passionate, and self-indulgent, so that he never avoided shedding and leaking [*qi*].

People of later generations have tended to just admire the luster of this book and took it as its root, never actually looking at its application for perfection. It is most regretful that the sagely pointers of the Most High were never properly understood in myriad generations. For this reason, I draft a commentary today, completing it in one scroll. In outline, it divides into three parts, its pattern assembling myriads of spirits. I very much hope that

---

[1] *Huangting waijing jing*, with commentaries by Liangqiuzi in *Xiuzhen shishu* 58 (main source of text and division) and, after the asterisks, by Wuchengzi from YQ 12. The two are reprinted in Zhou and Sheng 2015, 3-19 and 90-107. Variants in the main text are presented in brackets. The preface appears in YQ 12.
[2] *Daode jing* 6.
[3] About this story, see Wang 2010, 169; Yu 1991, 331.

due to this the teachings of the sages will not be obliterated but remain in the future.

Part One

1   老子［君］閑居作七言
Laozi [Lord Lao], living in seclusion, composed the seven-word [text],

Laozi was born before heaven and earth; he has always been present since heaven and earth came to be. He has thirty-six transformations and seventy-two names. He took refuge in the womb of Mother Li and was born after eighty-two years. He composed the *Huangting* [*jing*] to transmit his teaching to later generations. Through countless revolutions, he completed his task. Naturally he got special people to kneel before him and receive his instructions. If he had not got anybody, he would not have spoken even for ten thousand generations.

* * *

Laozi is the essential cloud spirit agent of heaven, the lord of naturalness. He created and established spirit immortality and has been always present for ten thousand generations. He composed this seven-word text to reveal his teachings to posterity.

2   解說身形及諸神
Explaining clearly the body and physical form and their relation to the spirits.

Laozi rests quietly in naturalness, yet at the same time floats about the eight ends of the universe. Like Dao he is vague and obscure, and cannot be fathomed. Continuously changing on and on, he holds the sacred talismans, controls the registers of life and death, and orders about the host of the spirits. Dao does not have two families—to the end it supports its servants. Dao does not have two kin groups—invariably it remains with the good.

* * *

The lord says that all is originally one continuous process. The whole body, from head to feet, can be brought to life. It is a single network and, as a whole, can be at peace. Dao is not twofold. Whoever practices it is wise.

3   上有黃庭下關元
Above there is the Yellow Court; below is the Pass Primordial.[4]

---

[4] Lines 3-17 and 34-35 are also translated in Puett 2010, 245-46.

The Yellow Court is in the head. The Hall of Light, the Grotto Chamber, and the Elixir Field are its three key locations. Enter between the eyebrows, and after one inch, there is the Hall of Light; after two inches, there is the Grotto Chamber; after three inches, there is the Elixir Field. These three constitute the upper primordial One.

The Yellow Court is paired with the Grotto Chamber. Together they bring forth the Infant [Red Child], who is their resident perfected. Always think of him! Be careful not to lose him!

The Infant transforms into a perfected and comes to reside in the Hall of Light. Then he is called Child Cinnabar. Thus, those knowing the One concentrate most on the Hall of Light as its key location.

Practice guiding *qi* and healing exercises, close your eyes and turn your vision inward, calm your mind and stabilize your will. Merge with chaos in the limitless! Get essence to move upward and flow into the Niwan Palace to reach the perfected, who is Child Cinnabar.

In the Hall of Light, the two are lord and minister. Further behind, in the Grotto Chamber, they are father and mother. In the Elixir Field, they are husband and wife.

According to another explanation, the Yellow Court is the spleen. It is over one inch long and located above the Great Storehouse, about three inches above the navel. The spleen is the seat of the Yellow Lord Lao, the spirit of the center. He rules from here.

The Pass Primordial is three inches below the navel. The gate of primordial yang is suspended in front of it. When essence here is clear like a mirror, it brightly radiates through the entire body. Never slacken in your practice of this Dao.

* * *

The Yellow Court is the eyes, the father and mother of Dao who raise and nourish the Infant. On the left resides Raised Yang (Luyang 陵陽), also known as Blossoming Brightness (Yingming 英明). On the right is Great Yin (Taiyin 太陰), also known as Mystery Radiance (Xuanguang 玄光). All three together complete potency, supporting each other as they ascend.

4   後有幽闕前命門
Behind there are the Dark Towers; in front, the Gate of Destiny.[5]

---

[5] The location of the Gate of Destiny has varied over the years. In early medical texts, it was placed between the kidneys; later it was identified with the right kidney. Unique to the Daoist tradition is its association with the six viscera as found here. See Robinet 1993, 79; Wang and He 2012; Gong 1997, 3:58-59.

The Dark Towers are the two kidneys. Like overturned cups standing on their rims, they are three inches off the navel, small on top and large below. Near then there is another universe, with its own sun and moon. The Gate of Destiny is below the navel.

* * *

The kidneys are the Dark Towers. They are linked with the eyes. The navel is three inches from the Gate of Destiny. When the sun rises and the moon sets, yin and yang are both present. Inhale and exhale primordial *qi* to nourish the Numinous Root.

5   呼吸廬間入丹田
Inhale and exhale through the Hut and into the Elixir Field.

"Inhale and exhale" means to take breath. *Qi* leaves: this is exhalation; *qi* enters: this is inhalation. The Hut is the nose. This expresses the core of expelling the old and drawing in the new. Entering three inches between the eyebrows is the Palace of the Elixir Field. The text says that one should draw *qi* in through the nose and enter it into the Elixir Field.

* * *

Exhaling, *qi* leaves; inhaling, it enters. As one inhales and exhales primordial *qi*, it assembles in the Elixir Field. The Elixir Field is three inches below the navel, the doorway of yin and yang. Ordinary people use this to generate children, while Daoists use it to generate themselves.

6   玉池清水灌靈根
The clear fluid of the Jade Pond drips on the Numinous Root.

The clear fluid in the Jade Pond is the saliva of the mouth. The Numinous Root is the tongue. Always click the teeth, rinse with saliva, and moisten the tongue.

* * *

The mouth is the Jade Pond, the Palace of Great Harmony. The saliva is the clear fluid, always beautiful and fresh. Saliva collected in the esophagus makes the sound of thunder and lightning. The tongue is the Numinous Root. Always keep it well watered.

* * *

This refers to eating and drinking spontaneously. [6] The Jade Pond is the saliva in the mouth. Breathe as prescribed and swallow it accordingly, and you will never be hungry. To begin, first avoid grain for three days or seven days. This is a small completion. Take care not to get dizzy in your head or eyes. Then continue for twenty-one days and thus complete your training. Your *qi* and vigor will increase daily. Then, if you want to eat you can eat; if you don't want to eat you can just breathe. Avoiding grain by following yin and yang, you will never run out of essence of lose your *qi*. Then it is fine, too, if you eat some grain.

7   審能修之可長存
All who can practice this can live long.

This tells people to practice cultivation day and night without slackening. Then they can attain long life.

* * *

Practice this day and night to eliminate the deathbringers, kill the three worms, and expel the hundred forms of wayward [*qi*]. Flesh and skin will blossom; proper *qi* will return, while wayward demons no longer pursue you. Then you can live long and your face will develop a bright radiance.

8   黃庭中人衣朱衣
The persons in the Yellow Court wear vermilion robes.

Visualize and think of mother and child in the spleen. See how they enter the spleen from the stomach, wearing red robes.

---

[6] This additional commentary appears after a citation of the last two lines in the *Shenxian shiqi jin'gui miaolu* 神仙食氣金櫃妙錄 (Wondrous Record of the Golden Casket on the Spirit Immortals' Practice of Eating *Qi*, DZ 836, SV 355, trl. Kohn 2012, 79-94). The text is listed in the *Suishu* 隋書 (History of the Sui Dynasty) as consisting of 9 sections and 23 scrolls (34.1048) and goes back to the Six Dynasties. The comment appears on p. 3b (Kohn 2012, 89). The same lines are also cited in the *Yangxing yanming lu* 養性延命錄 (Record on Nourishing Inner Nature and Extending Life, DZ 838, SV 345-46; trl. Kohn 2012, 165-76), a work associated with the Daoist master physician Sun Simiao 孫思邈 (581-682). Here a commentator called Ming adds: "Take food and drink in natural rhythm. The more natural it is, the more it becomes the Flowery Pond. The Flowery Pond is the saliva in the mouth. Inhale and exhale as prescribed, then swallow it down and you won't be hungry any more" (Kohn 2012, 183).

30 / OUTER SCRIPTURE

* * *

The tiny pupils in the eyes are husband and wife. The left is the King Father, the right is the Queen Mother. In capes and robes of vermilion color, they wander about to feast with the divine assembly in many places, especially in the elixir fields. Day and night visualize and think of them, never slackening or resting!

9   關門 [元] 壯 [茂] 籥合兩扉
The Pass Gate [Primordial] has a strong [strong] lock to join the two door leaves.

The gate of the lower Elixir Field has to be locked. Don't open it recklessly.

* * *

Close your eyes and turn your vision inward, making sure there is no place you do not look at. Close your mouth and curl your tongue back to feed on the mother, assembling and swallowing the jade glow [saliva]. Doing this, you will be free from trouble to the end of your days. Nonbeing [primordial] refers to *qi*. The teeth are strong; the tongue is the lock.

10   幽闕使 [俠]之高巍巍
The Dark Towers support [match] it: lofty and eminent.

The two kidneys are located at the gate of the Dark Towers, i. e., the building of the bureau of earth. They are the office of living *qi*. Above they connect to the ears. The ears are on the two sides of the head; hence the text says, "lofty and eminent."

* * *

Dao has Three Pimes, where volition and intention arise. The Dark Towers in the lower section are the mysterious spring that always flows. The Dark Towers in the middle section are the kidneys as they continue to transform. The Dark Towers in the upper section are the two ears as they look across to each other. As golden gate and the jade doorway, they connect to heaven above. Here Graceful Woman plays the zither and the flute, sounding and holding the notes *gong* and *shang*.

11   丹田之中精氣微
In the Elixir Field, essence and *qi* are subtle.

The Elixir Field is located three inches beneath the navel. It is about three inches square in size. Its *qi* is subtle and wondrous. Visualize it, and it is there; forget about it, and it is gone. It changes and disappears. Hence we say it is subtle.

* * *

The Elixir Field is the parlor of the One, located opposite the Hall of Light. Its essence and *qi* are subtle and wondrous, hard to distinguish. Hence we say it is subtle.

12   玉池清水上生肥
The clear fluid in the Jade Pond above develops opulence.

The Jade Pond is the mouth. Clear water is the liquid and fluid [saliva] in the mouth. "Above develops opulence" means that liquid and fluid collect above the tongue. Hence the text speaks of opulence.

* * *

Saliva in the mouth rests and moves. The tongue in the mouth is where white saliva accumulates and assembles. It appears rich and greasy like fat. Rinse with it and swallow it, and you can attain long life.

13   靈根堅固老不衰
The Numinous Root is firm and steady—one may grow old but never weak.

The Numinous Root is the root of the tongue. Always curl the root of the tongue, clicking the teeth to practice. Never let the root of the tongue wither or dry. Always visualizes its spirit, and you will live long and never decline.

* * *

The tongue is the Numinous Root. It governs and controls the four directions, balances and harmonizes the five flavors. It expels stench and invites fragrance. Click the teeth and swallow the *qi*, transforming it into nectar fit for drinking.

14   中池有士衣赤衣
In the Central Pond is a personage who wears a red robe.

Always visualize and think of the Infant in the heart. He is clad in a red, finely ornamented robe and resides in the [middle] Elixir Field. All exhaustion and inauspiciousness, all sloth and agitation, through him are made to go.

* * *

Residing in the esophagus as his capital is a primordial personage. Beneath central harmony, he rules the towers, matching the division of key principles. Garbed in robes of vermilion radiance, this spirit is a friend.

15   田 [橫] 下三寸神所居
Three inches below the Field [horizontal line] is where the spirits reside.

This refers to the spleen. Beneath it is the stomach; above it is the [triple] heater]. Nearby is the Numinous Root of the navel, where the spirits reside.

* * *

The palace of the Hall of Light is three inches square. This is where the spirits reside, in the very center between the eyes. The eyebrows are the Flowery Canopy: vibrant in five colors, they are shaped like scallions.

16   中外相距重閉之
When inside and outside are separate, firmly close them in.

This tells people to close in essence and guard it well. Never let it leak out recklessly. To close it in properly, use the golden tower and the jade lock.

* * *

Qi within should leave; *qi* without should enter. At the appropriate time, they move through the three passes. When the two *qi* are separate, the Dao of heaven is in a state of naturalness.

17   神廬之中當修理 [治]
The interior of the Spirit Hut should be kept cultivated and well ordered [regulated].

The Spirit Hut is the nose. There are little hairs inside, which should always be kept in order by removing them periodically. Guiding the *qi* carefully through the nose will expel all things wayward and nasty.

* * *

This teaches to remove the fine hairs in the nose to guarantee the coming and going of spirits and Dao. Hence the nose is called hut or residence. Practice continuously day and night, never stop or rest!

18   懸 [玄] 膺氣管受精符
The Hanging [Mysterious] Sphincter in the breath pipe receives the talisman of essence.

The lower part of the tongue is the talisman of essence. The esophagus is the breath pipe. Essence and *qi* move through it up and down. It is also where the Upper Prime harmonizes *qi* to be subtle and wondrous. It is the road on which the perfected travel up and down to connect to the spirits.

* * *

The center of the esophagus is the Hanging Sphincter. Primordial *qi* moves down along it, then rises up from there to move on. Hence the text says, "receives the talisman."

19   急固子精以自持
Strive to steady your essence so you can keep hold of yourself naturally.

This tells people to close in *qi* [hold the breath] and revert essence upward. Maintain this in a natural rhythm and never let it leak out recklessly. Reverting essence to supplement the brain—this is the way of no-death.

* * *

Maintain essence and never let it go.

20   宅中有士常衣絳
In the residence is a personage always wearing scarlet.

Continuously visualize and think of the spirit of the heart wearing a scarlet, cinnabar robe as he continuously leaves and enters. Doing this, you will be free from disaster and harm, expelling all wayward energies.

* * *

The face is the inch residence; the bureau of the perfected is in its center. His robe is red or vermilion; he radiates a fiery brilliance shining scarlet red.

21   子能見之可不病
When you can see him, you will be sick no more.

With strong concentration envision the spirit of the heart and think of him without stopping. Internally always see the Infant, and your body will be free from all sickness and disease.

* * *

This desires to get ordinary people to deeply realize Dao and perfection. Making the effort to envision this spirit, you will be free from sickness for the rest of your life.

22   橫立 [理] 長尺約其上

Horizontally positioned [placed], one foot long, it is just about above.

The spleen is horizontal, a bit over one foot long. It hovers above the Great Storehouse.

* * *

The spleen is one foot long and found just above the Great Storehouse. Its central area holds the Hall of Light. Lord Lao wanders and stops there in the morning.

23 子能守之可無恙
If you can maintain this, you can be free from ill.

Always maintain and nourish the spirit of the spleen. Think of him without stopping, and you will be free from disaster and disease.

* * *

Maintaining the spirit of the spleen, Lord Lao will harmonize and cleanse your knowledge. Knowing your intention, you can be free from ill.

24 呼噏 [吸] 廬問以自償
Breathe in and out through the hut, and you will naturally be fulfilled.

Use the nose to pull in *qi*, then enter it into the mouth and swallow it. In this manner, your primordial *qi* will be moist and glossy and thus you will receive benefits from heaven.

* * *

Close and seal the three passes, curve in your fingers and make fists. Breathe in and out [to activate] primordial *qi*. It will assemble in the head and from there sink into the mouth. There combine and swallow it. You will no longer feel any hunger or thirst and expel the three deathbringers, using your focused mind and intention.

25 保守 [子保] 完堅身受慶
Preserve and maintain [hold] it whole and stable: your body receives blessings.

Preserve essence and nourish *qi*, and your body and spirit will be radiant and glossy. Therefore, the text says, "receive blessings."

* * *

Each and every person has Dao, but they cannot maintain it. In those who preserve Dao, body and spirit are always at peace. Above they gaze at the three luminants, their shape like a string of pearls, scattered widely like rocks.

In their hearts, they remain solitary and full of goodness. Thus, they are naturally blessed.

26   方寸之中謹蓋藏
In the square inch, cover and contain it carefully.

Focusing on the square inch of the Elixir Field, recollect essence and maintain *qi*. Carefully cleanse it and hold it tight, thus you contain it carefully.

* * *

What is neither square nor round is the eye. Close the gates and block the orifices. Even if there is no central prime [you see], maintain it. Maintaining it, you attain the peace of Dao.

27   精神還歸老復壯
Essence and spirit revert here: even if old, you recover vigor.

Revert essence and refine spirit to strengthen brain *qi*. Then your teeth will be strong, your hair black, and your body will not age.

* * *

Essence and spirit always want to leave, they are much like floating clouds. Above, make sure essence does not leak; below, do not release it. Maintain the cloud (*hun*) and white spirit agents (*po*) within and even over years you remain full of vigor at all times.

28   使以 [心結] 幽闕流下竟
Guide [from the heart connect] it to the Dark Towers and let it flow to the lower region.

Pull out the Infant from the Hall of Light and guide him down to the Scarlet Palace right near the navel. Also visualize him changing and transforming, allowing essence to flow into the Elixir Field to nourish the physical form. In addition, think of the *qi* between the two kidneys, making it move from above to below. As you inhale, *qi* naturally moves up and reaches the Yellow Court. According to one explanation, this is between the eyebrows. The Dark Towers are in charge.

* * *

The ears are the hearing aspect of the mind. They connect and link to the Dark Towers. As the nose smells fragrance, their coverage is strengthened. The mind arrives, the will opens, and you can let it flow to the lower region.

29   養子玉樹令可壯 [仗]
Nourishing your jade tree, you can make yourself strong [vigorous].

You should always maintain the lower prime. Essence and *qi* are firm like jade. Close in essence and maintain spirit and you can make the branches strong.

* * *

Your body is the jade tree. Always keep it strong and healthy. Yin is the jade stalk. Revolve [*qi*] to create mutual harmony and integration. Revert essence to supplement the brain, and you can be free from disease. You live in eternal happiness, completely free from sorrow.

30   至道不煩無旁午
Utmost Dao remains untroubled, without sides or center.

Without any trouble or disturbance whatsoever, calm the mind and stabilize intention. Sit up straight to practice, oriented toward the center. That is, your back is turned toward *wu* {north}, your hips and belt to *you* and *mao* [east and west].

* * *

Great Dao is naturally free from troubles and worries. It radiates and reflects radiant and bright, forming the base and root of all human beings. Utmost Dao is hard to attain but easy to practice.

31   靈臺通天臨中野
The Numinous Terrace connects to heaven, near central wilderness,

The heart is the Numinous Terrace. Above, its *qi* connects to the brain gate, below it connects to the center of the spleen. If this *qi* is firm, it encompasses the entire body.

* * *

The head is a lofty terrace; the intestines form a wide wilderness. As primordial *qi* connects to heaven, the Mysterious Mother comes down and nourishes my self.[7]

32   方寸之中至 [間] 關下

---

[7] According to the *Dadong jing*, the Mysterious Mother is paired with the Primordial Father. The two symbolize heaven and earth and direct a group of five deities (Robinet 1993, 102).

From the square inch to [between] below the pass.

The esophagus is one inch wide. The perfected in the Hall of Light moves down to join the Elixir Field, then moves up to revert to the Hall of Light.

* * *

In the very center of the eyes, see jade florescence grow to the size of a chicken egg with the yellow on the outside. It sinks down and enters the mouth, where it gives rise to the five flavors. Practice this morning and evening and you will have no limits!

33   玉房之中神門戶
The Jade Chamber contains the gates and doors of the spirits.

Yin and yang are the gates and doors of the spirits. They preside over essence and regularity. In men, it is called essence; in women, it is called regularity. Men utilize the storage of essence; women work with their monthly flow. Hence the text speaks of the doors and gates.

* * *

The Jade Chamber is also called the Grotto Chamber, the Purple Chamber, the Scarlet Chamber, and the Hall of Light. Jade florescence covers the area of the golden casket, where the gates and doors of the spirits in their brightness are. It is a place where the One comes and goes.

34   皆 [既] 是公子教我者
This is all [just] what the Prince is teaching me!

The heart is the master of all great internal offices [viscera]. Matching this, the left kidney is the master of supervising empty spaces while the right kidney is the master of supervising open spaces. They all contain essence and *qi* which must not be allowed to leak out. If one can maintain the One, this becomes obvious.

* * *

On the left is the Prince [Blossomless]; on the right is White Prime. They nourish and nurture me and always want me to attain spirit immortality. They are the father and mother raising and nurturing the elixir child. Matching the sun and the moon, they are three inches apart.

35   明堂四達法海源
The Hall of Light extends in the four directions, modeling itself on the ocean's fonts.

Between the eyebrows, about one inch inside the head is the Hall of Light. *Qi* in all cases flows from there like the prime power of the ocean.

* * *

Three inches and three levels in size, it appears both in front and back. It causes the sun and the moon to return to the center. They duly ascend to reach out in all four directions, then flow into the ocean.

36   真人子丹當吾前
The perfected Child Cinnabar manifest before me.

The Infant is a perfected. His other name is Child Cinnabar. He resides in the Hall of Light. If one is able to always think of him, longevity can be extended.

* * *

About one inch tall, he rests between the two eyebrows. If one looks up and envisions him, the heart remains untroubled.

37   三關之中精氣深
Within the three passes, essence and *qi* are deep.

Passes appear in three sections. The Pass of Heaven is the mouth; the Pass of Earth is the lower section [feet]; and the Pass of Humanity is the hands. Always make tight fists to close and seal all three, so wayward *qi* cannot arise.

* * *

The mouth is the Pass of Heaven; the feet are the Pass of Earth, and the hands are the Pass of Humanity. Keeping them firmly closed, numinous pearls arraign themselves in a linked string. Subtle and wondrous, this is hard to know. Closed is what the text means by "deep."

38   子欲不死修崑崙
If you want to reach no-death, cultivate Kunlun.

Kunlun is the head. Anyone who nourishes the Niwan center in the brain will not die and attain long life.

* * *

The head is Kunlun. Dao is regulated there: its weft at the *wu* hour {noon}, the woof during the *mao* and *you* hours [5-7 am, 5-7 pm]. Then sun and moon shine brightly, [Child] Cinnabar wanders about playfully, and the hundred officials stand guard.

39   絳宮重樓十二級 [環]
The Multi-storied Tower near the Scarlet Palace has twelve stories [rings].

The esophagus has twelve rings. The area above the heart is the Scarlet Palace.

* * *

The golden building has five walls and twelve surrounding areas. Cinnabar and yellow form its circumference, the five colors assemble around it like clouds. The jade hall in Scarlet Palace is where the One comes and goes.

40   宮 [瓊]室之中五氣 [色] 集
In the palace [jasper] parlor, the five *qi* [colors] assemble.

Among the *qi* of the five organs, the heart is the emperor. He resides in the very center, where the host of the spirits come to assemble, right on the side of the Infant.

* * *

The Armillary Sphere or Jade Balancer, in charge of all, resides in the very center. Here the five colors and potent jades come to the height of yin and return to yang. It is a palace with a golden parlor.

41   赤城 [神] 之子中池立
The child of the Red City [spirit] appears in the Central Pond.

The Red City is the heart. The tongue is its child. The mouth is the Central Pond.

* * *

The spirit of the throat presides over the essence of the Pond. He receives an appropriate amount and turns it around repeatedly, then transmits it to the Great Storehouse.

42   下有長城玄谷色
Beneath is the Great Wall, colorful like the mystery valley.

The small intestine is the Great Wall. It pulls *qi* and enters it into the womb.

* * *

The intestines constitute the Great Wall. They have color, while the kidneys are dark. They are in a valley, arranged from south to north.

43   長生要妙 [慎] 房中急

To attain long life, be focused and meticulous [careful] with the urges of the bedchamber.

To nourish inner nature, be focused and meticulous: close and tighten the gate of essence.

* * *

The chamber is the Jade Chamber. The key is to maintain it always. Combine and assemble the six harmonies. What exactly happens in the six harmonies is hard to explain. If you wish to attain Dao, firmly close off compass and square.

44   棄捐淫慾 [欲] 專守 [子] 精
Do away with all lascivious desires, concentrate and keep [your] essence.

Living long is essential and wondrous: maintaining essence is top priority.

* * *

The wise nurture their essence; the ignorant nurture their wealth. They disperse and lose [essence], getting tied up with all sorts of things. Once gone, how can it be recovered? Better to revert essence to supplement the brain, letting it moisturize and enhance hair and whiskers.

45   寸田尺宅可理 [治] 生
The inch-size field and the foot-square residence: here you can regulate life.

The eyes are the inch-size field; the face is the foot-square residence. Regulating life means looking up to observe the one spirit in the upper section.

* * *

The inch-size field is the Elixir Field. The foot-square residence is the face. They are the weft and woof of Dao and must never be abandoned or ignored. Pursue them with dedicated effort and you inevitably will attain long life.

46   繫 [雞] 子長留心安寧
Hold it tight [like a chicken egg], always retain it: your heart-mind is at peace and calm.

Always observe the body and physical form of the Infant. Then your cloud and white spirit agents will always remain and the myriad spirits will not go astray. Quiet and bland, free from desires, your heart knows no fear or terror: thus it is naturally calm and restful.

* * *

With great Dao in chaos complete, you are naturally nebulous and confused, shaped just like a chicken egg. Concentrate your heart-mind and unify your intention, maintain it at all times and never let it go. Then you can be calm and restful.

47   觀 [推] 志遊神三奇靈
Observe [retain] your will, let your spirits wander, find the three marvelous numinous forces.

Maintaining the Numinous Root of the upper section means [working on] the tongue. Maintaining the Numinous Root of the middle section means [working on] the navel. Maintaining the Numinous Root in the lower section means [working on] the chamber of essence.

* * *

In great Dao wander and frolic, playing with great pleasure. Powerful and strong, hold on to your will and keep on observing and visualizing the perfected of Dao. Then the three numinous forces will serve and come to your side, sounding zithers, drums, and pipes.

48   閑暇 [行間] 無事心太平
At leisure [between activities], free from affairs, the heart-mind rests in great peace.

Quiet and bland, serene and absorbed, maintain emptiness and be free from emotions: body and organism are calm and restful; the heart is at great peace.

* * *

Be quiet, bland, and without desires, and Dao is naturally attracted. Engagements and profit-making much reduced, the spirits in their brightness are present in great numbers. This is great peace.

49   常存玉房神明達
Always visualize the Jade Chamber, and the spirits in their brightness will arrive.

The Jade Chamber contains the gates and doors of the spirits [=1/33]. Always visualize essence and *qi* coming and going from here, and the spirits in their brightness arrive naturally.

* * *

The Jade Chamber is the parlor of the One. Lying on the west side of the mountain and resting on the east side of the mountain, it is located in darkness and obscurity. Always envision it without end so that within and without can find mutual accord. Hence the text says, "brightness will arrive."

50 時念 [思] 太倉不飢渴

At all times, envision [think of] the Great Storehouse: no longer feel hunger or thirst.

The Great Storehouse is the stomach, the kitchen that processes the five grains. Always think of and envision it, and you will never again feel hunger or thirst.

* * *

Sucking and chewing on Great Harmony, the spirits descend and take up residence in the Great Storehouse. The spirit of the stomach is called Master of Yellow Constancy (Huangchangzi 黃常子). Address him and say: "Master of Yellow Constancy, let me have the Dao of long life so I can feel satiated without eating!" Make sure to not practice it erratically but stay with it. Eventually you reach a stage when you fully attain the ability to avoid grain and be free from hunger.

51 役使六丁神 [玉] 女謁

Command and order the spirit [jade] maidens of the Six Ding to present themselves.

Always think of the perfected in the Yellow Court, and the jade maidens of the Six Ding will naturally come and stand guard, yours to command.

* * *

Living in solitude, clear and pure, you come to control the realm of the Six Ding. Calling out their holy names, the jade maidens come to serve you.

52 閉子精路 [門] 可長活

Close your path [gate] of essence and you can live forever.

Eliminating all wayward *qi* and abolishing all connection to ordinary life, firmly close off the path of essence, and you can attain long life.

* * *

When yin and yang copulate and intermingle, essence and spirit desire to leave. Lascivious interaction causes their loss! Raging passions are like wild horses: they cannot be stopped. With your hand, press the inside of the strings [at the perineum], then pull in the jade stalk, and close the golden gate.

53   正室之中 [堂前] 神所居 [舍]
In the straight-lined parlor [in front of the hall] is where the spirits dwell [reside].

The straight-lined parlor is the Hall of Light or the Grotto Chamber. Always think of the Infant living there as a perfected. As you visualize him, he will be present. If you don't think of him, he will be gone.

* * *

In the straight-lined parlor, the five colors intermingle. The Armillary Sphere or Jade Balancer is where Dao establishes itself. Residing in the Hall of Light, it wanders to the Scarlet Palace and there transforms into a perfected who then stays in the Elixir Field.

54   洗身 [心] 自理 [治] 無敢污 [無身理]
Cleanse your body [heart] and it will be naturally regulated: no defilement dares approach [rest in a state of no-self].

Living in solitude, clear and still, burn incense and think of perfection. The perfected of the Scarlet Palace and the host of jade maidens all will come. Envision their form as you converse with ordinary people.

* * *

Revere and honor heaven and earth, get away from and avoid all jealousy and doubt. Close your eyes and engage in inner vision, think of the spirits coming and going. Never mingle with ordinary beings and you will not suffer defeat or defilement.

55   歷觀五臟視節度
Passing through all, observe the five organs, seeing them with their sections and measures.

Always think of the five organs and the many spirits will not leave your self and body.

* * *

The five organs and six viscera each have their ruler. Cultivate the body, cleansing it to be pure white. Cut off all grain and stop eating, instead ingesting and drinking Great Harmony. Move it all around, then start again at the beginning. Thus, you do not lose the rhythm.

56 六府修治潔如素
The six viscera cultivated and regulated: cleansed to raw simplicity.

The six viscera consist of: one, the gall bladder; two, the stomach; three, the bladder; four, the large intestine; five, the small intestine; and six, the navel. These are the viscera. All six of them must be kept clean and pure.

* * *

The mind must not engage in wrong thoughts; the mouth must not engage in wrong speech; the eyes must not engage in wrong seeing; the ears must not engage in wrong hearing; the hands must not engage in wrong taking; the feet must not engage in wrong walking. These six types of action constitute the base of the six viscera. If you can do away with all of them, Dao is complete and potency achieved. Thus, cleanse yourself to raw simplicity.

57 虛無自然道之故 [固]
Emptiness, nonbeing, and naturalness form the ground [base] of Dao.

Emptiness and nonbeing consist of twelve kinds of *qi*, among which naturalness is foremost. As people separate from Dao and move further away, they do not know its perfection.

* * *

Emptiness and nonbeing means being vague and obscure. If Dao is not there, naturalness cannot happen. Look up and down in self-vision and always maintain mystery and simplicity, working ever earlier. As you know the male and maintain the female, your cloud and white spirit agents will not leave your body.

58 物有自然事不煩
If beings have naturalness, affairs won't trouble them.

Know naturalness and the perfected will be present. Then the ten thousand generations vanish in an instant. As you maintain this always, what could possibly be troublesome?

* * *

Naturalness is the great spirit of heaven and earth. Even without visualization or imagination, its *qi* comes and goes naturally.

59 垂拱無為身體安

Relaxed and reverent, in deep nonaction, body and organism are at peace.

Quiet, bland, and in a state of nonaction, you live clod-like in solitude, Calming the mind and stabilizing the will, properly flowing *qi* naturally comes to stay. Body and organism experience great peace.

* * *

Sitting upright you naturally maintain deep vastness and primordial Dao. Never violate the heavenly prohibitions, and your body will be free from disasters and problems. Forever you remain deeply at peace.

60   虛無之居在幛[廉]間
Dwelling in emptiness and nonbeing is like being in screened [reserved] idleness.

Being in a tent, naturally protected, close the Grotto Chamber and cultivate Dao. Always dwell in this space and never contend with other people. Hence the text speaks of dwelling between screens.

* * *

It is the nature of emptiness and nonbeing to delight in clarity and purity. Cultivating harmony while living in solitude, you can talk speak with the spirits. Setting up screens and awnings, you never hear the sounds of other people. Observe and see mysterious potency, the five colors flitting back and forth. Examining all by the bright light of the sun and moon, let them move east to west and make the three and five recover and return. Therefore, they revolve through the organs and pivot around the body's matrix.

61   寂寞曠 [廓] 然口不言
Serene and solitary, vast [wide] and open, the mouth does not speak.

Residing in leisure and naturally resting, envision Dao and think of perfection. Seeing them, you are not startled: your mouth does not speak.

* * *

Hidden and secreted away behind the Flowery Canopy, harness the will and connect to emptiness. Serene, you widely envision the sun like a disk and the moon like a pearl. Immersed in darkness, breathing in solitude, you never desire luxury or praise.

[61 A   修和獨立真人宮][8]

---

[88] The rhyme here does not match the other lines. It is quite possibly a later addition.

Cultivating harmony, standing solitary in the palace of the perfected.

The palace of [the spirit of] Great Harmony is located in the Hall of Light, suspended below the Flowery Canopy: he wears a vermilion robe. The Hall of Light extends in all four directions. Those who know what perfected resides there see him as a little lad wearing resplendent, glittering garb. He says, If you want to know where I reside, ask Great Tenuity!

62 恬淡無欲游德園
Quiet and bland, free from desires: wander about the garden of high potency.

When cold, you need no clothes; when hot, you will not sweat. Quiet, bland, and without desires, you live clod-like in solitude. Deeply hidden in the mountains, you never desire glory and great wealth.

* * *

On the outside, let go of all error and doubt; on the inside, harbor jade brilliance. Quiet and tranquil, you are full of happiness and joy, never desiring anything of the ordinary world.

63 清淨香潔玉女存 [前]
Clear and pure, fragrant and chaste: jade maidens appear [before you].

Clear and pure, you live in solitude. Concentrating the heart-mind, you naturally observe the prohibitions. Offering fragrant incense, fasting to purity, jade maidens come to serve.

* * *

Do away with the ordinary world and live in the wilderness where there are no people. Burning incense and offering fragrance, you invoke the jade maidens of the Six Ding. They naturally come to serve.

64 修德明達道 [神] 之門
Cultivating potency, brightness arrives: the gate of Dao [the spirits]

To properly maintain the Gate of Destiny, people should sit upright and straighten out their thoughts, never looking at anything off or wayward. Cultivating Dao to a bright pure white, observing the outside to know what is within, the spirits naturally open the door of Dao for you.

* * *

As potency overflows, the body is rich. When it overflows the dwelling, the mind reaches far, the will pervades all, and in spirit radiance you see multi-storied buildings, wondrous doors, golden gates, and jade halls.

Part Two

1 作道優游深獨居
To practice Dao, wander widely, deeply live in solitude.

To practice Dao, you should enter an oratory. Reach out to your womb, refine your physical form, and revert essence and spirit.

***

Seclude your body, hide your physical form, and sever all ties with the ordinary world. Harbor *qi* and nourish essence, and your face will be glossy like cinnabar pearls.

2 扶養性命守虛無
Support inner nature, nourish destiny, maintain emptiness and nonbeing.

Emptiness and nonbeing constitute naturalness. Maintain Dao, nourish physical form, and cultivate alignment, and naturalness never leaves your body.

***

Decisively relinquishing all forebears and ancestors, avoid the ordinary world and live in seclusion. The Director of Destiny settles the registers. To be removed from the ledgers of the dead, change your name and alter your surname. In this manner, you can firmly maintain emptiness and nonbeing.

3 恬淡無為 [自樂] 向思慮
Quiet and bland, in nonaction [naturally joyful], attend to thoughts and worries.

Serene and bland, clear and pure, nourish the spirits and cherish your physical organism. Get ten thousand miles away from harm, and you will be free from thoughts and worries.

***

Serene and bland, in full obscurity, rejoice in Dao and maintain poverty. Don't engage in memories or worries, and you reach a state completely free from trouble.

4 羽翼已成 [具] 正扶疏 [骨]
Feathered wings already complete [formed], rightly support their spread [your bones].

As the study of Dao nears completion, bjadeody and organism get lighter and lift up. Vague and obscure, it is as if you had fur and feathers. When this happens, you lift up and ascend. Hence the text speaks of supporting their spread.

* * *

Cultivating Dao and practicing benevolence, the physical organism soars and the flesh gets lighter. When Dao is complete and potency achieved, a chariot of clouds comes to receive you. Jade maidens supporting its axle, it rises up and ascends to Great Clarity. You do not sprout fur or feathers.

5   長生久視乃飛去
Reach long life and eternal vision:[1] take off flying.[2]

Attaining Dao, you do not die; going beyond the world, you live forever. Then, in bright daylight, your cloud spirit agents fly off and enter Great Clarity.

* * *

Always alive for ten thousand generations, you become close friends with the One. Jade maidens pick mushrooms and sprouts to chew on. Ingesting them, you immediately sprout fur and feathers. The Highest Spirit issues a summons and you fly off to enter the azure ocean.

6   五行參差同根節 ［帶］
The five phases, joined and separate, merge at root and joints [belt].

The five organs pattern themselves on the five phases, at times moving up, at times moving down. Joined and separate, the merge into oneness at the esophagus.

* * *

The five colors soar and rise, at times joined, at times separate. Merged in chaos, they cannot be distinguished; together they bring forth root and stalk.

---

[1] This expression goes back to *Daode jing* 59.
[2] These five lines are highly poetic and outline the core program of the text:

> To practice Dao, wander widely, deeply live in solitude.
> Support inner nature, nourish destiny, maintain emptiness and nonbeing.
> Quiet and bland, in nonaction, attend to thoughts and worries.
> Feathered wings already complete, rightly support their spread:
> Reach long life and eternal vision: take off flying.

7   三五合氣要 [其] 本一
The three and five merge their *qi* in [their] original oneness.³

Above and below, the three and five join into oneness in the chamber. When the three and five are destroyed, they revert to oneness.

* * *

Three times five makes fifteen. In their very center, the two friends are hidden. They come and go to form the three yang. Full of mysterious potency, they are subtle and wondrous. Their shape is like a dragon. When you see this, laugh softly to yourself and never tell a living person.

8   誰與共之斗日月
All support them: Dipper, sun, and moon.

The left eye is the sun: the King Father rules within. The right eye is the moon: the Queen Mother rules within. The Dipper is the constellation of the seven stars. They are also called the seven regulators.

* * *

The female resides at the North Culmen; the male resides in the Southern Palace. The perfected are not far off but close by inside the Dipper. The three luminants shine forth everywhere, heaven and earth observe each other. If you want to attain the One, ask the two lads.

9   抱玉懷珠和子室
Embrace jade, clasp the pearl: harmonize your parlor.

Rough and irregular like jade, scattered widely like rocks, guide the *qi* and hold it in tightly. Your thoughts are like a string of pearls.

* * *

Glittering like jade, strung like pearls, balance and harmonize [*qi*] in your parlor and chamber, floating along forever with the generations.

10   子能知之萬事畢
If you can know all this, the myriad affairs are done.⁴

Cultivating Dao and maintaining the One, you absorb *qi* and extend your

---

³ According to the pantheon of the *Dadong jing*, these are the Five Spirits and Three Ones, representatives of the five directions and three elixir fields (Robinet 1993, 101).
⁴ This closely echoes *Zhuangzi* 12.

years, turn your destiny around and become a spirit immortal. Then the myriad affairs are done.

* * *

The One is the greatest of spirits, at the root of heaven and earth and the source of people's original destiny. If you can know this, the myriad affairs are naturally done.

11   子自有之持勿失
You naturally have it: hold on and never lose it.

Close in essence and naturally maintain it. Keep envisioning the Infant.

* * *

Each and every person has the One. Having the One but not knowing how to maintain simplicity, they lose their base and root in favor of receiving wealth and treasures. The wise attain it and make it their friend.

12   即得［欲］不死入金室
Then you attain [desire] no-death as you enter the golden parlor.

To cultivate Dao, by all means enter the parlor of the nine divisions and return to the womb to refine the physical form. Cultivate and regulate the perfect *qi*, mysterious and white. Serenely close off and seal the three passes, and no wayward *qi* will arise.

* * *

Then you enter the three-inch space to create the golden parlor in the Grotto Chamber. Connecting to the Dark Towers, I change my physical form into a perfected. The perfected then resides in the Elixir Field.

13   出日入月是吾道
Rising with the sun, setting with the moon: this is my Way!

The sun and the moon are the two eyes. Placed to the left and right, they regulate all. Residing in the palace of the Purple Chamber, they emerge and appear as perfected of Dao.

* * *

When the sun rises, there is greater yang. When the moon sets, there is greater yin. Revolving and circulating, they return again and again. Matching them, keep on practicing.

14   天七地三迴相守
The seven of heaven and the three of earth revolve and maintain each other.

Heaven has the seven stars, while earth has the three *qi*. Primordial *qi* moves by revolving evermore without end or pinnacle.

* * *

The seven of heaven and the three of earth are bound and interlocked. Draw in earth *qi* through the nose, then let it be subtle above. Thus, the two revolve and maintain each other.

15   昇降進退合乃久
Ascending and descending, advancing and retiring, I merge [with them] and live forever.

Primordial *qi* keeps on ascending and descending, moving up and down. Part of cosmic chaos, it has no physical form or visible end. Heaven and earth attain it and thus they can live long.

* * *

Earth *qi* moves up and ascends; heaven *qi* sinks down and descends. Yin and yang in proper alignment, they merge in the Scarlet Palace. At times advancing, at time retiring, straightforward *qi* is at ease, One can attain eternal life.

16   玉石珞珞［落落］是吾寶
Jade and rocks aligned like ornaments [scattered widely]: such are my treasure.

Jade white like rock resides in the lower section.

* * *

Strings of pearls and jade rings are scattered widely like rocks. Emerging from great yang, *qi* is like fire and smoke. Restrain it and you cannot attain it: treat it like a valued treasure.

17   子自有之何不守
You naturally have it, so why not maintain it?

Close in essence and naturally maintain it. Receive *qi* and nourish the spirit.

* * *

All people naturally have the One, but they don't know how to maintain it. Those who know how to maintain it, keep revolving it every day. The day they lose track of it, their destiny dissolves.

18 心曉根基養華采 [彩]⁵
The heart-mind knows the root and foundation: it nourishes flowery blossoms [shine].

The expression "root and foundation" refers to refers to people knowing how to maintain the One. "Blooming blossom" means that, if people's face and eyes are joyful and glossy, the entire organism radiates in florescence.

* * *

Widely attending to Dao and the perfected, deeply understanding the non-ultimate, you can retain your years and ward off old age. Naturally maintaining the base and returning to the root, you open and close yin and yang in proper rhythm. Healthy color and flowery glow spread and you always look like a young person.

19 服天順地合藏精
Absorb heaven, follow earth: merge [them] and contain your essence.

Heaven *qi* sinks down and descends; earth *qi* moves up and ascends the two merge and form potency. Changing and transforming, they bring forth each other. Close in *qi* and maintain essence, nourish the spirits and refine the material form.

* * *

The head is heaven; the feet are earth. Absorb and ingest heaven *qi*, allowing it to drip down and moisten the entire body and physical form. Merge them in your Elixir Field, contain them in your brain with door locked. With dew from heaven and rain from clouds, which herb would not flourish.

20 九原之山何亭亭 [= 22]
The Mountain of Nine Springs: how high and eminent!

In the Niwan, the *qi* is kingly and of radiant color. The perfected Great One resides within. "High and eminent" refers to the heart.

* * *

The heart is the Nine Springs. The perfected Great One resides within. Without ever going out the door and gate, he knows [all in] the four directions.

---

⁵ As Thomas E. Smith points out (personal communication), the rhyme scheme for the next ten lines is rather erratic, suggesting later editing and/or additions. This is also suggested by the variation in line arrangement between the editions.

21   中住 [有] 真人可使令 [= 23]
Inside resides [there is] a perfected: you can command and direct him!

The perfected Infant can be commanded and directed. Without going out the door, you know the world; without looking out the window, you know heaven's Dao.

* * *

The perfected is the Great One, a little lad deeply hidden in the golden building. He submits and does not rise. When he is secreted away and hidden in the Nine Springs, he cannot be ordered about.

22   七日之五 [午] 迴相合 [= 20]
The seven suns and five [For seven days at noon] revolve and join together.

The seven orifices and five inner organs come together and merge in harmony, assembling in the parlor of the One.

* * *

Practicing Dao, one should merge them once every seven days.

23   崑崙之山 [上] 不迷誤 [= 21]
The mountain [on top] of Kunlun: do not mistake or misplace it!

Kunlun is the head. The perfected wander and frolic there. The sun and moon revolve in their orbits, cold and heat keep on changing, never failing to the very end.

* * *

Kunlun is the head. Above, it connects to heaven. As it is widely endowed with primordial *qi*, do not mistake or misplace it.

24   蔽以紫宮丹城樓
Hide in it the Purple Palace with its cinnabar walls and tower.

The Elixir Field above connects to the Purple Palace. It contains five walls as well as the Twelve-storied Tower. The perfected wander and frolic there.

* * *

It has golden towers and jade walls, surrounded by cinnabar and yellow suburbs. The hundred officials lodge there to guard it. The One is its priority guest. The Scarlet Palace with its jade halls is where the perfected reside

25 俠以日月如連[明]珠
Clasp the sun and moon like a string of [bright] pearls.

This refers to the two eyes. Mysterious *qi* shines brightly through them, issuing like a string of pearls. The five colors are blurred and indistinct. Always envision them and you will have longevity and life without end.

* * *

Left is the sun, right is the moon, their merged essence in the center. The five colors blur in chaos: in the morning like bright stars, in the evening like bright pearls, brilliant and dazzling, luminous and glittering. Never ever stop!

26 萬歲昭昭非有期
For ten thousand years they shine forth brightly, there is no time limit.

Once the perfected attain Dao, for ten thousand years they never change their physical form. Men eight, women sev: they take birth in this rhythm. Maintaining themselves jointly with the sun and the moon, they preserve themselves along with heaven and earth.

* * *

Bright pearls come floating down: firmly maintain them within. The talisman of long life, they shine forth brightly for ten thousand years: there is no time limit ever again. The Director of Destiny settles the registers, and you are already removed from the ledgers of death.

27 外本三陽神自來
On the outside, provide a basis for the three yang, and the spirits will naturally come.[6]

The three yang are three times nine calendar phases. When a baby is born, the spirit of the One in the form of the cloud and white spirit agents comes and enters the physical form.

* * *

The three yang are the three forms of essence. Their shape is like tassels on a headdress. Based on mystery, they have no ruler. Using harmony as their root, they come naturally without ever being called, always soft and silent.

28 內養[拘]三陰[神]可長生
On the inside, nourish [embrace] the three yin [spirits], and you can live long.

---

[6] Lines 27-30 are also rendered in Puett 2010, 246.

Pull in yang *qi* through the nose, then collect it to nourish the Infant, the perfected, and the baby within. These are called the three yin. Doing so, you also feed the spirits. Yang here refers to primordial yang. It is white. It continuously changes and transforms, containing the essence of long life. You should always maintain the spirits of the three *qi*.[7]

* * *

The three spirits are the three internal masters. Embracing these three spirits, all ways of life are done.

29   魂欲上天魄入泉
The cloud spirit agents want to rise to heaven as the white spirit agents want to enter the [Yellow] Springs.

The cloud spirit agents are yang; the white spirit agents are yin. This says that in ordinary people who do not have Dao and potency, the cloud and white spirit agents leave the body [at death] and disperse to return to their origin.

* * *

When you lie down to sleep at night, the cloud spirit agents rise up to wander about heaven. When the three-legged crow inside the sun crows like a rooster, it abruptly hides and comes back to hide in the body. The white spirit agents represent the physical body. When a person gets to be seventy or eighty years old, the white spirit agents desire to enter the [Yellow] Springs. They cause people to grow old, develop strong yearnings, and wish to separate from the physical form and human appearance.

30   還魂返魄道自然
If you make the cloud spirit agents return and the white spirit agents come back, Dao will come naturally.

Embrace the cloud spirit agents and control the white spirit agents, making sure they do not move or get active. As the spirit emperor resides in the body, Dao follows naturalness.

* * *

Embrace the cloud spirit agents and control the white spirit agents, so they cannot leave your person. If you get skilled at maintaining naturalness, you won't need to use muscle strength.

---

[7] The same line also appears as 21A in the *Xiuzhen shishu*. This is its commentary.

Part Three

1   璇璣懸珠環無端
The Jasper Sphere's hanging pearls form a ring without end.

Just like the stars of the Jasper Sphere [in the Dipper] revolve in a string, *qi* in the conduits flows and connects all, never resting or stopping. Close the mouth and nourish spirit, rising to refine with sweet spring like floating pearls.

* * *

[庶幾結珠固靈跟]
Just about like stringing pearls, steady the Numinous Root.

Stringing pearls means pearls in a row. Allow them to enter the mouth and settle within. Then essence is steady and drips into the Numinous Root.

2   迅牝 [玉枝]金籥常 [身]完堅
The swift female [jade branches] and golden lock: always [the body] whole and firm.

Yin is the female; yang is the lock. The two never hurt each other. If you attain the *qi* of central harmony, use it to revert essence and refine the physical form. Then you can be whole and firm.

* * *

Jade branches are the teeth; the golden lock is the tongue. Open the mouth, curl the tongue, ingest the mother's *qi*, and never speak bad words. Then your body can remain whole and firm.

3   載地懸天周乾坤
Carried by earth, suspended from heaven, revolve through Qian and Kun.

Earth carries people who are in turn suspended from heaven. Dao is neither above nor below. Subtle and wondrous, it is in the center of Qian and Kun. Therefore, it revolves and flows all through Qian and Kun.

* * *

When people are born on earth, Dao comes and support them. Therefore, it says, "carried by earth." The Mysterious Mother nourishes the myriad beings all over the world without applying particular mechanisms or restrictions. The spirits in their brightness are subtle and wondrous, not what ordinary people hear about. They always desire that I attain spirit immortality. Urged on by Qian and Kun, I must never trespass or slip up.

4   象以四時赤如丹
In image they activate four seasons: red like cinnabar.

The Hall of Light extends in the four directions and blesses the four seasons. It is where the perfected Child Cinnabar resides. If you can always think of it and regularly swallow its *qi*, your longevity will be without limit.

* * *

The four seasons and five phases complete one revolution, then immediately begin anew. The perfected Child Cinnabar transforms in a moment to become one with yourself. His cloak and garb are studded with red pearls; their form resembles cinnabar.

5   前仰後卑各異 [列其]門
Raised in front, low behind: each with a different [arranged by its] gate.

This refers to the head and the feet, the kidneys and the heart. The heart is red while the kidneys are black. When the base is stable and firmly rooted, water and fire overcome each other. Thus, they can be different or the same.

* * *

"Raised" means high. High in front and low behind, the kidneys face the middle. The right one is yin; the left one is yang. They are separate buildings, each with gates and doors.

6   送 [選]以還丹與玄泉
Send [choose] [*qi*] to revert the elixir and join the mysterious spring.

"Elixir" here refers to the blood. As you transform and move it downward, it changes to become white essence. As this time, you should contract the nostrils and revert it upward into the Niwan as well as downward into the mouth. There it transforms into jade spring.

* * *

"Choose" means to pick. By contracting and pulling upward, you revert the elixir until it turns into the *qi* of the mysterious spring. What the text talks about here is having it move up and ascent to the Niwan where it refines the root of the hair. By all means keep on breathing subtly, and Dao [the procedure] will become fully natural.

7   象龜引氣至 [致]靈根
Like a turtle drawing in *qi*, guide it to the Numinous Root.

Pull in *qi* through the nose and guide it to the root of the tongue, then swallow it to send it into the belly, where it makes a matching sound like thunder. At this point, perfect *qi* will flow naturally.

* * *

Like a turtle, use the nose to inhale *qi*. When full, stop and breathe out subtly. Close the mouth and swallow it all the way to the Numinous Root.

8   中有真人巾金巾
In the middle is a perfected wearing a golden kerchief.

The Infant wears a scarlet robe and a golden kerchief.

* * *

The perfected in the golden parlor wears a golden kerchief.

9   負甲持符開七門
Clad in armor and holding talismans, he opens the seven gates.

Holding the talismans of the Six Jia, he wards off all wayward *qi* and dispels all wayward specters. As he spreads the *qi* through the seven orifices, eyes and ears become perceptive and keen. Another explanation says that one should have one's back to *zi* [north] while facing *wu* [south]. Hips and beltline match *you* and *mao* [east and west]. The talisman then is the *qi*.

* * *

Armor is *zi* [north], where the back is while facing *wu* [south]. Hips and beltline connect to *you* and *mao* [east and west]. To control and direct primordial *qi*, hold a talisman and practice repeatedly. Sovereign Heaven is the Lord of the Great Dao. Always look for him through the seven gates.

10   此非枝葉實是根
This is neither branch nor leaf: it is indeed the root!

Naturalness is the core of Dao. It is not just an empty phrase.

* * *

The Highest Sovereign, Laozi, Lord of the Great Dao is Great Harmony. Always hold on to him on the right and left and see how he transforms into the myriad beings. They are not mere leaves and branches.

11   晝夜思之可長存
Day and night, always think of it and you can live forever.

Morning and evening think of Dao, never slackening. Open the eyes to see the perfected; close the eyes to think of the spirits. In this way, you can attain long life.

* * *

Always with focused intention think and be aware of it, and naturally you will see the three luminants. The utmost and most wondrous expression of Dao, they are near the center of the Dipper.

12   仙人道士非有神 [異有]
Immortals and Daoists do not have inherent divinity [anything different].[1]

Dao does not have two clans, but is complete and integrated, joining and merging all at the root without recovering the spirits of the earth. Harmonize the mind and stabilize the will, and Dao will rise anew each day.

* * *

Immortals have gone beyond the world: they have no special divinity. Maintain the One and keep it firm and steady, then essence from above does not leak out and essence from below does not disperse. Essence and spirit well maintained within, one can live for a thousand years and not die.

13   積精所致為 [和]專年 [仁]
Rather, by accumulating essence they can concentrate their years [become harmonious, concentrated, and benevolent].

Do not activate yin and yang recklessly nor waste and release essence and spirit. Rather, accumulate essence and hold on to *qi*, and your longevity can reach ten thousand [years].

* * *

Nurture essence and nourish *qi*, focus the mind and unify the intention, thus harmonizing the *qi* in benevolence and righteousness. Thus, potency merges with Dao and perfection.

---

[1] Lines 12-16 are also translated in Puett 2010, 247.

14   人皆 [晝]食穀與五味

Ordinary people constantly [exhaustively] eat grain and take in the five flavors.

Ordinary people eat the essence of soil and earth, and their body dies to recompense earth. Sages eat the *qi* of primordial harmony and their body becomes immortal to recompense heaven.

* * *

Ordinary people all devour the fruit of the hundred grains, the essence of soil and earth. The five flavors and their fragrance continue to make them feel satiated. As they eat their diets, there is no perfect Dao on the inside and consequently they eventually return to the Yellow Springs.

15   獨食太和陰陽氣

Just ingest the *qi* of Great Harmony, matching yin and yang,

Those who study Dao ingest yang *qi* in the morning and eat yin *qi* in the evening. In addition, they also take in primordial *qi*.

* * *

Yin *qi* rises up while yang *qi* sinks down. They meet and assemble in the midst of the six harmonies and bring forth the five flavors. If you always and naturally ingest and eat these, heaven will keep you well supplied.

16   故能不死天相既

And you can reach no-death and align with heaven.[2]

Attain Dao and be in a state of no-death. Years and destiny without end, you match heaven and earth. "Align" means connect.

* * *

Eating and drinking great harmony is the foremost medicine of no-death. If you ingest it without slackening, heaven will naturally keep you well supplied.

17   試 [誠]說五臟各有方

I now try to [truly] explain the five organs and how they each have their direction.

---

[2] The last five lines (12-16) are cited in chapter 4 of the early Tang collection *Sandong zhunang*, in a section on dietary practices (Li 2010a, 114; 2010b, 817).

The fine inner organs are replicas of the five phases. The four limbs match the four seasons. Earth is their chief, situated in the very center.

∗ ∗ ∗

The five inner organs are replicas of the five phases. The six pitchpipes [viscera] are placed around the intestines and stomach.

18   心為國主五臟主［王］
The heart is like the ruler [king] of a country: it rules the five organs.

The heart is like a chicken: unruly and hard to calm down. Each country has wise men who strive for great peace. When the heart is joyful and clear, the body is calm and at peace.

∗ ∗ ∗

The body contains 360 spirits, among whom the heart is chief. Without ever going out the door, it knows all about the world. Without ever stepping down from its hall, it knows all in the four directions.

19   意中 [受意]動靜氣得行
Intention focused [hold intention] in activity and stillness: *qi* attains full function.

This says to visualize and maintain the spirits within, so body and mind are still and at peace. Never startling or moving them recklessly is the reason why *qi* continues to flow smoothly.

∗ ∗ ∗

What follows along with the will never comes to an end. In clear fragrance and pure goodness, *qi* flows naturally.

20   道自持我神明光
Dao naturally supports me: the spirits in their brightness are radiant.

By maintaining the One and envisioning Dao I can fully protect my essence. Then the spirits in their brightness are radiant.

∗ ∗ ∗

Seated firmly, the spirits and I are together. As my breath rises, they are with me, clothing me and feeding me. They stay within and do not pass as guests. Then the sun, moon, and three luminants always protect and maintain each other.

21 畫日昭昭夜自守

Throughout the day they shine forth brightly, at night they naturally rest.

This says that, as long as one thinks of the Infant in the heart, *qi* shines forth brightly. The myriad spirits are well maintained and sun and moon radiate. Thinking of the root in the two kidneys, throughout the day I maintain radiance; at night I maintain the spirits.

* * *

Throughout the day, it is bright outside and the eyes can see. At night when the stars are out, all is murky and vague, and all returns to me.

22 渴自飲 [可得] 漿飢得飽

When thirsty, I just drink [can get] sweet dew; when hungry, I find satiation.

When hungry, I eat the *qi* of pure naturalness; when thirsty, I drink the spring water from the Flowery Pond. In this manner never hungry or thirsty, I can attain long life. [YQ: Never hungry or thirsty, I can attain long life.]

23 經歷六腑藏卯酉

Passing through all six viscera, store it at *mao* and *you*.

The ears are the root. They bring forth the *qi* of the six viscera as it is stored and emerges during the hours *mao* and *you*. Essential and wondrous, it reaches everywhere and cannot be attained.

* * *

The two spirits of the kidneys are the foremost rulers of essence. The left is the King Father; the right is the Queen Mother. The two *qi* intermingle and circulate through the six viscera. Above they meet in the eyes: the left is in the position *mao*; the right in *you*.

24 轉陽之陰藏於九

Revolving yang into yin, store it right at nine.

Yang returns and latches onto yin. They revolve around the organism and overcome each other. It is best to store them at nine. Nine indicates the head. Hence the scripture says: "Left is two, right is seven, store at nine, and dwell at one.

* * *

When yang rules within yang, it multiplies its kind. Yin brings forth the wheat and millet, while yang brings forth flaming fire. As the two *qi* keep turning into each other, they mutually embrace and contain one another. Nine is located in the mouth.

25 常能行之不知老
If you always can practice this, you will never know old age.

Always, at cock crow, lie flat on your bed, unbind the hair, click the teeth thirty-six times, gather the saliva, and swallow the *qi*. This is the way to get rid of death.

* * *

Knowing the male and maintaining the female, their potency will not leave. Knowing the self and maintaining *qi*, constant potency will not be exhausted.

26 肝之為氣修而長
The liver as *qi*: cultivate and lengthen it.

This says to cultivate *qi*, guide it upward to reach the head and supplement the Niwan.

* * *

The liver is the green dragon; the lungs are the white tiger. Above, they penetrate into heaven. Once they connect, they can be lengthened.

27 羅列五臟生三光
Move through the five organs in the right order: generate the three luminants within.

The five palaces and six offices each have their chief. The kidneys, both above and below, each have a sun, moon, or three luminants. The three luminants are and expression for the lords of sun, moon, and stars.

* * *

The heart-mind concentrated and the intention focused, the five inner [powers] never waver. Sit up straight or lie down peacefully and look up to observe the three luminants.

28 上合三焦飲 [下]玉漿
Above merge with the Triple Heater, drink [below] the jade nectar.

The Triple Heater is the prime source of the three passes. When hungry, eat natural *qi*; when thirsty, drink from the spring of the Flowery Pond. You will never again experience hunger or thirst.

"Above merge with the Triple Heater" means to harmonize the six in the center. Then potency will spread to the four limbs and sweat will rise like dew on jade.

29   精候天地長生道 [not in YQ]
Essence attending to heaven and earth: such is the way of long life.

Essence is my spirit; *qi* is my Dao. Hanging on to essence and always thinking of *qi*. Moving it up and down and ingesting it in the directions is the way to regulate it.

* * *

30   我神魂魄在中央 [= 29]
My spirits, cloud spirit agents, and white spirit agents reside in my very center.

The two kidneys are the very center of the cloud and white spirit agents. The cloud spirit agents are on the left; the white spirit agents are on the right. During the day use the cloud spirit agents to maintain the white spirit agents; at night use the white spirit agents to maintain the cloud spirit agents. Embrace the cloud spirit agents and control the white spirit agents, so neither ever moves and acts up.

* * *

Embrace the cloud spirit agents and control the white spirit agents, so neither ever moves and acts up. Both should rest and rise together, never stopping in their rhythm. The Hall of Light is the very center.

31   精 [津]液流泉去鼻香 [= 30]
Liquids [essence] and fluids flow from the source, removing all fragrance from the nose.

When yin and yang intermingle and engage, there is a leak of fluids and loss of essence. Then, when eating and drinking, you have no sense of the five flavors and your nostril lose all sense of smell.

* * *

Essence flowing and fluids issuing is like having a constant source or spring. During the day and at night, whether awake or at rest, widely rinse the mouth and teeth, remove all stench and take in fragrance. In this manner, you can regulate the hair and teeth.

32   立於玄 [懸] 膺含明堂 [= 31]
Centered in the Hanging [Mysterious] Sphincter, there is the Hall of Light.

Below the tongue is the Hanging Sphincter; the lungs are the Hall of Light. Gather *qi* and swallow it, letting it drip into the Hall of Light. Then the fluids will move throughout the body.

* * *

In the Hall of Light, there is three-inch space, both round and square. It is the root that brings forth Dao. About the size of a chicken egg, it is yellow like an orange. Passing through the Mysterious Sphincter, it is sweet like honey.

33   通我華精調陰陽 [= 23A]
It connects my flowery essence as it balances yin and yang.

This says one should nurture essence and nourish spirit. Carrying yin and embracing yang one can balance essence and spirit.

* * *

Yin and yang lined up and spread are like floating stars. Floating stars and the seven regulators enhance flowery essence.

[雷電霹靂往相聞] [= 32][3]
Thunder and lightning, claps and bolts come forth to be heard.

[右酉左卯是吾室] [= 33]
Right *you*, left *mao*: such is my parlor.

In the very center between *wu* in front and *zi* behind, pay proper respects to the Great One. Under the bright glow of the Flowery Canopy, yang *qi* sinks down and rests in the Scarlet Palace.

34   伏於玄 [志] 門候天道
Submit to the Mystery [Volition] Gate and attend on heaven's Dao.

The Gate is the nose. It attends on the one spirit of the upper section.

* * *

The Volition Gate is the Mystery Gate. It attends on heaven's Dao and maintains the dark and white.

---

[3] These two lines are only found in the *YQ* version, with only one line of commentary.

35   近在我 [子] 身還自守
It is close within my [your] body: reverting, it is naturally maintained.
Order and maintain spirit and essence, naturally thinking of them at all times.

* * *

Great Dao is not far off. It is quite close, within the body. You naturally have it, there is no need to pursue it elsewhere.

36   清淨無為神留止
Clear and pure, in nonaction, the spirits rest and remain.

To cultivate Dao on the inside, practice nonaction. To cultivate Dao on the outside, practice being free from desires. When the heart-mind is free from trouble and disturbances, essence and spirits rest and remain.

* * *

Dao is something the wise undertake; it is not something the ignorant practice. Focus the mind and stabilize the will, and the spirits in their brightness will rejoice.

37   精氣 [神] 上下關 [開] 分理
As essence and *qi* [spirits] move up and down, all gates [orifices] are evenly regulated.

When *qi* is well matched and essence always thought of, the upper and lower sections of the body all maintain the spirits in oneness.

* * *

As essence and spirits move up and down, they are vague and obscure and without constancy. Thus, you pursue the mysterious and again mysterious.

[37A   精候天道長生草]
Essence attends on heaven's Dao and becomes a long-life herb.

Above know the heights of heaven; below inspect the patterns of earth. Then you can stay your years and master your destiny. White hair returns to be inky black: this is the long-life herb.

38   七孔 [竅] 已通不知老
The seven orifices fully permeable: you never know old age.

The seven orifices in the head and face are the gates and doors of essence and spirit. As they connect to and benefit body and consciousness, one will never know old age.

***

The ears hear the five tones; the eyes observe the dark and yellow; the nose receives clear *qi*; the mouth tastes the five flavors—thus you never know old age.

39   還坐天門候陰陽
Revert and sit at heaven's gate: attend on yin and yang.

In the morning, ingest yang *qi*; at night, take in yin *qi*. Both assemble in the mouth.

***

Heaven's gate is the gate of the One of great yang. Yin and yang, male and female are subtle and wondrous and hard to observe. Thus, you must sit and carefully attend to them.

40   下於喉嚨通神明 [神明通]
Moving down through the esophagus, it connects to the spirits in their brightness [the spirits in their brightness connect].

The esophagus has twelve hour-pavilions, complete with guards who all hoist jade halberds for its protection. The perfected of the esophagus resides within. He is in charge of the upward and downward movement of *qi*.

***

The esophagus is the throat. As long as you eat and ingest the *qi* of harmony, the spirits in their brightness descend from above.

41   過華蓋下清且涼
Passing to below the Flowery Canopy, all becomes clear and fresh.

The eyebrows are the Flowery Canopy. A spirit resides in them.

***

Below the Flowery Canopy, the five colors are clear and vibrant. In the abyss of clear numinous force, all is "clear and fresh."

42   入清虛 [淵] 見吾形
Entering the clear and empty enclosure [abyss], I see my own form.

Entering through the brain gate, one sees the Niwan Lord.

***

The clear and empty abyss is subtle and wondrous, always connected to the mystery. Close the eyes and engage in inner vision and you can see rivers and oceans attending to and moistening my physical form. At times they seem to look at each other like reflections in a bright mirror. As the deep wells come to face each other, I see them and feel happiness without limit.

43　期成還丹 [年] 可長生
When the period is up, I revert the elixir [years] and attain long life.

Letting go of all naturally assigned years, my body does not decline or age and I attain long life.

* * *

When one gets to be forty or fifty years old, things don't naturally go backwards. Those who understand this pattern can increase vitality every day and attain eternal life. Those who never realize this will inevitably be mired in suffering.

44　還過華池 [下] 動腎精
Reverting [*qi*] to flow [down] past the Flowery Pond, I activate kidney essence.

From the brain gate move it along the spine until you reach the kidneys.

* * *

Below the Flowery Canopy are many hidden springs. The myriad spirits meet and assemble here. Let them repeatedly welcome each other, then pull the kidney *qi* and move it upward into the Purple Palace.

45　望 [立] 於明堂臨 [望] 丹田
Gazing up [standing] at the Hall of Light, I approach [gaze up at] the Elixir Field.

One inch moving in between the eyebrows is the Hall of Light. Three inches further in is the Elixir Field.

* * *

The Hall of Light and the Elixir Field are not far from each other. They are mutually visible.

46　將使諸神開命門
Commanding and directing all the spirits to open my Gate of Destiny.

Pull in perfect *qi* through the nose, continuously day and night. The nose is the root of heaven.

***

One calls this the great spirit, the leader of the myriad beings. Directing and commanding the host of the spirits, one can rescue and safeguard the myriad people, always entering and leaving through the Gate of Destiny.

47   通利天道藏 [存] 靈根
Connecting to and engaging with heaven's Dao, I hold [visualize] the Numinous Root.

The head is round, a replica of heaven; the Numinous Root is the tongue.

***

Nine times nine is eighty-one. To begin, the body divides into two sections, with primordial *qi* flowing continuously from head to feet and circulating all around the body. The Numinous Root should be firm and stable. Maintain it without stopping.

48   陰陽列布如流星
Yin and yang align and spread like floating stars.

The face has seven orifices, which are a replica of the seven stars. As yin reaches its extreme and moves into yang, observe the sun and look out to see the stars arranged above. Then essence is active while *qi* spreads out and you can enter the mysterious court.

***

The three *qi* ascend and descend, opening and closing the three passes, the hundred conduits and nine orifices. *Qi* attends to them, making them shiny and lustrous, radiant and bright, as it arranges itself and spreads throughout the skin like sprinkled stars.

49   肝氣似環 [周還] 終無端
The liver *qi* is like a ring [circles and reverts], without end or beginning.
Liver *qi* revolves and flows through the body. It resembles a ring without end.

***

The liver is the green dragon; it issues on my left. The lungs are the white tiger; they reside on my right. The Dao of spirit is vague and obscure, without beginning or end.

50   肺之為氣三焦起
The lungs as *qi* rise from the Triple Heater.

Lung *qi* issues from the three passes. The Pass of Heaven is the mouth; the Pass of Humanity is the chest; and the Pass of Earth is the lower section of the body.

* * *

The lungs have three leaves. They rise from the Triple Heater. Also called the Flowery Canopy, their color is a purplish red.

51   伏於 [上座] 天門候故道
Submit to [above rest at] heaven's gate and attend on the Dao of old.

"Heaven's gate" is the mouth and throat. "Dao" is the door that connects to the brain.

* * *

The Dao of heaven passes through the male gate; thus it constitutes the root and base. Visualizing the root and maintaining the base, one can attain long life.

52   清 [津] 液醴泉通六府
Clear [liquids and] fluids as sweet spring connect to the six viscera.

Rinse and wash the Flowery Pond, letting its liquid drip to soak the root of the tongue, then have it flow further to connect to the large intestine, small intestine, gall bladder, stomach, bladder, and Gate of Destiny. They are the six offices/viscera.

53   隨鼻上下開二 [兩] 耳
Moving up and down through the nose, it opens both the ears.

Primordial *qi* leaves and enters through the nose. Moving up and down, it connects to the ears. Going along with it allows it to function.

* * *

Close in *qi* and contract the nostrils. After a long time, begin to breathe very subtly, inhaling and exhaling primordial *qi*, moving it up, then moving it down. As you keep on contracting the nostrils, you will open the ears.

54   窺視天地存童子
Examining heaven and looking at earth, visualize the lad [within].

Heaven is the head; the earth is the lower section. The lad should be visualized and envisioned: thus you maintain the one spirit.

* * *

Look up at heaven's gate and see the three luminants. Look down at the patterns of earth and see the little lad.

55 調和精華理髮齒
Balancing and harmonizing flowery essence, regulate hair and teeth.

This tells people to breathe in the five *qi*, click the teeth thirty-six times, and swallow the saliva thirty-six times. In this manner you can regulate the dark and white.

* * *

As regards essence and fluids in the Flowery Pond, always at cock crow click the teeth thirty-six times, then swallow the saliva. Always activate the throat to open and close the nine orifices. All this reaches up into the head and regulates hair and teeth.

56 顏色光澤老不 [不復] 白
Color radiant, complexion glossy, even if old there is no [more] white [hair].

This tells people to ward off white [hair] and stop the years. Then their eyes and facial complexion generate radiance and glossiness. Their hair will never again be white.

* * *

Gates and doors wide open, essence and spirits spread and harmonize. Then color and complexion are radiant and moist, hair and beard are lustrous and shiny, never again turning white.

57 下于喉嚨何落落
Moving down through the esophagus, how can it possibly be scattered?

The esophagus has twelve pavilions, whose chiefs hoist jade halberds for its protection.

* * *

Visualizing and attending to the Dao of heaven, there will never be any trouble. *Qi* scattered like rocks, the heart is singularly joyful.

58 諸神皆會相求索
All the many spirits assemble jointly: with them pursue close linkage.

This says that all the spirits assemble and meet. With mind and intention visualize them in the eight extremes.

* * *

Great Dao wanders and frolics as the numerous spirits meet and assemble. They interchange and flow about, moving freely to and fro in Great Simplicity.

59　下入絳宮紫華色
Then move down and enter the Scarlet Palace, in its purple flowery color.

This speaks of the spirit of the heart being of red *qi* and purple color.

* * *

Moving down, they enter the Scarlet Palace, with its cinnabar walls and buildings of gold and purple awnings. They move freely to and from in all its four quarters.

60　隱藏華蓋通神 [觀通] 廬
Hide and store it in the Flowery Canopy, connect it to the Spirit [observe it connecting to the] Hut.

The eyebrows are the Flowery Canopy. Below they connect the *qi* all the way to the nose.

* * *

At night contained in the Flowery Canopy, during the day it wanders to the Hall of Light. Observing and looking at the Spirit Hut, the golden casket is my home.

61　專守心神傳相呼
Concentrate the heart-mind, maintain its spirit, matching them with every exhalation.

Visualize and envision the spirit of the heart and think of him as the ruler of the country. The various other spirits are the people. Using the exhalation, you can summon them. None will refuse to come.

* * *

The heart-mind is the ruler of the country, residing in the Palace of the Great One. Concentrating the heart-mind and unifying the intention, one gets closer to great yang. Tightening the will and keeping all clear and pure, the host of spirits are happy and joyful. Call upon them, and they all come.

62 觀我諸神 [神明] 辟除 [諸] 邪
I observe all the spirits [in their brightness], driving out and eliminating anything [all] wayward.

Focus your will and reach out internally to see the spirits in their brightness. Then wayward *qi* will never again dare to affect you.

* * *

The One settled in the center, the many spirits are stable and stand guard. At this time, look up to observe the radiant spirits in their state of primordial yang. Child Cinnabar will drive out the myriad forms of wayward *qi*.

63 脾神還歸依大家
The spirit of the spleen reverts and returns, close to the great homestead.

The Infant reverts and enters the Yellow Court. The spleen is the ruler of the center, in charge and control of all in the four directions. He represents the depth of Dao.

* * *

The spirit of the spleen in the morning comes to the Hall of Light and at night returns to his palace. Therefore, he is close to the great homestead, that is, the Great Storehouse.

64 藏養靈根不復枯 [= 65]
Contain and nourish the Numinous Root, never again allow it to wither.

This tells people to nourish the Numinous Root and never allow it to dry up or be parched. Underneath the tongue is a sweet spring that issues like a string of pearls. Always contain and swallow it, never expelling it recklessly.

* * *

To contain and nourish the Numinous Root, gradually moisturize and balance *qi*, filling the mouth [with saliva] and swallowing it. Doing so, the interior will never wither or dry up.

65 至 [致] 於胃管通虛無 [元] [= 64]
Reaching through the stomach duct, connect to emptiness and nonbeing [primordiality].

The original text lacks this one sentence. I add it based on the Lin edition.

* * *

The stomach duct is the entrance to the Great Storehouse. The Palace of Emptiness and Nonbeing is in Great Antecedence.

66   閉塞命門似 [如] 玉都
Close and seal the Gate of Destiny as if it were [just like] the Jade Capital.

People's life is linked with destiny through tied-up essence. Always love and nourish this tied-up essence, never activating or leaking it recklessly. Rather, essence should be coagulated it like jade, resting in the lower section.

* * *

Shut the gate and close the door, and you can know the Dao of heaven. The yang side of the jade halls, the capital city of the spirits, is where the myriad beings are valued and counted.

67   壽傳萬歲將 [年] 有餘[4]
Receive longevity of ten thousand years: there [years] will be a surplus.

This tells people to abandon all leanings and stay their years. As they revert the elixir and nourish destiny, their body does not grow weak or old and they can attain long life.

* * *

Ordinary people have excessive wealth; sages have excessive years. Their longevity and destiny are without limit.

68   脾中之神遊 [住] 中宮
With the spirit in the spleen, I wander through [rest in] the Central Palace.

The spleen is located above the Great Storehouse. It is the hall where Lord Lao holds audience every morning. Then, he wanders up to the palace of the Hall of Light, where he becomes the Lord of the Great One.

* * *

The Central Palace in the position *wuji* presides over the earth office. The myriad beings arise as the children of earth and soil. The spleen is the Hall of Light. Its spirit rules the Central Palace.

---

[4] As Thomas E. Smith points out (personal communication), Lines 60-67 follow the rhyme of the beginning of *Neijing* 35, while lines 68-92 more or less follow the rhyme of its long second part.

PART THREE / 75

69   朝會五神 [藏] 和 [列] 三光
In audience, I encounter the five spirits [organs] and [plus] the three luminants.

The palace of the spleen is the central office where all the various spirits assemble. Underneath its towers, the three luminants, sun and moon, shine forth.

* * *

The five organs and six offices all serve as residences for the spirits in their brightness. The sun and the moon assemble each morning in proper order. Look up to observe the three luminants: sun, moon, and Dipper.

70   上合天氣 [門] 及 [合] 明堂
Above I merge with heaven's *qi* [gate] and [with] the Hall of Light.

Once *qi* has moved up and ascended, it moves down and reverts to the gall bladder, then it assembles in the Hall of Light.

* * *

As heaven's gate opens and closes, *qi* issues as male and female and the three luminants are generated. It is close to the Hall of Light, round above and square below. All exists in its midst.

71   通利六府調五行
Connecting with and engaging the six viscera, I balance the five phases.

The five organs and six viscera each have their rulers. The five phases below are patterned on the five constants [virtues]. Above they form preside over the five planets.

* * *

Calm the spirit and nourish the self, and the six viscera will be connected and wide open. Wayward *qi* is expelled and leaves, while proper *qi* maintains the essence of the five phases within. Metal, wood, water, fire, and earth and their expressions.

72   金木水火土為王
Treating them all—metal, wood, water, fire, and earth—as kings.

Metal is white; wood is green; water is black; fire is red; and earth is yellow. Those are the rulers in charge and control of the four directions.

* * *

The five phases generate each other, with earth being their chief. The myriad beings in their many different species all return to earth.

73 通利血脈汗為漿
Connecting and engaging with blood vessels and [*qi*] conduits, sweat becomes sweet nectar.

When the five inner [organs] are calm and at peace, the blood vessels are not agitated. Then there are sufficient sweat and body fluids, a sign of the spirits in their brightness.

* * *

Harmonizing *qi* and nourishing essence, the blood vessels and [*qi*] conduits are vibrant and full. The bones are glossy and the tendons strong, while the skin is lustrous and moist, and sweat issues like sweet nectar.

74 二神相得下 [化] 玉英 [= 75]
The two spirits join to attain it, descending as [transforming into] jade blossoms.

This says that Dao has male and female who revolve around each other and mutually join to form jade. The two never harm each other.

* * *

The spirits of the sun and the moon revolve according to yin and yang. During the day, they dwell in the Hall of Light, where they transform to generate a yellow glow. This then flows down into the mouth, filling it as if with the flavor of nonbeing. Keep on applying this without stopping.

75 上稟元 [天] 氣年 [命] 益長 [= 76]
Moving up, they gather primordial [heavenly] *qi*: my years are [destiny is] ever longer.

This says that by ingesting primordial *qi*, you will not harm the inner [organs] and essence and *qi* will be in harmony with spirit. Then you can live as long as 300 years and become an earth immortal, wandering freely among people.

* * *

Sit upright and raise the head to look up, so the nose can receive the *qi* of Highest Clarity. Step with your feet on firm soil, so you can follow pure yang, and the four limbs will be calm and at peace. Respect and honor the prohibitions of heaven, and your destiny will increase tremendously.

76   循 [修] 護七竅去不祥 [= 74]
Moving along, I guard [cultivate] the seven orifices, eliminating all that's inauspicious.

The face has seven orifices that all should be open and connected. The ears and eyes should be keen and perceptive, sound and voices should be pleasing and beautiful. Wayward *qi* does not arise; joyful *qi* comes about naturally.

* * *

The same cavities yet different orifices, each divide into east and west. Always cultivate and guard what the spirits in their brightness depend on, releasing and eliminating all that is not conducive, and the myriad beings naturally transform.

77   日月列布張陰陽
The sun and moon align and spread, extending yin and yang.

This speaks about the two eyes. The left eye is the sun, the King Father in charge of yang. The right eye is the moon, the Queen Mother in charge of yin.

* * *

The sun and the moon radiate and illuminate the myriad beings. Look up to see how yin and yang establish themselves and expand widely, making sure the four seasons are in balance and harmony. All these four activities are also present in the physical body.

78   伏於太陰成其形 [= 79]
Yield to great yin to complete the physical form.

This speaks of the baby in the womb, deeply hidden and carefully protected. Yin completes its form.

* * *

The little lad of great yin is the Infant deity in the [constellation] Dark Warrior. Hide him and never let him rise up. Rather, I circulate yang into yin and thus complete my physical form, always visualizing the old child in Great Simplicity.

79   五臟之主腎為精 [= 78]
The ruler of the five organs, the kidneys, brings forth essence.

The kidneys are attached to the spine and located about three inches below the navel. Their ruler expels essence and *qi*. On his head he carries the sun and moon, stars and chronograms.

* * *

The *qi* of the kidneys should be clear and fragrant. The right is the Queen Mother; the left is the King Father. The left is the green dragon; the right is the white tiger. Both connect to heaven.

80　出入二竅入 [合] 黃庭
In and out through the two orifices, it enters [merges with] the Yellow Court.

This says that primordial *qi* moves through the nose and mouth, issuing and entering through these two orifices and from there connects to the Yellow Court. The Yellow Court is the spleen.

* * *

Moving in and out through the two orifices between the two hands, the personage in the Yellow Court, in charge of spirits and immortals, desires to attain residence within me, as I enter the towering mountains.

81　呼吸虛無見吾形
Inhaling and exhaling [in a state of] emptiness and nonbeing, I see my physical form.

Make tight fists and refine the physical form and you will naturally come to envision the form of emptiness and nonbeing.

* * *

Emptiness and nonbeing are vague and obscure, hard to express in words. Inhaling and exhaling primordial *qi* circulates around without end. I desire to see my physical form as if standing close to an abyss.

82　強我筋骨血脈成 [盛]
Strengthening my tendons and bones, my blood vessels and [*qi*] conduits complete [all full].

This says that the bones get lighter and the flesh soars. Flesh transforms into bones while intestines transform into tendons. Blood transforms into essence while spirit transforms into the elixir. Then you become a spirit immortal.

* * *

Essence and *qi* not leaking out, bones and marrow are complete and dense. Always, I am naturally strong and vigorous; blood vessels and [*qi*] conduits are smooth and full. As they move along like oxen and horses, the entire body never gets tired.

83 恍惚不見過清靈
Vague and obscure, I see nothing as I pass through clear numen.

This says to sit and completely let go of all, pass through the brain gate to change and transform along with nonbeing and [original] constancy.

* * *

In the midst of vagueness and obscurity, there is a being; in the midst of clear numen, there is a form, its image vague and obscure. In the midst of great Dao, there is the One: none can see its light.

84 坐於廬下觀 [見] 小童
Sitting below the Hut, I observe [see] the little lad.[5]

The nose is the Hut. Below it, observe the little lad.

* * *

Below the Spirit Hut, in the wilderness of the golden casket, look to observe the perfected and see how the little lad searches out the area beneath the Flowery Canopy.

85 日夕 [內息] 存在 [思存] 神明光
Morning and evening [as I breathe in] I visualize [imagine] the spirits in their brightness fully radiant.

At sunrise and sunset visualize the spirits, never letting them leave the body. Their radiance and glow are always before my eyes.

* * *

Close the eyes and engage in inner vision, visualize the spirits in their brightness and come to see my own radiance. Looking up and down, they appear to me in green, red, white, and yellow.

---

[5] In the YQ edition, this line repeats again after line 90, with *yingjian* 鷹間 (in the Sphincter) replacing *luxia* 廬下 (below the Hut). The commentary here says: "The jade spirit of the golden casket is the little lad. He sits inside the Hut matching the way of the immortals. See the little lad and attend on him. When I see him firmly, my Dao is complete."

86   出於無 [天] 門入無戶 [間]
Emerging through nonbeing's [heaven's] gate, I enter without doors [space].

Once people have attained Dao, they can conceal themselves whether emerging or entering, acting or walking. They do not move through gates or doors.

* * *

Emerging through heaven's gate, see the four neighborhoods. Entering into the spaceless, see Great Mystery. In Great Mystery is the gate to all wonders.

87   恬淡無欲養華根 [莖]
Quiet and bland, free from desires, I nourish the Flowery Root [stalk].

As one is quiet and bland, free from desires, Dao naturally comes to stay. Cultivating and practicing the dark [mysterious] and white, I nourish the root of black hair.

* * *

Leisurely residing in a quiet location, deeply stabilize the numinous pearl. In simplicity, discard all that is worldly and ordinary; with strong push and hard strength, pursue what is deep. Harbor and nourish the jade stalk, and your complexion will be like peach blossoms.

88   服食玄氣可遂生
Absorbing and ingesting mysterious *qi*, I can follow life.

This speaks of absorbing and ingesting the white *qi* between the two kidneys. Hence it says "mysterious *qi*."

* * *

On the outside there is Great Mystery; on the inside there is the Great Abyss. If you let it flow like ordinary people, it will merge with the four seas. But if you always absorb and ingest it, you can attain continuous aliveness.

89   還返 [過] 七門飲太 [大] 淵
Reverting and returning [passing through] the seven gates, I sip from the Great Abyss.

This says that there are seven orifices in the face that should all be connected and open. Sipping from the Great Abyss means to swallow and ingest the sweet spring in the mouth.

                      * * *

The jade nectar of the Great Abyss is sweet like honey. It is close within my own body, but you won't know where exactly. Obtain it: the well of Penglai.

90   通 [道] 我喉嚨 [懸鷹] 過青靈

Connecting [moving] through the esophagus [Hanging Sphincter], I pass the green numinous force.

Qi is Dao. *Qi* moves down from the esophagus and settles in the gall bladder.

                      * * *

The abyss of Great Clarity is cool and clear in accordance with the times. The Numinous Terrace extends to the four directions. Observe the Hanging Sphincter and see the *qi* descend all the way to the Great Storehouse.

91   問於仙道與奇功

I ask about the Dao of the immortals and all the marvelous powers.

The immortals have 3600 different methods that relate to myriad ends. They include many arts of attaining Dao, being endowed with *qi*, maintaining naturalness, and not dying. Each of them, moreover, comes with marvelous powers.

                      * * *

"Dao of the immortals" refers to emptiness, nonbeing, and naturalness. Without moving, one arrives; raising a foot, one covers ten thousand miles. Sitting, one is present; standing, one is gone. Its marvelous recipes are the medicines of not dying.

92   服食靈芝 [芝草] 與玉 [紫華] 英

I absorb and ingest numinous mushrooms [mushrooms and herbs] as well as jade [purple flowery] blossoms.[6]

---

[6] The word *zhi* 芝 refers to a form of mushroom that grows in soft soil as well as on trees. It is particularly associated with immortality, since "it is said to absorb the earthy vapors and to leave a heavenly atmosphere" (Stuart 1976, 271). G. A. Stuart suggests the translation "moss," then specifies *zhi* of different colors associated with the five sacred mountains and effective for particular health conditions (1976, 271-72). "Numinous mushroom" (*lingzhi*) is Ganoderma Lucidum, used widely in medicine and Daoism. See Wachtel-Galor et al. 2011; Lu 2015.

Not only famous mountains grow mushrooms, herbs, and jade blossoms. They are also present within the five organs. Always absorb them from within the organs and you can live as long as heaven and earth.

* * *

Cut off the five grains and eliminate the core starches, and the jade maidens of the Six Ding naturally arrive and serve you. They help you obtain mushrooms and herbs, golden and purple, flowery and shining. Get and ingest them.

93   頭戴白素足丹田
On my head I wear the white and undyed; my feet step on the Elixir Field.

With the moon as a cap and the sun for slippers, I revert essence to supplement the brain. This is called the Dao of refining the physical form, living long, and not dying.

* * *

The perfected have come to stay. They always desire to get people to attain spirit immortality. During the day their heads are black, at night they take on a white sheen like pure simplicity. Their feet step on the Elixir Field.

94   沐浴華池灌 [生] 靈根
I bathe and rinse the Flowery Pond, letting it drip to [grow] the Numinous Root.

The Flowery Pond is the mouth. The Numinous Root is the tongue. Always rinse and wash with its sweet spring, letting it drip to soak the root of the tongue.

* * *

"I bathe and rinse the Flowery Pond" means to refine the body in the Elixir Field. To do so, it is essential to moisten the Numinous Root. The Flowery Pond is the Jade Pond.

95   三府相得開命門
The three offices all evenly matched, I open the Gate of Destiny.

The Grotto Chamber, Flowery Canopy, and Hall of Light are the main offices. The Gate of Destiny is the nose. Open and connect it to yin and yang, they come together at the ears and eyes. This causes them to be keen and perceptive.

* * *

Laozi and Great Harmony each represent one office. Together they wait upon the Lord of the Dao. Always open and close the Gate of Destiny, and yang brightness persists without end.

96   五味皆至善氣還
The five flavors all attained, good *qi* reverts.

Rinsing and filling the mouth with sweet spring, the five flavors are attained. Reverting the elixir and refining the physical form one can attain long life.

* * *

In the six harmonies, the five flavors arise naturally. Expand and ingest them, and proper *qi* comes of itself.

97   大道蕩蕩心勿煩 [= 98]
The great Dao vast and open, my heart is free from trouble.

The great Dao is like a river or the sea: reaching for it, there is no end. Keep on thinking of the practice and maintain the One, never letting the manifold thoughts and worries frighten or disturb the spirit.

* * *

"The great Dao vast and open" means that it is radiant and expansive. Centered in Dao one is not troubled; troubled, one cannot be centered in Dao. Hence it is important to pursue the formless.

98   被髮行之可長存 [= 97]
Unbind the hair to practice this and you can remain forever.

Dividing the hair and ingesting the essence of the sun and the moon, you can engage in mutual protection with them. This means, you attain long life.

* * *

The great Dao has ten thousand ends in skin and hair. Lying down to sleep, one can refine the body in all five colors. This way, one can attain long life.

99   吾言畢矣勿妄傳
Thus, my words end. Do not transmit them recklessly.

This Dao must not be transmitted recklessly to the wrong people.

* * *

The "I" in this is the Central Lord Lao. He has explained how the Dao of heaven can be generated from head to foot. Do not transmit this to the wrong people lest Dao will be obscured. Be very, very careful!

The Inner Scripture

Preface by Liangqiuzi[1]

Now, the myriad things [dharmas] take the human being as their ruler, while human beings take the heart as first patriarch. Without a ruler, the myriad things do not arise; without the heart, the human body is not established. Both things and the heart have numerous gates: their usage and application are not one. They function in the mode of being and nonbeing, going along with events and according with universal workings. For this reason, there are the distinctions of ordinary and sagely, shallow and deep, ignorant and wise, perfect and false. None of them is not distinguished and recognized by heart and spirit: they are the cause of all ongoing functions.

Now, the Dao of the world is such that all the different paths return to the same root, and all the hundred thoughts arrive at the same point. From the gross to the wondrous, there are in fact two steps: matching traces and tallying with perfection, right and wrong are joined in one view. The *Huangting neijing jing* (Inner Lights Scripture of the Yellow Court) contains the secrets of Eastern Florescence, bears witness to the essential wonder of learning how to become a feathery being.

As long as there are excessive folds and the [internal] circuit is not yet complete, one observes and imagines only crude gains, calculating the myriad numinous items and actively molding the unified form. The meaning has four patriarchs, meeting brightness in seven characters. It points at things using images and metaphors, speaking both on the inside and outside. More than driving out perception and destroying the organism, in leisure going along with *xu* and following *si*, I lick my brush and rub my ink, abruptly bequeath original divination.

---

[1] The two prefaces are translated from YQ 11.1ab and 1b-9b, respectively. They do not appear in the *Xiuzhen shishu*.

Preface by Wuchengzi

The Lord Great Emperor of Fusang ordered the Divine King of the Valley of the Rising Sun to transmit [the teaching] to Mistress Wei [Wei Huacun].[2] The Divine King of the Valley of the Rising Sun is a minister of the Great Emperor. When he handed over this scripture, he arrived together with the Lord Green Lad. The Mistress at the time was in Xiuwu 修武 district.

According to the *Huangting neijing* (Inner Lights [Scripture] of the Yellow Court), the spleen is the Gate of Destiny of the Yellow Court, the Hall of Light in the central section [of the body]. Lord Lao resides there; thus, the text says, "The inner person of the Yellow Court wears a robe of brocade" [4.1]. Three inches behind the navel, this area is known as the Gate of Destiny of the Yellow Court, which is why it is also said that deep within the Gate of Destiny there are the Primordial King of the Yellow Court and the Great Lord of the Mysterious Towers. It is just like in the head they call it the Niwan and locate it in the Grotto Chamber.

This scripture takes emptiness and nonbeing as its chief theme, and uses the Yellow Court as their main marker. As for "lights," this indicates the spirits. There are thirteen major spirits in the text, all indicating the inner lights of the body and called by specific names.

Beyond this, there is also the *Laojun waijing jing* (Lord Lao's Outer Lights Scripture). Thus, the various perfected speak of the *Neiwai Huangting* [*jing*]. Juanzi 涓子 says,[3] "The *Neiwai Huangting* [*jing*] are separate texts. The names of the spirits and the eight major lights are not the same."

Also, there are gaps in the transmission and handing down, so applications and functions vary in places. Names and garb being different, the source and root are also separate. For example, The Great Ultimate and Great Tenuity are items that name regions.

The work is also called *Taishang qinxin wen* 太上琴心文 (Text of the Most High on Strumming the Heart).

"Strumming" means harmonizing. Reciting the text, one can establish harmony among the six viscera, calm the heart and spirit, and set the cause

---

[2] In ancient mythology, Fusang is the tree where the ten suns rest and rise. The Valley of the Rising Sun is where they bathe, located on the shores of the Eastern Sea (Kim 1999, 250-51; Kamitsuka 1990).

[3] Juanzi, according to the *Liexian zhuan*, was an ancient immortal who received divine instructions and compiled the *Qinxin*, an alternative title of the *Huangting jing* (Kaltenmark 1988, 68).

for attaining spirit immortality. This [sentence of] seventeen words is commentary to the original scripture.

Another name is *Dadi jinshu* 大帝金書 (Golden Book of the Great Emperor).

The Lord Great Emperor of Fusang recited it in his palace every day and had it carved on golden tablets. Therefore, it is also called *Golden Book*. These twenty-one words are commentary to the original scripture.

Yet another appellation is *Donghua yupian* 東華玉篇 (Jade Chapters of Eastern Florescence).

Eastern Florescence is the name of the All-square Palace [Fangshu gong 方諸宮], the residence of the Lord Green Lad in the eastern sea. There jade maidens and immortals all recite and chant this text. It is carved in jade writing and therefore called *Jade Chapters*. These thirty-three words are commentary to the original scripture.

Now, if you recite the text just like the spirit immortals in these two palaces, you will not just expel wayward *qi*, but properly speaking harmonize the spirits. Once you have completed ten thousand rounds of recitation, you attain full comprehension of the scripture. However, if you don't rely on the following observances, you will face a major obstacle.

Undergo a cleansing fast for ninety days and chant the text ten thousand times.

That is to say, first fast for ninety days, then proceed with the recitation. Without the ninety-day fast, how can you recite the text ten thousand times? As for the actual recitation, the number of days has no set limit. Concentrating fully on the method, you can do twenty rounds in one day and night. If you are still engaged otherwise and have affairs to deal with, you can use your leisure time and maybe complete four or five rounds. To count ten rounds, you can also use bows and prostrations. Once you have finished the set number of rounds but feel that you are not yet connecting to its original impulse, you can also recite it in your heart without stopping.

Doing so, you will balance and harmonize the three cloud spirit agents, control and refine the seven white spirit agents, eliminate and expel the three deathbringers, pacify and harmonize the six viscera. The five organs will generate florescence, your complexion will return to that of a young child, the hundred diseases can no longer harm you, and disasters and misfortunes will no longer affect you.

Once you finish ten thousand rounds, you will naturally connect to and observe ghosts and spirits, internally see your intestines and stomach, and gain a clear vision of your five organs. At that time, there will be the perfected of the Yellow Court and jade maidens of Central Florescence who come to teach you how to become a spirit immortal.

Working with this path of no-death, as you open your eyes and look outside, you will see ghosts and spirits approach your body; as you fold your hands and turn your vision inward, you will find your organs and viscera pervaded and separate. At this point you get to a stage where there is no more boundary between inside and outside and sojourning perfected descend in their divine presence. Soon they bestow the mysterious teaching upon you and give you wondrous instructions for practice. This is called no-death: it means that you will live as long as heaven and earth. What else can you possibly ask for?

Once you have the characteristics of an immortal, you can get this book from me.

"Me" here is the way the Divine King of the Valley of the Rising Sun refers to himself. This text describes the arrangement of the divine parlors in the physical form and the exact location of the embryonic spirits. There are many spirits in the physical form, and they cannot all be exhaustively explained. However, you can envision their parlors and residences, and prepare to penetrate their trusty secrets.

The embryonic spirits are the three Lords Lao in the Hall of Light, generally called the great spirits of embryonic numen. They represent is the key root of the *Huangting* [*jing*]. Constantly reciting and chanting it, the spirits' parlors are bright and proper, the embryonic perfected are calm and at peace, the numinous fluids flow freely, and the hundred passes are lucid and clear.

Also, blood and marrow are stocked to overflowing and the intestines and stomach are empty and plenteous—empty since they are free from dregs and defilements, plenteous since are always full of liquids and fluids. We call this state the six *qi* being plenteous and full, the spirit bright and numinous. The five organs combine their florescence, ears and eyes are perceptive and keen, decayed teeth will grow again while white hair returns to blackness.

The reason you can eliminate the disorder and likeness of all wayward *qi* and maladies is that I have [in this text] provided the personal and family names of the cloud spirit agents' essences as well as of the six weblines.

Disorder and likeness are like chaos and confusion. The five organs and the gall bladder form the six weblines: they support the essence and vibrancy of the spirit and cloud spirit agents. When the physical form is stocked with the cloud spirit agents' essence, even if someone says they want to die, this cannot possibly happen. Thus, the *Inner Lights of the Yellow Court* outlines the path of no- death.

Death in people is always the separation of the spirits from the physical form. Now, if the physical form is permanently stocked, the spirits stay and do not wander off. If the spirits are always calm, the physical form is complete and free from destruction. As long as the two maintain each other, where could death sprout from? Even though someone may say that they want to depart, how can that happen?

If you follow this path, even if you cannot quite control the lights and climb up into emptiness to attend high banquets in Highest Clarity, you are completely free from the affliction of death. Physical form is steady and spirit is spotless. On the inside, you penetrate the numinous forces in the body; on the outside, you meet glowing sages as they descend. Living in seclusion, you attain great pervasion and once you reach this to the utmost, when you sit upright [in meditation], you can summon the perfected, no longer waiting to wander beyond the fish trap and rabbit snare.[4] How can there be anything more than that?

In order to receive the text, you must fast for nine, seven, or at least three days, and only then can you receive it. The one bestowing it should be a teacher; the one receiving it should venerate this teacher. If there are multiple disciples, they should combine their fasts. The number of fasting days depends on their bodily condition and social circumstances. If they walk about a lot in the dust and grime of the world, they must fast for an accumulation of days to get themselves properly cleansed. If they reside in the clear and orderly world of the mountains, three days should be sufficient. When they bind themselves in the covenant and swear their oath, they must be careful not to divulge anything.

In the old days, when there was a covenant, disciples pledged ninety feet of mysterious, cloudy brocade plus forty feet of gold-threaded, phoenix-patterned gauze and nine pairs of golden knobs. They also had to cut off their hair and drink blood to represent their commitment to not divulge anything. The objects given show rare silks from the homestead of the spirits, not commonly available in the red district of this world.

Today, instead of brocade, you can use white silk; for gauze you can use green cloth; and for the knobs you can use golden buttons. These are sufficient as pledges for the nine heavens as long as they are reported properly to the three bureaus. Numerous scriptures also mention pledges in the form of

---

[4] This refers to the passage in *Zhuangzi* 26: "The fish trap exists because of the fish; once you've gotten the fish, you can forget the trap. The rabbit snare exists because of the rabbit; once you've gotten the rabbit, you can forget the snare." The two are metaphors for technical tools and concrete instructions.

gold dragons and jade fish. All these are precious and valuable, things that can be managed in a cold space, which is why one can also hear about other comparable objects.

Now, gauze and brocade are different types but one must select the most concentrated and clear ones that in their nature go beyond ordinary people's work and in principle match established representations. The nine yards of silk should be woven in one piece; the buttons should be smaller and more delicate than the knobs. To submit them, one should use nine ounces of gold and make nine pairs, matching both richness and leanness. All this should be offered to venerate the teacher who holds the scripture, then scattered in a cold space.

If you violate the covenant or betray the contract, your ancestors of seven generations will be judged at the [Yellow] Springs in the Valley of the Rising Sun and you yourself will become a lowly ghost and be beset by wind and knives.

This is in accordance with the oral instructions of the spirit immortals of the Valley of the Rising Sun. These seven words are commentary to the original scripture.

Anyone who receives this book can transmit it to nine others. Most scriptures frequently mention that transmission is limited to three people every 700 years, but this is not the actual standard of the world. Today, although there is a limit with regard to the number of people, there is no regulation about the time span involved, but many say that one should stop with once in a lifetime.

Generally, when inspecting the physical form and *qi* [of a transmission candidate], he or she must be compassionate and benevolent, loyal and honest, dote on the mystery and focus fully on perfection. If he never jeopardizes perfection and proper order but shows deep respect for and delight in spirit immortality, he can be shown the book. Anyone who does not naturally have the right aptitude is bound to leak and divulge it.

Diligently measure who you can give it to, even though finding clear testimony may be difficult. Quite possibly someone may not be able to protect it always, either starts out diligent and ends up lax or is good about it in the beginning and turns bad later on. However, if in her true disposition she is compassionate and benevolent, focused and honest, dotes on the mystery and relishes immortality, she is bound to not again encounter misfortune and punishment. On occasion, when you cannot fully see these six virtues, follow what the text says later, and better be cautious and keep it secret.

Also, it is most excellent to first look for impulse and response, inspect and question emptiness and numinous force. In general, if there is a person you can transmit [the text] to, you should also have a dream that declares and awakens. As the time gets closer, you should in addition feel a mysterious sense of liberation in your heart. The formalities of disclosure are severe and the process is quite like walking on the edge of a precipitous ravine. As a master of the *Huangting neijing*, in all cases better be cautious and keep it secret, in accordance with the instructions of the perfected of clear emptiness.

Now, the *Huangting neijing jing* is the *Jinshu* (Golden Book) of the Lord Great Emperor of Fusang. It contains secret words on how to refine perfection. These twenty-six words are commentary to the original scripture.

According to these two works, the outline of the observances and standards regarding transmission is not part of the original text of the golden book written in jade characters revealed by [the lords] Fusang and Eastern Florescence. Rather, they are oral instructions issued by two technicians at the time transmission to the Southern Perfected. For this reason, they contain both main text and words of commentary.

To declaim the *Huangting neijing jing*, always use a separate parlor, burn incense, and undergo proper cleansing, then take hold of the book. Whenever you wish to declaim this scripture, always act like this. Set up a high seat and face east, burn incense, bathe and cleanse yourself, tie your sash, and open the scripture on top of the table. Soften your voice and sound as you sing and intone, recite and chant, never allowing yourself to hesitate or make a mistake.

When you hesitate or make a mistake, proceed according to the rites for dissolving friction and once again declaim the previous thirty words. When you notice you have completed ten rounds, get up and perform a prostration. As long as you are in possession of this scripture, you can avoid the hundred forms of wayward *qi*.

If you ever enter a mountainous or forested, uninhabited or dark place, and in your heart feel trembling and terror, straighten your heart by facing north and declaiming the *Neijing* for one round. Stop once your spirit is still and your intention level, and you feel as if you were traveling together with a thousand people.

As all forms of wayward *qi* are eliminated, the spirits are at peace. At that point you will no longer face any afflictions caused by doubt or fear. If you manage to declaim the text ten thousand times, you will naturally see your five organs, intestines, and stomach as well as the various ghosts and spirits in all under heaven. You can control and order them to rest within yourself. Once you see them clear and lucid, the outside will mirror this and be equally pervaded. Jade maidens will come to you, descending to supervise the ghosts and spirits. What else would you need to control and order them about?

If you ever face hardship or disease, declaim the text by visualizing it in your mind, and you will be healed even if close to death. You may be unable to hold the actual book, that's why you should declaim the text by visualizing it in your mind. If you don't have the stamina to recite it from head to tail, just pick out the names of the spirits and chant the relevant passages.

Juanzi says, "Numinous Prime is the spirit of the spleen. He is four inches long and sits on top of the spleen, looking like an infant, wearing a yellow robe. His position is that of Lord Lao in the Hall of Light of the central section."

If there is sickness in your body and if ever hunger and satiation are not happening appropriately, merely visualize the color of the robes of this Lord Lao in the central section, seeing him move about in the spleen. Call his name three times, then stop. Swallow the saliva seven times, and the myriad diseases will do as you wish. This matches when the text says, "Call my name three times, and the spirits will naturally come" [15.7].

Generally, there is a comprehensive taboo against eating the six domestic animals as well as fishy-smelly meat. The six domestic animals are oxen, horses, pigs, sheep, chickens, and dogs. "Fishy-smelly" is an expression for generating a fetid stench, which is why such substances are taboo. In addition, is also prohibited to consume the five pungent vegetables: onions, garlic, scallions, chives, and coriander.

If you face a situation where you have to take impure [foods], handle it as best as you can while in the world. However, any situation where you have to take filthy [foods] you must avoid at all cost. This is not open for discussion. If you have to take off your slippers [at a meal] and take some impure [foods], bathe and cleanse, wash and rinse, burn incense to your left, and declaim the scripture for one round. This will eliminate the hundred diseases. There are more taboos regarding food and drink beyond this, but the scholars have not put them into words.

If, during your travels, you encounter a situation where you have to take filthy [foods], you can use peach and bamboo to dissolve the evil. Again, burn incense to your left, so that yang can dissolve yin. If you don't follow these instructions, you will attract stale *qi* and the hundred diseases are hard to eliminate. As the *Scripture* says later, "Enter the chamber, face east, and chant the *Jade Chapters*" [36.2]. Also, its preface has, "Face east and declaim the *Neijing* for one round." This holds true particularly for times of dispelling wayward *qi* and cutting off evil, but it is also appropriate when harmonizing the spirits and summoning the numinous forces.

Now, if you continuously declaim the scripture in accordance with the prescribed method, it is best to work with the previously cited commentary and begin by facing east. Also, the Lesser Lord spoke of the method Shan Shiyuan received from Master Meng,[5] noting that it is good to declaim the *Huangting neijing* once before going to sleep in the evening. This causes people's cloud and white spirit agents to be naturally controlled. Practice like this for twenty-one years, and you become immortal.

This is the same as chanting it for ten thousand rounds. The optimal situation is to do three or four rounds each night. As Mistress Jiang of the Northern Peak says, "Declaiming this scripture also makes a person free from disease: it is the way of no-death." Like this, in the evening, as you get close to lying down, burn incense facing east, then lie on your bed and recite it. If you just do one round each night, it will take you twenty-seven years to reach the full ten thousand.

If some version says twenty-one years, that is actually a mistake. If people do not complete the course, it is because they did not continuously practice one round each night. Thus, it is correct to speak of three to four rounds as being optimal. Also, after ten rounds have been completed, it is good to get up and bow. The mention of ten thousand rounds is a way to indicate a final limit. If you declaim the text but do not bother to count the repetitions, it means you cannot exert due diligence in the process.

Explanation
The word "yellow" (*huang*) in *Huangting neijing* indicates the color of the center. The word "court" (*ting*) refers to the center of the four directions. The things referred to as "outer" are in heaven, among humanity, or on earth. The things referred to as "inner" are in the brain, in the heart, or in the spleen. Therefore, "in the yellow court" means the heart. "Lights" are images.

Metaphors involving outer images include sun and moon, stars and planets, clouds and the empyrean. Those involving inner images are things like blood and flesh, muscles and bones, organs and viscera. The heart-mind resting deep inside the body, one visualizes and observes the entire organism with its various images and colors: thus, the text speaks of "inner lights."

---

[5] The Lesser Lord is the youngest of the three Lords Mao, but according to the *Zhengao*, the actual speaker was Lord Pei (9.23b). Master Meng also appears in *Zhen'gao* 13.13 and *Dengzhen yijue* 3.1a-3b. I am indebted to Thomas E. Smith for pointing this out (personal communication).

Instructions for Reciting the *Huangting jing*[6]

Before entering the oratory to recite the *Huangting neijing yujing*, first burn incense, undergo a cleansing fast, and don the garb and cap of the divine law. Once you have entered the doorway, prostrate yourself four times to the north, then kneel upright, click your teeth twenty-four times, and announce:

> I hereby announce to the lofty and highest myriad perfected,
> To the Jade Chronogram, Most High and Great Lord of Dao:
> Your servant today enters this oratory to recite the *Jade Scripture*
> Refine my spirit and protect my organs.
> I pray: Let my stomach palace be glowing and lustrous,
> So that I in my body get to stride upon emptiness
> And above worship at the imperial court.

Once this is done, face east and greet the four great emperors. Click your teeth another twelve times and announce:

> I hereby announce to the Great Emperor of Fusang,
> The Divine King of the Valley of the Rising Sun:
> Your servant, so-and-so, today enters this oratory
> To chant the *Jade Scripture*.
> I pray: Let divine mushrooms grow naturally in this oratory,
> Let jade florescence rise in precious splendor,
> And the three luminants pervade all with their brightness.
> After ten thousand times, let my immortal embryo arise
> And grant me the same numinous power as the emperor.

Once the incantation is complete, face east and chant the scripture ten times to make one round. After this, again face north and prostrate yourself four times, then face east and give four bows, but there is no need to repeat the announcement.[7]

---

[6] The overall instructions here, but not the specific incantations, match the *Tuisong Huangting neijing jing fa* 推誦黃庭內景經法 at the end of YQ 12, translated below.

[7] The pattern to chant ten times, then give four bows north and east is also found in *Dengzhen yinjue* 3.1b.

One[1]

1.1   上清紫霞虛皇前
In the purple aurora of Highest Clarity, before Sovereign Emptiness,[2]

The realms of the Three Clarities are Great, Highest, and Jade Clarity. They are where all the great sages reside. The *Yutai jing* 玉臺經 (Jade Terrace Scripture) says, "Sovereign Emptiness is the area regulated by the Great Lord Dao."[3] Therefore, the region ruled by Great Dao is part of the Three Clarities. Also, the "Ten Names of Mystery Metropolis" notes, "The great numinous Sovereign Realm of Emptiness refers to the Heavenly Venerable." This means it is the original appellation of Primordial Beginning. The Lord of the Dao desires to illuminate how the seven-word [lines] originated in the Palace of the Purple Empyrean. This is also known as the Palace of Purple Jasper, or again, the Residential Palace of White Purple.

1.2   太上大道玉晨君
The Most High, Great Dao, Lord of Jade Morning Light,

Most High refers to the Venerable. The *Benxing jing* 本行經 (Scripture of Original Conduct) says, "It is an appellation of the five old lords of Primordial Beginning."[4] Lord of Jade Morning Light is therefore another title of the Yellow Lord.

---

[1] *Huangting neijing jing*, with commentary by Liangqiuzi in *Xiuzhen shishu* 55-56, the prime source for the main text (also in Zhou and Sheng 2015, 26-87). After three asterisks—mainly in sections 1 to 3— follows the commentary by Wuchengzi in YQ 11-12. After that, the two commentaries are the same, with some textual variants, presented in brackets and marked "YQ." Unmarked additions in brackets are for clarification of content. Chapters in the book divide after six verses each of the original to allow for easier access.

[2] YQ combines this and the following line before offering its commentary. The first four stanzas are also translated in Kroll 1996, 151-55.

[3] The YQ variant in the commentary to *Neijing* 22.13 has this as *Yuli jing* 玉歷經, an alternative title of the *Laozi zhongjing*. This text does not contain these words. A similar statement, though, appears in chapter 2 of the Tang encyclopedia *Miaomen youqi* 妙門由起 (Entrance to the Gate of all Wonders, DZ 1123, SV 442-44).

[4] A text of this title appears in DZ 345 (SV 242-43). A Lingbao document, it speaks at great length of the five elders or emperors of the five directions as well as about Primordial Beginning, but does not have a sentence that matches this fully.

* * *

Highest Clarity is a name of one of the Three Clarities. Sovereign Emptiness is an inner appellation of the Dao Lord of Triple Prime, Purple Clarity and Great Simplicity, Highest Emptiness and Pervasive Radiance. The Most High is therefore the Great Lord of the Dao, Mysterious Sovereign and Eminent Sage of Great Perfection of Jade Morning Light. He governs in the pearl-studded chamber of Highest Clarity, from where one can observe all the planets. Here purple aurora spreads brilliantly and auspicious *qi* radiates widely.

1.3 　　閑居蕊珠作七言 [= 1/1][5]
Living in seclusion in the pearl-studded [chamber], composed the seven-word [lines].

The *Biyao jing* 祕要經 (Scripture of Secret Essentials) says, "In the palaces of the immortals, there are halls of vast yang, towers of medicinal pearls, and chambers of verdant clouds."[6] The Dao Lord was here when he revealed this scripture, because he wanted to prepare people to also have them in their bodies.

* * *

"Pearl-studded" is the name of a palace tower in the realm of Highest Clarity. When he created this scripture, he used seven-word verses throughout.

1.4 　　散化五形變萬神
Dispersing and transforming the five-part physical form and changing with the myriad spirits,

This says that he can change and transform: drive out perception and understanding, cast off form, do away with understanding, and make himself identical with the Great Dao.[7] Placing the root first, then attending to the traces, he could rely on the spirit and apply it wisely. Spirit here is what follows and accords to all. Dispersing the body in five ways means one can change with the spirit in myriad modes.

* * *

---

[5] Numbers in brackets after the main text refer to matching parts and lines in the *Waijing*. I use a slash rather than a period to distinguish this numbering from that of verses in the *Neijing*. In most cases, they are only partially identical.

[6] This may refer to the *Shixing biyao jing* 施行祕要經 (Scripture of Practice Essentials, DZ 1363, SV 594), a text close to *Zhen'gao* 9-10. The citation is not found there.

[7] This cites *Zhuangzi* 6, the classic passage on sitting in oblivion.

Dispersing and transforming the physical form and organism, one can change in connection with the spirit in ten thousand modes. This illustrates the secret and wondrous nature of this scripture.

1.5   是為黃庭曰內篇
He produced this, the *Yellow Court*, called the *Inner Chapters*.

The title derives from the center [of the body].

* * *

The perfected words are spoken beautifully: thus they are the *Inner Chapters*.

1.6   琴心三疊舞胎仙
Qinxin (Strumming the Heart) in three folds: it lets your immortal embryo dance,

"Strumming" means harmonizing; "folds" are layers. It means to visualize the three elixir fields and harmonize their layers into oneness. "Immortal embryo" means to breathe like an embryo in the womb. The embryo being in the belly, it utilizes *qi* and does not require regular breath.

* * *

"Strumming" means harmonizing. The "three folds" are the three elixir fields. It says that the various palaces are arranged in layered folds. The immortal embryo is the Great Spirit of the Numinous Womb, also called the perfected embryo. He resides in the Hall of Light. What is called the Triple Lord Lao is the ruler of the Yellow Court. When the heart is harmonized, the spirits rejoice, thus the text speaks of "letting the immortal embryo dance."

1.7   九氣映明出霄間
As the nine *qi*, glinting and bright, emerge from the empyrean.

In the three elixir fields are the nine *qi*: brilliant and lustrous, none of them fails to shine. The *Dadong jing* 大洞經 (Scripture of Great Pervasion) says, "The three elixir fields, the Three Primes, and the three grotto chambers together constitute the nine bureaus. Each bureau is ruled by a heavenly sovereign. Their nine white spirit agents change into nine *qi* and transform into nine spirits."[8]

* * *

---

[8] Chapter 9 mentions the nine white spirit agents in relation to the nine heavens and says that they are no different from the spirits of the three elixir fields.

The *qi* of the nine heavens enters the person through the nose, then circulates and flows into the brain palace. Glinting and bright, it arrives at the top, thus the text says "emerge into the empyrean." The *Jiutian shengshen jing* 九天生神經 (Scripture of the Spirits Generated in the Nine Heavens) says, "As the Three Primes raise and nurture [the person], the nine *qi* bind the physical form."[9]

1.8   神蓋童子生紫煙
The pupils under the spirit canopy generate a purple haze:

Observe the radiance as you visualize and meditate, making it your business to activate your eyes. The text below says: The eyebrows are called the Flowery Canopy; they cover all like bright pearls.

* * *

The divine canopy is a way of referring to the eyebrows. The lads are the spirits of the eyes. The purple haze is the radiant *qi* of the eyes.

1.9   是曰玉書可精研
This is how the *Jade Book* is best studied with diligence.

The text originated following the traces but its power connects to all.[10]

1.10   詠之萬過昇三天
Chant it ten thousand times, and you can ascend to the three heavens,

Essence well prepared and spirit full, your name is entered in the Three Clarities above.

* * *

This scripture is also called *Jade Book*. The text says, it should be studied and read with concentrated heart-mind. Chant it the full ten thousand times and you will naturally ascend into heaven. The three heavens are Great, Highest, and Jade Clarity.

---

[9] A text of this title appears in DZ 318, SV 220 but the present edition does not contain these words. The same passage is found, cited from the same scripture, in YQ 36 as well as in the ordination text *Shangqing jing bijue* 上清經秘訣 (Secret Instructions from the Scriptures of Highest Clarity, DZ 1291, SV 465).

[10] YQ combines this and the following line before offering its commentary.

1.11   千災以消百病痊
The thousand disasters all dissolve, the hundred diseases are well healed.

The reason for all this lies in essence and spirit.[11]

1.12   不憚虎狼之兇殘
You do not shrink from the nasty ravings of tiger or of wolf,

There will be no more injury.

1.13   亦以卻老年永延
But hold off old age and extend your years forever.

This stanza contains the entire way of the *Yellow Court*.

* * *

The perfected scripture is venerable and serious. If you hold it tight and chant it well, you will be covered in blessings, while all disasters and diseases are naturally eliminated and neither tigers nor wolves attack you. In your declining years, you revert to youthfulness, longevity and destiny extending for long periods. The *Daojing* 道經 (Scripture of Dao) says: "As for those skillful in managing life, poisonous insects and fierce beasts will not attack them."[12] This stanza initially explains the key points of the *Scripture*, which was recorded by a direct disciple of the Most High. It is much like the *Xiaojing* 孝經 (Classic of Filial Piety) or the *Liji* 禮記 (Book of Rites), said to have been compiled when Confucius was living in seclusion.

Two

2.1   上有魂靈下關元 [= 1/3]
Above is the cloud spirit agents' numinous force, below the Pass Primordial.

The cloud spirit agents above represent the division of heaven; the pass below represented the division of earth. The cloud spirit agents' numinous force has no form, but the Pass Primordial has material substance. Human beings match heaven and earth in their physical form and image.

* * *

---

[11] YQ combines this and the following two lines before offering its commentary.
[12] *Daode jing* 50.

The cloud spirit agents here stand for both the cloud and white spirit agents, while numinous force is the inherent power of the womb. The cloud spirit agents reside in the liver, the white spirit agents sit in the lungs, and the numinous force of the womb is in the spleen. The Pass Primordial is the navel, which is the palace that harbors destiny. This being so, the cloud and white spirit agents are above, while the Pass Primordial is below.

2.2   左為少陽右太陰
Left is lesser yang; right is greater yin.

Left is east; right is west. *Mao* is life; *you* is death.[13]

* * *

Lesser yang is the left eye, while greater yin is the right.

2.3   後有密戶前生門 [= 1/4]
Behind are the Secret Doors; in front, the Gate of Life.

In front is south; behind is north. Behind the Secret Doors are two orifices, described as hidden and secret. In front of the Gate of Life there are seven orifices, described as open and generative. Together they are the nine orifices.

* * *

The Secret Doors are the kidneys, the palace of essence among the organs. Maintain them carefully, never letting them be rushed or leaking. The Gate of Life is the Gate of Destiny.

2.4   出日入月呼吸存 [= 1/5]
With rising sun and setting moon, inhale and exhale as you visualize them.

The sun and the moon are the essences of yin and yang. They rise on the left and set on the right. The body, too, has the *qi* of yin and yang. In its image, it matches the *qi* of heaven and earth. Rising is inhale; setting is exhale. As you inhale and exhale, visualize them in your mind.

* * *

This says that one should always visualize the sun and the moon in the two eyes, letting their radiance merge with the entire body and thereby connect to perfection.

---

[13] *Mao* and *you* are two of the twelve earthly branches, designators of the ancient Chinese calendar. Numbers 4 and 10, respectively, they are associated with east and west, sunrise and sunset.

The *Jiuzhen zhongjing* 九真中經 (Central Scripture of the Nine Perfected) says: "At midnight, when *qi* first rises, or at cock crow, kneel upright, close in the *qi*, and visualize the sun rising from the left eye and the moon emerging from the right. They move above the two ears and form a high window for the six harmonies.

"From here make the sun and moon radiate through the entire body, deeply penetrating into the Niwan above and widely illuminating the five organs below. Throughout the stomach and intestines, you can see all widely pervaded. Suffused on the inside and in harmony on the outside, the entire body shines forth jointly with the radiance of the sun and moon. Practice this for a long time, then click your teeth nine times, swallow the saliva nine times, and softly intone the following incantation:

> Most High Mysterious One:
> Let the Nine Sovereigns spit forth essence
> And change through three, five, and seven
> So I can pervasively observe all that's hidden and dark.
>
> Let the sun and the moon radiate jointly,
> Sink down to suffuse my spirit court
> So they illuminate the six harmonies.
> Let the Great One rest in yellow calm,
> And the Imperial Lord command the ledgers,
> Making sure the golden books are not askew.
>
> As the five Lords Lao offer talismans,
> Heaven and earth join in sincerity.
> Let me be free from death
> And attain perfect numinous force,
> Eliminate all myriad forms of wayward *qi*,
> Let all misfortunes and harms be resolved.
>
> Above I bow to you, Heavenly Sovereign,
> Let me revert old age and recover youth.
> As you, Great Emperor, have control over all:
> Let the hundred spirits listen with respect!"[14]

---

[14] The *Jiuzhen zhongjing* is contained in DZ 908 and 1376 (SV 102, 144-45) but the quoted passage does not appear there. Rather, it is found in YQ 1, under the heading "Methods of Absorbing the *Qi* of the Sun and the Moon." Solar and lunar essences play a key role in Shangqing practice. See Robinet 1993; Esposito 2004.

2.5　元 [四]氣所合列宿分
Primordial [YQ: the four] *qi* is [are] well blended, the arrayed mansions are distinct.

Primordial *qi* is the One. This says to merge the heart with Dao, visualize the numinous radiance of sun, moon, stars, and planets, their brightness properly arrayed, as the entire body shares the light and merges with heaven.

* * *

The four *qi* are the numinous *qi* of the four seasons. The arrayed mansions are the three lights [sun, moon, stars]. This says that one should always visualize the primordial *qi* merged with the body and continuously think of the sun, moon, and Dipper stars spreading their brightness and shining forth luminously. Doing this for a long time, one can connect to pure numinous force.

2.6　紫煙上下三素雲
Purple haze moves up and down: the clouds of the three simplicities.

Purple haze is the *qi* of the eyes' essence. Visualize a white *qi* moving up and down in the three elixir fields, flowing from there to connect to the entire organism. Another explanation has: the radiance of the eyes comes in three colors, purple, blue, and green. They are the clouds of the three simplicities. The *Xianjing* 仙經 (Immortals' Scripture) says, "The incantation of Mistress Cloud Forest has, 'The lads of the sun and the moon represent the essence of the perfected lord of three clouds and two eyes.'"[15]

* * *

The three simplicities are purple, white, and yellow.[16] Always visualize these three wondrous forms of primordial *qi* moving up and down through the body, and your physical form and spirit will connect and respond closely.

2.7　灌溉五華植靈根 [= 1/6]
Dripping moisture on the five florescences, plant the Numinous Root.

The cloud-*qi* of the three simplicities forms jade fluid in the mouth. As you swallow it, visualize it dripping down. The five florescences are the glowing

---

[15] Citation unclear. Quite a few texts have the appellation "Immortals' Scripture."
[16] As described in the *Dadong jing*, these are three female deities, the mothers of the three central gods Blossomless, White Prime, and Central Yellow (Robinet 1993, 101).

flowery energy of the five organs. The Numinous Root is the root of destiny, all life is planted there.

* * *

The five florescences are the glowing flowery energy of the five directions. The Numinous Root is the root of the tongue. This says to rinse with fluids and swallow saliva, inhaling to pull in the five *qi* and absorb them. Doing so, the Numinous Root will continue forever and the offices of the spirits will be clear and lustrous.

2.8   七液洞流衝廬間
The seven fluids connect in their flow, pushing through the Hut.

The fluids of the seven orifices move up and down, flowing everywhere. Moving up, they penetrate; moving down, they circulate, settling eventually between the Hut [YQ: forehead] and the jowl, right in the Hall of Light.

* * *

The top of the Hut, between the two eyebrows, is what we call the forehead. The seven fluids indicate the four *qi* and Three Primes coming together to form numinous fluids. They flow and moisten the organs and viscera, their *qi* pushing up to fill the brain.

2.9   回紫抱黃入丹田
Circulate the purple and embrace the yellow, so they can enter the Elixir Field.

These are internal images and metaphors. The *qi* of the spleen is yellow, that of the eyes is purple. As the seven fluids flow around the body, embracing the yellow and circulating the purple means to move them in and out of the Elixir Field in coordination with inhalation and exhalation. There are three elixir fields, forming the root of numinous destiny.

    The *Dadong jing* says, "Moving in between the eyebrows for three *fen* there is the double elixir field; moving into the bone segment for three *fen* there is the terrace tower. The green chamber is on the left, the purple door is on the right. Two spirits reside there.

    "Moving in between the eyebrows for one inch, there is the Hall of Light. On the left is the Lord Bright Lad (Mingtong jun 明童君); on the right is the Honorable Bright Lady (Mingnü jun 明女君); in the center is the Divine Lord Bright Mirror (Mingjing shenjun 明鏡神君). Moving in between the eyebrows for two inches, there is the Grotto Chamber. On the left is Lord

Blossomless (Wuying jun 無英君); on the right is Lord White Prime (Baiyuan jun 白元君); in the center is the Yellow Lord Lao (Huanglao jun 黄老君).

"Moving in between the eyebrows for three inches, there is the upper Elixir Field, also known as the Niwan Palace. On the left is the Lord Infant of the Upper Prime (Shangyuan chizi jun 上元赤子君); on the right is the Lord Imperial Minister (Diqing jun 帝卿君). Moving in between the eyebrows for four inches, there is the Palace of Flowing Pearls. The Perfected Lord of Flowing Pearls (Liuzhu zhenjun 流珠真君) resides there. Moving in between the eyebrows for five inches, there is the Palace of the Jade Emperor. The Perfected Mother of Jade Clarity (Yuqing zhenmu 玉清真母) resides there.

"One inch straight above the Hall of Light, there is the Palace of the Heavenly Court. The Perfected Lady of Highest Clarity (Shangqing zhennü 上清真女) resides there. One inch straight above the Grotto Chamber, there is the Palace of Ultimate Perfection. The Imperial Lord of Great Ultimate (Taiji dijun 太極帝君) resides there. One inch straight above the Elixir Field is the Palace of Cinnabar Mystery. The Lord of the Great One and Central Yellow (Zhonghuang Taiyi jun 中黄太乙君) resides there. Two inches straight above the [Palace of] Flowing Pearls is the Palace of the Great Sovereign. The Most High Lord (Taishang jun 太上君) resides there.

"Men work with the Male One; women work with the Female One. Both men and women can cultivate equally."[17]

* * *

The Elixir Field mentioned here is the upper Elixir Field. It is a palace located three inches moving into the head from between the two eyebrows. The Perfected One of Upper Prime resides there. Yellow and purple refer to the numinous *qi* of the Three Primes.

2.10   幽室內明照陽明 [門]

Let the Dark Parlor be bright within, shining with yang brightness [YQ: through the Gate of Yang].

In the Dark Parlor, deeply secret, naturally meditate and visualize the heart. The eyes become a bright mirror, just like the sun and the moon. Spirit is an expression for that which is boundless. Both heart and spirit have no bounds:

---

[17] This passage appears in the beginning of the Tang text *Jiugong zifang tu* 九宮紫房圖 (Chart of the Nine Palaces and Purple Chambers, DZ 156, SV 612-13). The arrangement of deities matches that outlined in the *Dadong jing*. Robinet 1993, 100-01.

when you visualize them, they become present; when you let them go, they vanish.

* * *

The Dark Parlor is the kidneys. The Gate of Yang is the Gate of Destiny. This says to visualize and envision the organ of the kidneys and make its interior light up. Hold on to *qi* and guard essence, never letting them leak out or disperse. Bright and radiant both inside and out, persistently maintain the Gate of Destiny. This stanza first explains the location of the various palaces in the *Yellow Court* system as well as the circulation and flow of *qi* and fluids, how they move up and down and connect with each other.

Three

3.1   口為玉池太和官
The mouth is the Jade Pond, the Bureau of Great Harmony.

The fluid in the mouth is jade liquid, also called sweet spring or jade nectar. When this water is stored, it forms a pond. The hundred joints balanced and supple, the five organs harmonious and aligned—they all report to the mouth as their bureau chief. One version calls it the Palace of Great Harmony, but this does not match the proper rhyme structure.

The *Dadong jing* says, "In your mind visualize the entrance of the stomach, seeing there a female with the physical form of a baby but without any clothes or garb. Standing right at the stomach duct, she opens her mouth and issues cloud-spirit fluid. Looking up, she exhales the five *qi* which then collect and fill the mouth, inside and out, with liquids and fluids. Once they fill your mouth, swallow them, and send them directly into the mouth of the mysterious female. Do this five times. Once complete, click the teeth three times and subtly intone the following incantation."

> Most High Ninefold Numinous Force of the
> Nine Heavens of Jade Clarity:
>
> Transform and become a divine female,
> Descend into my stomach clarity
> With your golden harmony and jade luster.
>
> My mind at ease with the spirits in their brightness,
> Let me absorb and ingest pure solar essence,

So the golden flower fills me up completely.[18]

3.2   漱咽靈液災不干
Rinse and swallow its numinous fluid: disasters can encroach no longer.

With numinous fluid and perfect *qi* present, wayward energies no longer come about.

3.3   體生光華氣香蘭
The organism generates a radiant florescence [shine], the *qi* is fragrant like an orchid.

If you do not eat the five grains, the organism is free from dregs and filth.

3.4   卻滅百邪玉煉顏
As you eliminate and extinguish the hundred forms of wayward *qi*, your features are refined in jade.

Your flesh and skin are like ice and snow, meek and modest like a young girl.

3.5   審能修之登廣寒 [= 1.7]
Decisively cultivate in this manner and you will ascend to Vast Coldness.

Vast Coldness is the name of an immortal palace in the far north. The day of the winter solstice is when the moon reclines in the Palace of Vast Coldness. At this time, nourish the cloud spirit agents in the Area of Vast Coldness. The celestials pick essential, flowery threads to distinguish the radiance of the sun and the moon.

* * *

Vast Coldness is the name of an immortal palace in the far north. Another version notes that it is the name of a mountain, which is also called Vast Mist. The *Dongzhen jing* 洞真經 (Cavern Perfection Scripture) says, "The day of the winter solstice is when the moon reclines in the Palace of Vast Coldness. At this time, one should nourish the lunar spirit agent in the Pond of Vast Coldness. The celestials pick pure flowery lines in the forest to harness the radiance of the sun and the moon."[19]

---

[18] For the first four lines of this stanza, YQ offers the same commentary as the text in the *Xiuzhen shishu*. Citation unclear.

[19] The title refers to the scriptures of Highest Clarity in general. The citation appears in the Eastern Jin document, *Shangqing huangqi yangjing sandao shunxing jing* 上清

3.6   晝夜不寐乃成真
Day and night never resting, you achieve perfection.[20]

By cultivating when active and stabilizing when resting you will become a perfected.

3.7   雷鳴電激神泯泯
Though thunder sounds and lightning spurs, the spirits remain placidly at rest.

Balance the spirits and regulate the *qi*, and your essence and white spirit agents will be serene and joyful. Even though there may be claps of thunder, you will not be startled or afraid. Another interpretation says that "thunder sounds and lightning spurs" refers to clicking the teeth and practicing visualization and meditation. That is, the passage refers to the activation of the spirits and should not really speak of "placidly at rest."

Four

4.1   黃庭內人服錦衣 [= 1/8]
The inner personages of the Yellow Court wear robes of brocade,

The inner person of the Yellow Court is the Mother of the Dao. The perfected of the Yellow Court is the Father of the Dao. Each body contains them, complete with their robes of five-colored brocade. They are also described as the perfect *qi* of the five organs that should be kept in the three courts.

4.2   紫華[霞]飛裙雲氣羅
A flying skirt of purple florescence [YQ: mist], gauze of cloud-like *qi*.

The *Shifang jing* 十方經 (Scripture of the Ten Methods) says, "The Most High Jade Sovereign wears a brightly patterned skirt of flying clouds."[21] Such is the garb of the immortals.

黃氣陽精三道順行經 (Highest Clarity Scripture on Following the Three Orbits and [Absorbing] Yellow Qi and Yang Essence, DZ 33, SV 148-49), 3a. For more on the celestial palace, see Smith 2013, 248n40.

[20] The two versions, to a very large extent, have the same commentary from here on. Wuchengzi's notes appear after asterisks. Variants are added in brackets and marked "YQ."

4.3 丹青綠條翠靈柯
It is cinnabar and cerulean, with green trim and cyan-blue numinous lines.

The variegated *qi* of the five colors comes together to generate the base of the garb of the immortals with their trim and lines.

4.4 七蕤玉籥閉兩扉 [= 1/9]
Its two sides held together by a jade pin of seven leaves.

This is an external image ormetaphor. The way the seven orifices open and close is like the lock on a gate. Use the lock in accordance with the instructions and do not open it recklessly. A leaf is an ornament on a lock. To visualize the spirits, you must close the eyes. Hence the text speaks of closing the two door leaves.

4.5 重扇 [掩] 金關密樞機
Doubly join [YQ: shut] the golden pass, the secret hinging mechanism

Gold here stands for being firm and strong. Laozi's *Scripture* says, "A well-shut door needs no bolts and yet it cannot be opened."[22] This stays that, in cultivating life, one should well maintain essence and spirit, never letting them leak out recklessly.

4.6 玄泉幽闕高崔巍 [= 1/10]
The mysterious spring is at the Dark Towers, high like rocky summits.

The mysterious spring is the fluid in the mouth. It is also called jade nectar, jade fluid, or jade spring. The area between the two eyes is the tower court, while the two kidneys are the Dark Towers. Like the left and right wings of a door, they resemble summits. The way of central naturalness rests in the

---

[21] This statement appears in *Taiping yulan* 675 as cited from the *Shangqing jing*, either a generic term for the entire corpus or an alternative title of the *Dadong jing* (Robinet 1993, 97). It also appears in chapter 17 of the 6th-century compendium *Wushang biyao* 無上祕要 (Esoteric Essentials of the Most High, DZ 1138, SV 118-19; Lagerwey 1981) as cited from the *Bianhua qishisi fangjing* 變化七十四方經 (Scripture of the Seventy-four Methods of Transformation). The latter is cited at length in the *Shangqing zhongjing zhu zhensheng bi* 上清眾經諸真聖祕 (Secret Books of Sages and Perfected of the Host of Highest Clarity Scriptures, DZ 446, SV 603). It presents mostly a list of deities with their various names, but does not specify their garb.
[22] *Daode jing* 27.

kidneys, thus they are called the Dark Towers. As regards the kidneys being located at the lower end of the five organs yet described as high, this is because when visualizing their spirit in the physical form, he is located above the Elixir Field. For this reason, they are high.

4.7　三田之中精氣微 [= 1/11]
In the three fields, essence and *qi* are subtle.

This refers to internal affairs. In the Elixir Field, spirit and *qi* change and transform. In impulse and response following the heart, they are neither there nor not there and cannot be pinned down. In image overflowing, they enter the wondrous; sealed and grounded, they have distinct lines. For this reason, when working with *qi*, use the heart as the ruler. Establish it in the proper image and enter a state of extreme stillness, extreme subtlety to the point where you cannot follow or count [the breath]. The *Daoji jing* 道機經 (Scripture of Dao Mechanism) says, "Heaven has the three luminants: sun, moon, and stars. Humans have the three treasures: the three elixir fields. The qi in the elixir fields is green on left, yellow on the right, white above, and black below."[23]

4.8　嬌女窈窕翳霄暉
Graceful Woman, modest and retiring, screens the empyrean luster.

The *Zhen'gao* 真誥 (Declarations of the Perfected) says, "Graceful Woman is the name of the spirit of the ears."[24] This says that the hearing of the ears is keen, penetrating brightness and able to close off darkness and luster.

---

[23] Ge Hong 葛洪 lists a *Daoji jing* in 5 *juan* in his *Baopuzi*, ch. 19. The passage appears in the *Jinque dijun sanyuan zhenyi jing* 金闕帝君三元真一經 (Scripture of the Three Primes and Perfect One, by the Imperial Lord Goldtower, DZ 253, SV 595), which is also contained in YQ 50 as well as in the *Suling dayou miaojing* 素靈大有妙經 (Wondrous Scripture of Great Existence of Simple Numen, DZ 1314, SV 187-88), 27a-38b.

[24] This quote does not appear in the *Zhen'gao*, which speaks of ear goddesses in 9.11a-12b. Comparable passages are found in the *Suling jing* (DZ 1314, 1.17a) and Tao Hongjing's *Shangqing wozhong jue* 上清握中訣 (Highest Clarity Instructions to Be Kept at Hand, DZ 140, SV 6283), 3.6. I am indebted to Thomas E. Smith for these references.

4.9   重堂煥煥明八威

The Multi-storied Hall, glowing iridescent, illuminates the Eight Daunters.[25]

The Multi-storied Hall is a name for the esophagus. It is also known as the Multi-storied Tower or Multi-storied Rings. The *Benjing* 本經 (Original Scripture) says, "The Multi-storied Tower near the Scarlet Palace has twelve stories."[26] The Scarlet Palace is the heart. The esophagus is above the heart; thus it is called the Multi-storied Tower. The esophagus is the main pathway for fluids and liquids. The flow through there, moving up and down, moistening and enriching the entire organism as they iridescently illuminate the eight directions. The spirits of the eight directions are the Eight Daunters.

4.10   天庭地關列斧斤

From the Heavenly Court to the Pass of Earth, all arrayed with axes.

The area between the eyebrows is the Heavenly Court. The incantation to the Lady of Purple Tenuity (Ziwei furen 紫微夫人) has: "Open and connect my Heavenly Court and let me attain long life."[27] "Arrayed with axes" indicates an appearance of courage.

4.11   靈臺盤固永不衰 [= 1/13]

The Numinous Terrace level and steady: you never ever weaken.

The heart is the Numinous Terrace. This says that a spirit of numinous power resides there. In stillness, maintain the One; in activity, visualize the spirits. When the spirits are fully present, the organism is at peace and there is neither weakness nor exhaustion.

---

[25] The Eight Daunters (*bawei* 八威) are a group of deities protecting the eight directions, closely connected to the eight trigrams and the Eight Phosphors (*bajing* 八景), cosmic lights that disperse fog, dispel darkness, and eliminate demonic forces. In their service, the Eight Daunters "attack all threats to benign travelers along the roads of Heaven" and serve as "guardians of the somatic organs and conduits" (Schafer 1985, 7).

[26] This title could refer to various titles. The citation is not found in this format, but the information reflects the classical understanding of Daoist body cosmology.

[27] The Lady of Purple Tenuity is a key revelatory deity in Highest Clarity. Associated with the north, she first serves as a matchmaker between Yang Xi and Consort An, then serves as teacher to Xu Mi and Xu Hui (Smith 2013, 16).

Five

5.1 中池內神服赤珠 [= 1/14]
The spirit in the Central Pond wears red pearls,

The gall bladder is the Central Pond, the tongue is the Flowery Pond, and the small intestine is the Jade Pond. Together they are called the three ponds. The *Danbu zhang* 膽部章 (Stanza on the Gall Bladder Section) says: "Dragon banners flying horizontally in the sky, wield the fire bell."[28] "Red pearls" refers to wearing the fire bell.

5.2 丹錦雲袍帶虎符
A cloudy wrap of cinnabar brocade, he has a tiger talisman on his belt.

A cloudy wrap of cinnabar brocade indicates the color of the heart and the lungs. They are located above the gall bladder; hence the text says, "cloudy wrap." It is complete with a tiger talisman. The *Jiuzhen jing* 九真經 (Scripture of Ninefold Perfection) says, "The Yellow Lord Lao wears a mysterious dragon and divine tiger talisman at his waist and a bell of flowing gold on his belt."[29] Such is the garb of the Lord of the Dao.

5.3 橫津三寸靈所居 [= 1/15]
Three inches below the horizontal ford is where the numinous forces reside.

This refers to internal affairs. The navel is above the womb. Hence the text speaks of the horizontal ford. Three inches below the navel is the Elixir Field, where the Perfected Infant resides.

5.4 隱芝翳鬱自相扶
Hidden mushrooms and screen-like thicket naturally come together.

This refers to the physical form and organism of men and women. "Hidden" and "thicket" engage in intercourse: such is the Dao of nature. The *Neiwai*

---

[28] Text and citation are unclear. The fire-bell is a potent talisman made from pure *qi* that glows red and is wielded widely by the celestials. See Smith 2013, 106.n.96; Robinet 1993, 164.

[29] A *Jiuzhen zhongjing*, cited above (2.4), appears in DZ 908 and 1376 (SV 102, 144-45). It does not contain this statement, but a similar description is found in *Zhen'gao* 9 and *Wushang biyao* 17.

shenzhi jijue 內外神芝記訣 (Recorded Instructions on Inner and Outer [Uses of] Divine Mushrooms) says, "The fluid of the five organs constitutes mushrooms."[30] Hence the text speaks of hidden mushrooms. Another name is internal mushrooms.

Six

6.1　　天中之岳精謹修
At the peak of the heavenly center, essence is diligently cultivated.

The peak of the heavenly center is the nose. It is also called heavenly terrace. The *Xiaomo jing* 消摩經 (Scripture of Dispelling Demons) says, "At the nose, you want to count [the breath] at the left and right [nostrils], making sure the *qi* is level."[31] "Dripping [*qi*] to moisten the peak of the center" is an expression found in various famous books and imperial records.

6.2　　雲宅既清玉帝游
Once the cloud residence is clear, the Jade Emperor comes wandering.

The face is the cloud residence, also known as the heavenly residence. Since spirits use the eyebrows, eyes, and mouth to reside there, it is called their residence. When essence is cultivated there so it connects with ease, the spirits and immortals come wandering. The *Dadong jing* says, "The face is the inch residence. Some also speak of it as the red marsh."[32]

6.3　　通利道路無終休
It is a path or way to pervasive prosperity that never rests nor ends.

The *Taisu danjing jing* 太素丹景經 (Scripture of Great Simplicity and Cinnabar Lights): "As regards the surface of the whole face, you always want massage and rub it with your two hands."[33] Follow its contours high and low.

---

[30] Citation unclear.

[31] A text of this titles appears in DZ 1344, SV 590-91. The citation is found in *Zhen'gao* 9.

[32] Not found in the *Dadong jing*. The same sentence also appears in YQ 51, as cited from the *Dongshen jing* 洞神經 (Cavern Spirit Scripture), which is a generic term for the texts of the Three Sovereigns in the Daoist Canon.

[33] A text of this title appears in DZ 1424, SV 1245. However, this is a philosophical treatise of unknown date or provenance. The citation, attributed to the same source, is found in the *Shixing biyao jing*.

without stopping, and keep the *qi* conduits of ears, eyes, and mouth connected and usable.

6.4   眉號華蓋覆明珠
The eyebrows are called the Flowery Canopy. They cover the bright pearls.

The bright pearls are the eyes.

6.5   九幽日月洞空無
The nine realms of darkness as well as the sun and the moon are all pervaded by emptiness and primordiality.

The *Wuchen xingshi jue* 五辰行事訣 (Instructions on How to Practice with the Five Planets) says, "Entering into the head above the eyebrows by one inch, there is the Flowery Hall of the Purple Towers. The left eye is the sun, the right eye is the moon."[34] The *Yuli jing* 玉曆經 (Jade Calendar Scripture) says, "Great Clarity has [brilliant clouds of] five colors and a Flowery Canopy of nine layers."[35] The human body has these as well. Always visualize the lads of the eyes as bright as the sun and the moon.

6.6   宅中有真常衣丹 [= 1/20]
In the residence is a perfected always clad in cinnabar.

The perfected is the spirit of the heart, Lad of the Red City, also known as Perfect One, Infant, Child Cinnabar, or simply the Perfected. Visualize him always in front of your eyes, in close accordance with the heart. He is clad in cinnabar, representing the red color of the *qi* of the heart.

6.7   審能見之無疾患 [= 1/21]
When you can see him, you will be free from sickness and afflictions.

Yuanyangzi 元陽子 says, "Always visualize the spirit of the heart, and you will be free from sickness."[36]

---

[34] YQ 52.15b.

[35] *Laozi zhongjing* 1.5.

[36] Yuanyangzi, according to YQ 104, was a celestial from the North Culmen, raised in emptiness. He received the *Huangting jing* from Lord Lao and commented on it.

6.8 　赤珠靈裙華蒨粲 ［倩榮］

[He wears] a numinous skirt with red pearls, ornamented brilliantly with flowery plants [YQ: pretty and lustrous with flowery patterns].

This illustrates the colors of the heart spirit's robe.

6.9 　舌下玄膺生死岸

Beneath the tongue is the Mysterious Sphincter: the shore of life and death.

This refers to internal affairs. The Mysterious Sphincter is the shore, along which fluids and liquids pass. The *Benjing* says, "The Mysterious Sphincter is the energy duct, the receptacle of essence."[37]

6.10 　出青入玄二氣煥

Issuing from the clear and entering the dark, the two *qi* shine forth.

This says as you expel and take in the two *qi* of yin and yang, they shine forth brightly.

6.11 　子若遇之昇天漢

If you match them properly, you can ascend to the heavenly shores.

In one gets good at matching the patterns of expelling and taking in [the breath], he becomes a celestial immortal.

---

[37] See above, 4.9.

Seven

7.1   至道不煩決存真 [= 1/30]
Perfect Dao remains untroubled: consistently visualize the perfected.

If you keep [your mind] focused, you will get there.

7.2   泥丸百節皆有神
The Niwan as much as the hundred joints all have their own spirits.

The spirits are the most wondrous among the myriad beings. Their names match their image [YQ: as explained below].

7.3   髮神蒼華字太元
The spirit of the hair is Verdant Florescence (Canghua), also known as Great Prime (Taiyuan).

White and black is called verdant. Since he resides at the highest part of the head, he is also called Great Prime.

7.4   腦神精根字泥丸
The spirit of the brain is Root of Essence (Jinggen), also known as Niwan.

The Palace of the Elixir Field is the equivalent of the Yellow Court. The ruler of the Grotto Chamber is the root of yin and yang. The Niwan is the key image of the brain.

7.5   眼神明上字英玄
The spirit of the eyes is Brightness Above (Mingshang), also known as Glowing and Mysterious (Yingxuan).

The eyes are like the sun and the moon. Located in the upper part of the head their spirit is called Brightness Above. Glowing and Mysterious refers to the essential colors of their lads [YQ: pupils]. This refers to internal affairs.

7.6   鼻神玉壟字靈堅
The spirit of the nose is Jade Mound (Yulong), also known as Numinous Firmness (Lingjian).

The bone of the eminent dike looks like jade. Here divine *qi* connects to heaven. It leaves and enters without ever getting exhausted, thus he is called Numinous and Firm.

7.7 耳神空閑字幽田
The spirit of the ears is Open Leisure (Kongxian), also known as Dark Field (Youtian).

In open leisure, dark and still, they hear all beings and evaluate them. Since a spirit resides in them, they are called Dark Field.

7.8 舌神通命字正倫
The spirit of the tongue is Connecting Destiny (Tongming), also known as Proper Cord (Zhenglun).

Swallowing saliva and using the tongue, inner nature and destiny are connected. Properly identifying the five flavors, in each case it matches their correct structure.

7.9 齒神崿鋒字羅千
The spirit of the teeth is Edge Point (Efeng), also known as Network of Thousands (Luoqian).

The teeth are firm and sharp like knife edges or choppers' points. Like a network they capture the host of being and eat them.

7.10 一面之神宗泥丸
The spirits of the entire face venerate the Niwan.

The spirit of the brain resides in the Elixir Field and is chief of the hundred spirits.

7.11 泥丸九真皆有房
The nine perfected of the Niwan each have their own chamber.[1]

The *Dadong jing* says, "The Three Primes transform secretly, forming the three officials. Three times three makes nine, thus we speak of the three elix-

---

[1] According to the *Dadong jing*, the nine perfected include the spirits occupying the five organs plus the gall bladder, stomach, blood-essence, and the Niwan. See Robinet 1993, 101.

ir fields. In addition, there are three grottoes who merge above into oneness. Combined with two primes, they make up the Nine Palaces. In them reside nine perfected spirits. Three times nine makes twenty-seven. Their divine *qi* creates harmony in human beings. You should always visualize them. They are also called the Nine Sovereigns. Their nine cloud spirit agents change into nine *qi* and turn into nine spirits. They each reside in their own grotto chamber."[2]

7.12   方圓一寸處此中
Square and round, one inch in size, they are empty within.

Each chamber is one inch in size. The brain contains the Nine Palaces.

7.13   同服紫衣飛羅裳
Their spirits equally wear purple robes and capes of flying gauze.

The garb of the nine perfected in all cases looks like colored *qi*. It is called "flying" because it is very light.

7.14   但思一部壽無窮
Only think of this one section and gain limitless longevity.

Visualize and think of the nine perfected: such is the way of no-death.

7.15   非各別住俱腦中
It is not that they each live separately: they are together in the brain.

The Elixir Field is where the source spirits live,

7.16   列位次坐向外方
Lined up by rank, seated in order, all face outward.

The spirits are joined in the Elixir Field, their faces turned outward to better ward off the inauspicious. The *Basu jing* 八素經 (Scripture of the Eight Simplicities) says, "The perfected have nine ranks. They all stand arrayed, facing outward. More specifically, the highest perfected face up, the lofty perfected face south, the great perfected face east, the divine perfected face west, the

---

[2] Not found in the *Dadong jing*. The citation appears in *Taidan yinshu* 太丹隱書 (Secret Scripture of Great Cinnabar, DZ 1330, SV 159-60), 9a.

mysterious perfected face north, the immortal perfected face northeast, the celestial perfected face southeast, the emptiness perfected face southwest, and the ultimate perfected face northwest. All these heavenly perfected can perceive sights without seeing and sounds without hearing. They have no need for speech to be upright and no need for action to be on track."[3]

7.17   所存在心自相當
As long as you visualize mentally, they will naturally attend on you.

Mentally visualize the mysterious perfected, and all without and within will be in accord.

Eight

8.1   心神丹元字守靈
The spirit of the heart is Cinnabar Prime (Danyuan), also known as Maintaining Numen (Shouling).

These are internal images. The heart is prime among all organs and viscera. It is associated with the direction of the south and the quality of fire. It is the residence of the spirit with the highest authority. Hence he is called Maintaining Numinous Force.

8.2   肺神皓華字虛成
The spirit of the lungs is Dazzling Florescence (Haohua), also known as Emptiness Complete (Xucheng).

The lungs are the Flowery Canopy, covering the heart, they shine forth like a brilliant flower. They are associated with the direction of the west and the quality of metal. The color of the lungs is white. Their substance is light and empty, thus they are called Emptiness Complete.

8.3   肝神龍煙字含明
The spirit of the liver is Dragon Smoke (Longyan), also known as Containing Brightness (Hanming).

---

[3] A text of this title appears in DZ 426, SV 141-42. It does not specify immortals' ranks. The latter appear in chapter 1 of the Tang compendium *Daojiao yishu* 道教義樞 (The Pivotal Meaning of the Daoist Teaching, DZ 1129, SV 442), by Meng Anpai 孟安排.

The liver is in the position of the phase wood. It is associated with the direction of the east and the quality of the green dragon. Among the organs, it rules over the eyes. Since the sun rises in the east [YQ add: and wood generates fire], it is called Containing Brightness.

8.4   翳鬱導煙主濁清
The screen-like thicket brings forth smoke: it rules the clear and turbid.

The screen-like thicket is an image for wood. It obtains fire and smoke is generated. It obtains yang and its *qi* is clear. When it is clear, the eyes are bright; when turbid, they are dark.

8.5   腎神玄冥字育嬰
The spirit of the kidneys is Mysterious Gloom (Xuanming), also known as Raising Offspring (Yuying).

The kidneys are linked with water; thus, they are called Mysterious Gloom. The essence of the kidneys brings forth children, thus their spirit is called Raising Offspring.

8.6   脾神常在字魂停
The spirit of the spleen is Always Present (Changzai), also known as Cloud Spirit Pavilion (Hunting).

The spleen occupies the position of the center and the phase earth, thus its spirit called Always Present. It is the Palace of the Yellow Court. The spleen is a grindstone that dissolves food, it has divine strength and appears highly vigorous, thus it is called Cloud Spirit Pavilion.

8.7   膽神龍曜字威明
The spirit of the gall bladder is Dragon Brilliance (Longyao), also known as Majestic Brightness (Weiming).

The color of the gall bladder is a clear radiance; thus, its spirit is called Dragon Brilliance. He rules over courage and fierceness; thus, he is called Majestic Brightness. On the outside, he is associated with the direction of the east and the green dragon. He matches the image of thunder and lightning.

8.8   六腑五藏神體精

The six offices [viscera] and five repositories [organs]: the spirits are essential to the organism.

Their substance protects the entire body, not leaving out even a single part, thus the text says "the spirits are essential to the organism." Heart, liver, spleen, lungs, and kidneys make up the five repositories. Stomach, large intestine, small intestine, bladder, Triple Heater, and gall bladder make up the six offices. The latter are called offices because they are like civil offices in towns, keeping order among all beings. Hence they are called offices.

As regards the organs, they are called repositories because they each manage one substance and keep it stored in the body. Hence they are called repositories. Many sources also speak of the Triple Heater, but are not clear about its perfected nature. In fact, it is located above the three organs of the heart, liver, and lungs and connects their functions. Hence it is called the Triple Heater.

The *Zhonghuang jing* 中黃經 (Scripture of Central Yellow) says, "At the head of the lungs sits [YQ: the heart, liver, and lungs make up] the Triple Heater."[4] It has its clear location. In addition, among the colors of the five directions, the spleen is yellow and is considered the ruler of the five organs. However, today people say the heart is their ruler. Why is that? The answer is: The heart is located in the center of the five organs; its substance is empty and receiving. Consisting of emptiness and nonbeing, it is seat of spirit and consciousness, the source of all circulation and application. Thus, it can bend in all directions and maintain its rulership, move and apply itself widely to keep the spirits under control. It is quite impossible to express it properly in words or images, nor can any being come close to it. It just represents the inherent patterns of nature.

8.9   皆在心內運天經

All assemble within the heart and from there revolve around the celestial passageways.

Each of the five organs and six viscera have their own jurisdiction. They all match and imitate heaven and earth, follow yin and yang, and accord harmoniously with the way of nature. Hence the text says, "revolve around the celestial passageways.

---

[4] In YQ 13.33a.

8.10 晝夜存之自長生
Visualize them day and night, and you naturally gain long life.

The five spirits in their garb and colors, think of and visualize them without stopping: this is the way of no-death. The *Xianjing* says, "Visualize the *qi* of the five organs, see it change into clouds of five colors, then have them hover above your head and envelope your entire body, See the sun residing in front of you, the moon behind you. The green dragon is on your left, the white tiger on your right, the red bird ahead, the dark warrior in back. Thus, you expel all wayward energies. This is the way of long life."[5]

Nine

9.1 肺部之宮似華蓋
The palace of the lung section resembles the Flowery Canopy.

The bureau of metal, the lungs are located at the top of the five organs. Their leaves are like a canopy. [YQ add: Their four hanging parts form a residence.]

9.2 下有童子坐玉闕
Below is a lad who sits in a jade tower.

The lad's name is Dazzling Florescence. The physical form of the lungs is like a canopy. Hence the text says "below." The jade tower is the white *qi* in the kidneys. It is linked with the lungs above.

9.3 七元之子主調氣
Master of the seven primes, he rules the balancing of *qi*.

Yuanyangzi says, "The Lord of the Seven Primes wears armor and carries talismans. He wards off and expels all misfortune and wayward energies, spreading good *qi* to the seven orifices and making the ear keen and the eyes perceptive." The seven primes, therefore, are the primordial *qi* outside the seven orifices.

9.4 外應中嶽鼻齊位
On the outside, he corresponds to the Central Peak, that is, the nose occupying the position of Qi.

---

[5] Unclear. See 2.6 above.

The Central Peak is the nose. It is also called Qi. Qi is Kunlun. The nose is the gate and doorway of the seven orifices. Its position is like that of the ruler.

9.5 素錦衣裳黃雲帶
Its spirit wears a robe and garb of undyed brocade with a belt of yellow clouds.

Undyed is the color of the membrane of the lungs. [YQ add: As regards the belt of yellow clouds], there are yellow membrane strands within the lungs, spreading out like gauzy threads. They look just like cloud *qi*.

9.6 喘息呼吸體不快
Panting and pausing, inhaling and exhaling, the rhythm is not fast.

It has to have proper timing.

9.7 急存白元和六氣
Hasten to visualize White Prime and harmonize the six *qi*.

Lord White Prime is the official in charge of the lungs. The *Dadong jing* says, "Lord White Prime resides in the right part of the Grotto Chamber."[6]

9.8 神仙久視無災害
As a spirit immortal, keep regarding him for long periods: you will be free from disaster and harm.

No wayward energy dares to show up.

9.9 用之不已形不滯
Use this without stopping, and your physical form will not be obstructed.

Always visualize in this way, and your physical form and *qi* will be glowing and flourishing. This is achieved by cultivating and refining [YQ: responding to spirit] with utmost sincerity.

---

[6] Not found in the *Dadong jing*. The citation appears in *Dongfang neijing zhu* 洞房內經注 (Inner Scripture of the Grotto Chamber with Commentary, DZ 133, SV 185-86), an early Highest Clarity work attributed to the immortal Zhou Yishan 周義山.

Ten

10.1 心部之宮蓮含華
The section of the heart looks like a blossoming lotus.

The bureau of fire, the substance of the heart organ resembles a lotus flower that has not yet opened.

10.2 下有童子丹元家
Below there is lad, called Cinnabar Prime.

The spirit of the heart is Cinnabar Prime, also known as Maintaining Numinous Force within the heart. [YQ add: He resides inside the heart and underneath clouds.] The texts says "below" because he is covered by the Flowery Canopy.

10.3 主適寒熱榮衛和
He rules and adjusts heat and cold, keeps the nutritive and protective [*qi*] in harmony.

Heat and cold indicate states of yin and yang, stillness and excitement. People should always harmonize and adjust them to nurture and protect their body. Laozi's *Scripture* says, "Excitement overcomes cold; stillness overcomes heat. Clarity and stillness are the proper way of being in the world."[7]

10.4 丹錦飛裳披玉羅
He wears flying garb of cinnabar brocade and a cloak of jade gauze.

The heart resembles the trigram Li (fire). His robe and garb of cinnabar brocade show outer yang; the cloak of jade gauze represents inner yin.

* * *

This presents an image of the color of the heart organ. It is just like the white *qi* of the lungs appears as jade gauze.

---

[7] *Daode jing* 45.

10.5 　　金鈴朱帶坐婆娑
Complete with a golden bell and vermilion sash, he sits like an old woman.

The golden bell is an image of internal medicine [muscle fibers]; the vermilion sash represents the blood vessels. Sitting like an old woman means that the spirit is in stillness and at peace. The *Jiuzhen jing* says, "The Yellow Lord Lao wears a bell of liquid gold."[8] Such is the garb of immortals.

10.6 　　調血理命身不枯
He balances the blood and regulates destiny, making sure the body does not wither.

When the heart is at peace and the organism in harmony, one is free from all disease.

10.7 　　外應口舌吐五華
On the outside, the heart corresponds to the mouth and tongue and issues the five florescences.

The heart rules the mouth and the tongue. It issues and takes in the fluids of the five organs and perceives the flavors of the five phases. Hence the text says, "on the outside, it corresponds."

10.8 　　臨絕呼之亦登蘇
Never stopping to [inhale and] exhale along with it, one can rise to a state of plenty.

Whenever people are faced with disease or danger, they should visualize the lad Cinnabar Prime with his vermilion robe and red cap, thereby to seek rescue and protection.

10.9 　　久久行之飛太霞
Practice this for a very long time and you can fly up the great empyrean.

Always practice in this manner and you can attain the state of a flying immortal.

---

[8] Same as 5.2 above.

Eleven

11.1 肝部之中翠重里 [裏]
The liver section has cyan-blue layers inside.

The bureau of wood, the liver has a verdant, cyan-blue color. It resembles big and small layers that face each other.

11.2 下有青童神公子
Below is the Green Lad, the divine Prince.

The liver is associated with the direction of the east and the position of the phase wood. It presides over the color green; thus its lord is called the Green Lad. Positioned on the left, he is the lord and master, also known as Containing Brightness. Above it is the Flowery Canopy, thus the text says "below."

11.3 主諸關鍵聰明始
He rules over all passes and locks, and represents the beginning of perception and understanding.

The liver rules the three months of spring [among the seasons], the origin and beginning of yang. Among orifices it rules the eyes, the pass and mirror of all the five phases. Hence it is "the beginning of perception and understanding."

11.4 青錦披裳佩玉鈴
Its spirit is clad in cape and garb of green brocade, complete with a jade bell.

Green brocade is the color of the liver. The jade bell is an image for the white channel hanging down. The *Shengxuan jing* 昇玄經 (Scripture of Ascension to the Mystery) says, "The five emperors of the three heavens all wear a big jade pendant on their belts."[9] The *Suling jing* 素靈經 (Scripture of Simple Numinous Force) has, "The lords of numinous luster wear cinnabar skirts and green brocade. Such is the garb of all spirit immortals."[10]

---

[9] The *Shengxuan jing* is an extensive cosmological and philosophical work of the early Tang, most of which survives in Dunhuang (DH 41 in Komjathy 2002), with one *juan* reprinted in the Daoist Canon (DZ 1122, SV 276). This statement does not appear there.

[10] Citation unclear. The *Suling jing* is found in DZ 1314, SV 187-88.

11.5　和制魂魄津液平

He harmonizes and controls the cloud and white spirit agents and makes sure the liquids and fluids are on an even keel.

This refers to internal affairs. The east and spring tend to be harmonious and warm; here the myriad beings arise.

11.6　外應眼目日月清

On the outside, the liver corresponds with the eyes, the clarity of sun and moon.

The liver on the outside rules the eyes: left is the sun; right is the moon.

* * *

The liver presides over and belongs to the eyes. They are images to show the brightness of the sun and the moon.

11.7　百痾所鍾存無英

If you are crowded by the hundred diseases, just visualize Blossomless.

If the various diseases encroach upon you, just visualize Lord Blossomless.

* * *

On the left is Blossomless. The spirit of the liver is on the left: therefore, you visualize him. One edition does not speak of Blossomless. Blossomless represents the generation of all beings.

11.8　同用七日自充盈

Equally apply this for seven days, and you will naturally feel full and satisfied.

Visualize the five organs all together, this is what is meant by "equally apply." In general, seven days make up one cycle, that is one round of practice. [The *Zhouyi* 週易 (Zhou Book of Changes) says, "In seven days he comes and returns."[11] That is just it.]

11.9　垂絕念神死復生

When close to quitting, envision this spirit; though you may die, you will come back to life.

---

[11] This appears in the Judgment of Hexagram 24. Sung 1971, 108; Wilhelm 1950, 97.

When close to death, visualize and envision the spirit of the liver, the green-robed lad, revert and gain increased vitality.

11.10 攝魂還魄永無傾
Restrain the cloud spirit agents and revert the white spirit agents: forever you are free from all upsets.

The *Taiwei lingshu* 太微靈書 (Numinous Book of Great Tenuity) says,[12]
Every month on the third, thirteenth, and twenty-third days, in the evening the three cloud spirit agents leave the body to wander about outside. To restrain them, always lie down facing up. Remove the pillow, extend your legs, and interlace your hands above the heart. Close your eyes, hold the breath in for three rounds, then click your teeth three times.

Once complete with this, in the heart visualize a red *qi* the size of a chicken egg. With each breath it enters and emerge through the throat, then evolves and grows to eventually envelope the entire body. From here, it turns into fire and burns the body several times. As you feel the organism getting slightly warmer, call out the names of the three cloud spirit agents: Vibrant Numen (Shuailing 爽靈), Womb Radiance (Taiguang 胎光), and Dark Essence (Youjing 幽精),[13] then softly intone the following incantation:

> Bureau of Great Tenuity,
> Central Yellow and Inaugural Green:
>
> Refine within my three cloud spirit agents,
> Let Womb Radiance be calm and at peace;
> All spirits, numinous forces,
> And jade treasures arise with me,
> None activated recklessly,
> All are under supervision of great emptiness.
>
> If they wish to go off flying,
> Let them visit only Highest Clarity.
> If they become hungry or thirsty,
> Let them drink mysterious water and jade essence.

---

[12] In *Lingshu ziwen* 靈書紫文 (Numinous Book in Purple Characters, DZ 639, SV 150-51), 9b-12a. The full passage, slightly abbreviated here, is translated in Bokenkamp 1997, 322-26.
[13] Bokenkamp gives these names as Bright Spirit, Embryo Light, and Tenebrous Essence (1997, 322).

Also, every month, on the days of the new, full, and last moon, the radiant white spirit agents gain fullness and start to interact and connect with outside entities. At this time, visualize and think of essence being refined, working with the methods of reversal and return. To do so, lie down face up, extend your legs, and with the palms of your hands cover both ears. Let the fingers surround the top of the head and hold the breath in for seven rounds, then click your teeth seven times. In your mind visualize a white *qi* at the tip of the nose, about as big as a small bean. Allow it to gradually grow bigger until it covers the body in nine layers above and below.

Suddenly this *qi* changes into two green dragons in the two eyes and two white tigers in the two nostrils. The red bird hovers above the heart while a verdant turtle lies under the left foot and a coiling snake under the right. Two jade maidens wearing robes of brocade come forth, their hands holding fiery radiance which they place close to the ear opening.

After you finish this, swallow the saliva seven times and call out the names of the seven white spirit agents: Corpse Dog (Shigou 屍狗), Subduing Arrow (Fuya 伏矢), Sparrow Yin (Queyin 雀陰), Devouring Robber (Tunzei 吞賊), Negating Poison (Feidu 非毒), Filth Expeller (Chuhui 除穢), and Stinky Lungs (Choufei 臭肺). Intone this incantation:

> With ninefold reverted simple *qi*,
> I control all wayward energies and encroachment of my white spirit agents.
>
> Let the [constellation] Heavenly Hound guard the gates,
> Graceful Woman hold the towers.
> Refine my white spirit agents to be harmonious and soft,
> Granting me deep peace.
>
> Let none be activated recklessly,
> But have them keep watch over the deep spring of my physical form.
> Should they be hungry or thirsty,
> Let them drink the yellow of the moon and the cinnabar of the sun.

Twelve

12.1 腎部之宮玄闕圓
The palace of the kidney section consists of towers, mysterious and round.

This is about the bureau of water. "Towers, mysterious and round" refers to the form and shape of the two kidneys. Dark is the color of water. It is an internal image or metaphor.

12.2 中有童子冥上玄
Inside is a lad, called Gloom, near the Upper Mystery.

The kidneys represent the lower mystery, their spirit is called Mysterious Gloom, also known as Raising Offspring. The heart is the upper mystery: dark and far away, its *qi* is linked to the kidneys. Hence the texts says, "Gloom, near the Upper Mystery."

12.3 主諸六府九液源
He rules all the six viscera and the source of the nine fluids.

The nine fluids link and intermingle, the [*qi* in the] hundred conduits flows and connects all—even if one fails, the system does not function. The five organs and six viscera are as explained above. The nine fluids are the fluids and liquids of the nine orifices.

12.4 外應兩耳百液津
On the outside, they [kidneys] correspond to the two ears plus the hundred fluids and liquids.

The bureau of the kidneys is in charge of the ears. When their *qi* declines, there is deafness, but when yin and yang merge in harmony, the fluids and liquids in the hundred conduits flow and connect all.

12.5 蒼錦雲衣舞龍蟠 [幡]
Its spirit wears a cloudy robe of verdant brocade and coiling [YQ: a pennant of] dancing dragons.

Verdant brocade is an image for the color of the kidneys. The cloudy robe is an image of their membrane. Coiling [YQ: the pennant of] dragons indicate the kidney conduit. The *Jiuzhen jing* says, "The Lord of the Dao always wears a robe of green brocade and a skirt of verdant florescence."[14]

12.6　　上致明霞日月煙
Above he reaches the bright aurora, the haze of sun and moon.

As long as kidney-*qi* is full [YQ: and sufficient], ears and eyes remain keen and perceptive, and [YQ: yin and yang] do not decline. This is an external image.

12.7　　百病千災急當存
If any of the hundred diseases and thousand disasters [arrives], quickly visualize him.

Yuanyangzi says, "Cold and heat generate each other, male and female complete [form] each other. In the kidneys, two spirits reside, their capes and robes of a flowery green color. On the left is a male holding up the sun; on the right is a female holding up the moon. Visualize and imagine seeing them, and forever you will be free from pause [disasters and afflictions]."

12.8　　兩部水王對生門
The king of water, in charge of the two sections, faces the Gate of Life.

The kidney organ consists of two matched parts; thus the text speaks of "two sections." The king of water residing in the kidney palace transforms into the Infant, thus the text says that he "faces the Gate of Life."

12.9　　使人長生升九天
He makes people live long and ascend to the nine heavens.

The Infant transforms into a perfected and ascends to the nine heavens. The nine heavens are commonly called the clear heavens of the nine *qi*. This *qi* rules all generative processes.

---

[14] Similar to the description of the deity's garb from the same source in 5.2 above.

Thirteen

13.1　脾部之宮屬戊巳
The palace of the spleen section belongs to *wusi*.

This refers to the bureau of earth. *Wusi* is the position of the center.

13.2　中有明童黃裳里
Inside is a bright lad, wearing yellow garb.

The bright lad is called Cloud Spirit Pavilion. The yellow garb signals the color of earth.

13.3　消穀散氣攝牙齒
He dissolves grain and spreads *qi*, assisted by the teeth.

The spleen is the pivot of the five organs; it grinds up food and dissolves it so that living *qi* can come forth [YQ: inner-nature *qi* can be complete]. They are known as Network of Thousands. Hence the text says, "assisted by the teeth."

13.4　是為太倉兩明童
He shows up in the Great Storehouse, one of two bright lads.

The Great Storehouse is the stomach among the viscera. The bright lad here is the spirit of the stomach. His name is Chaos Vigor (Hunkang 混康).

13.5　坐在金臺城九重
He sits on a golden terrace, a wall of twelve stories.

Envision him attentively, visualize and think of him, and the spirit will manifest himself.

13.6　方圓一寸命門中
Square and round, one inch in size: the center of the Gate of Destiny.

That is, he resides in the Yellow Court, the Palace of the Elixir Field.

13.7　　主調百穀五味香
He rules and balances the hundred grains with their five flavors and fragrances.

Budding flavors in the mouth arise because the spleen properly grinds up the food.

13.8　　關卻虛羸無病傷
It cuts of and eliminates all emptiness and fullness so you can be free from disease and harm.

This refers to internal affairs. [YQ: It works because food is dissolved.]

13.9　　外應尺宅氣色芳
On the outside, the spleen corresponds with the inch residence, where *qi* and complexion flourish.

The inch residence is the face. Hungry and satiated, empty and full match the physical form and show up in the complexion of the face.

13.10　　光華所生以表明
It is where radiance and florescence arise, spreading brightness outward.

This is because it knows the states of emptiness and fullness.

13.11　　黃錦玉衣帶虎章
He wears a jade robe of yellow brocade and has a tiger seal on his belt.

The ruler of the spleen is Central Yellow (Zhonghuang 中黃). Also known as Perfected of the Yellow Court, he wears a robe of brocade. The *Yuqing yinshu* 玉清隱書 (Secret Book of Jade Clarity) says, "The Most High Lord of the Dao as a pendant wears a jade seal with a spirit tiger."[1]

13.12　　注念三老子輕翔
Envision the three Old Ones attentively, and you will feel light and soaring.

---

[1] DZ 1355, SV 139-40. The text consists of exorcistic hymns and talismanic writings. It invokes the Most High Lord of the Dao and mentions wearing a jade seal with a spirit tiger, but not in the same passage.

The three Old Ones are the Old Lords of Nonbeing, Seniority, and Mystery. As you envision the perfected in the spleen, they naturally change and transform. "You" here refers to the student of the Yellow Court.

13.13   長生高仙遠死殃
A lofty immortal living long, you will be far away from death and destruction.

Zhuangzi says: "Where there is life, there must be death; where there is death, there must be life. Where there is acceptability, there must be unacceptability; where there is unacceptability, there must be acceptability."[2] Discussed from this perspective, the principles are equal. That is, those who live long do not die; those who find cessation in serenity [nirvana] do not live. Not dying and not coming to life: that is perfect long life; not living and therefore not dying; that is perfect cessation in serenity. Where would death and destruction reach?

Fourteen

14.1   膽部之宮六府精
The palace of the gall bladder section is the essence of all six viscera.

The six viscera were already explained above [YQ: gall bladder, stomach, large intestine, small intestine, bladder, and Triple Heater]. The *Taiping jing* 太平經 (Scripture of Great Peace) says, "Accumulated clarity forms essence" Therefore, the gall bladder is "the essence of all six viscera."[3]

14.2   中有童子曜威明
Inside is a lad, called [Dragon] Brilliance or Majestic Brightness.

The *Scripture* says: "The spirit of the gall bladder is Dragon Brilliance, also known as or Majestic Brightness."[4] These names indicate courage and ruthlessness [YQ: forbidding].

14.3   雷電八震揚玉旌
Thunder and lightning, the eight quakes, shake the jade flags.

---

[2] *Zhuangzi* 2, "Qiwulun."
[3] Contained in *Taiping jing* (Wang 1979, 190).
[4] This cites the text above, *Neijing* 8.3

Thunder and lightning of the eight directions are images for the majestic and violent qualities of the gall bladder. Jade flags express the shape [YQ: quality] of its *qi*.

14.4 龍旗橫天擲火鈴
Dragon banners streak the sky as he wields the fire bell.

The gall bladder is the color green [QU: of the green dragon]. Flags and banners are instruments that show majesty and war. Fire bell is an image of the pearls in the area around the gall bladder. When angry he rouses and shakes them, thus the text says "wields."

14.5 主諸氣力攝虎兵
He rules with force all kinds of *qi* and manages the tiger soldiers.

The gall bladder forcefully rules over all ruthlessness and hardship, thus it says, "manages the tiger soldiers."

14.6 外應眼瞳鼻柱間
On the outside, the gall bladder corresponds with the pupils of the eyes, the area of the pillar of the nose.

This refers to internal affairs. All joy and anger of the heart correspond to the area between the eyebrows [YQ: and eyes].

14.7 腦髮相扶亦俱鮮
Brain and hair support each other and become equally refreshed.

When people are upset or angry, their hair quivers and stands up like a cap.

14.8 九色錦衣綠華裙
He wears a robe of nine-colored brocade and a skirt of green florescence.

Green brocade is the color of the nine *qi* of the east. The skirt of green florescence is an image showing the membrane of the gall bladder.

14.9 佩金帶玉龍虎文
He wears a pendant of gold and a belt of jade, showing dragon-tiger patterns.

The spirit of the gall bladder wears adornments of Majestic Brightness.

14.10　能存威明乘慶雲
If you can visualize Majestic Brightness, you can ride up on felicitous clouds.

This is an internal image. Think of and visualize the spirit of the gall bladder without tiring, and you can attain on the way of immortality.

14.11　役使萬神朝三元
You can command and direct the myriad spirits and attend an audience with the Three Primes.

The spirit lords of the Three Primes live in the Three Clarities. The spirit immortals of all the heavens attend and honor them in audience.

Fifteen

15.1　脾長一尺掩太倉
The spleen is one foot long; it covers the Great Storehouse.

The Great Storehouse is the stomach. The *Zhonghuang jing* says, "The stomach is called the Great Storehouse."[5] Yuanyangzi says, "The spleen sits horizontally right above the stomach."

15.2　中部老君治明堂
Lord Lao of the central section rules here, from the Hall of Light.

The spleen is the bureau [YQ: palace] of the Yellow Court. It is the place from which the Yellow Lord Lao rules. Above it corresponds to the Hall of Light, found when entering one inch inside between the eyebrows.

15.3　厥字靈元名混康
His agnomen is Numinous Prime (Lingyuan), his proper name is Chaos Vigor.

The spleen grinds up food and dissolves it, corresponding properly inside and out. The large intestine is the son of the stomach. "Chaos" means that it receives and takes in primordial yang. "Vigor" means being at peace.

---

[5] The text appears in YQ 13. It speaks about the location of the various organs, including the stomach, but does not mention the term Great Storehouse.

15.4　治人百病消穀糧
It cures the hundred diseases in people, as it dissolves all grains and starches.

As long as the bureau [YQ: palace] of the stomach is glorious and flowery, you will be free from disease and harm.

15.5　黃衣紫帶龍虎章
Its spirit wears a yellow robe and purple sash with a dragon-tiger seal.

The spleen resides above the stomach; thus, the text says he wears a yellow robe. The purple sash and dragon seal as images show the energy lines of the stomach.

15.6　長精益命賴君王
To lengthen essence and increase destiny, rely on this Lord King.

Chaos Vigor of the Great Storehouse is the Lord King.

15.7　三呼我名神自通
Call my name three times, and the spirits naturally pervade all.

Visualize and think of the spirits of the stomach office, and your heart will be numinous and pervasively mirror all.

15.8　三老同坐各有朋
The Three Lao [Elders] all sit equally, each with his fellows.

Lord Lao of Upper Prime resides in the bureau [YQ: palace] of the upper Yellow Court together with the Lord of Niwan, the Lord of Verdant Florescence, and the Lord of the Green City. In addition, the lords and ministers who reside in the Hall of Light, the spirit father and mother in the Grotto Chamber, the perfected in the Heavenly Court, and others all are his fellows.

　　Next, Lord Lao of Middle Prime resides in the bureau [YQ: palace] of the central Yellow Court together with the Lad of the Red City, the Lord of the Elixir Field, the Lord of White Floresence, the Lord of Containing Light, the Lord of Mysterious Glow, and the Perfected of Cinnabar Prime. They and others all are his friends.

　　Again, Lord Lao of Lower Prime [YQ: The Yellow Lord Lao] resides in the bureau [YQ: palace] of the lower Yellow Court together with the Lord of the Great One, the Lord of the Cloud Spirit Pavilion, the Lord of Numinous

Prime, [YQ: the Lord of the Great Storehouse], and the Perfected of the Elixir Field. They and others all are his friends.

Always visualize the Three Lao, and the hundred spirits will flow and connect all positions in the different sections [of the body], nurturing and protecting them. Never stop or interrupt the practice

15.9　　或精或胎別執方
Whether essence or womb, do not hold tight to only one direction.

The *Yuli jing* says, "The lower Elixir Field is the root and base of primordial destiny. It is where the essence and spirit are stored, the prime source of the five *qi*. Located three inches below the navel, it attaches to the spine. Called the office of the Infant, it is where males store their essence and where females have their womb. It rules all harmony and, through the Infant, serves as the gate and doorway of yin and yang. The *qi* in this Elixir Field is green on the left and yellow on the right, white above and black below."[6]

15.10　　桃孩合延生華芒
Peach Child (Taohai), also known as Merge and Extend (Heyan), generates flowery abundance.

This are the personal and secondary names of the Lord of the Great One. In various places he causes spirit and *qi* to be rich and bountiful.

*　*　*

Peach Child is the name of the spirit of yin and yang. He is also called Uncle Peach (Botao 伯桃). The *Xianjing* says, "In the palace near the navel, the Gate of Destiny, is a great lord. His name is Peach Child, also known as Merge and Extend. He wears a vermilion robe together with a headdress of purple hibiscus. When you lie down at night, visualize him, and the Six Jia and Six Ding spirits will come to serve you."[7] The expression "generates flowery abundance" means that the *qi* of yin and yang does not decline.

15.11　　男女回九有桃康
When men or women circulate *qi* nine times, Peach Vigor (Taokang) appears.

---

[6] *Laozi zhongjing* 1.17.
[7] Unclear. See 2.6 above.

The spirit beneath the Elixir Field is called Peach Vigor. He rules the origin of people's essence and womb. If you can circulate *qi* and connect the three fields, you will complete the *qi* of the nine spirits.

* * *

When men and women come together, they must visualize the three elixir fields according to the right methods. Peach Vigor is the name of the spirit beneath. He rules all affairs of yin and yang. Three circulations [of the three fields] make nine, thus it says, "circulate nine times." The *Dadong zhenjing* says, "The Three Primes transform secretly and constitute the Three Palaces. In the Three Palaces are nine spirits."[8] These are the upper, middle and lower lords of the Three Primes, plus the Great One, the Prince, White Prime, Blossomless, the Director of Destiny, and Peach Vigor. Each have their own palace and chamber." This is what the text means when it refers to Peach Vigor.

15.12　道父道母對相望
Father and mother of Dao face and look at each other.

Yin and yang are two halves that make one, thus it says, "face and look at each other."

15.13　師父師母丹玄鄉
Father and mother teacher rest in the homestead of cinnabar mystery.

Dao and ancestral teachers are the rulers of yin and yang. The homestead of cinnabar mystery refers to the method of visualizing the Elixir Field.

15.14　可用存思登虛空
If you can use the right way to visualize and think of them, you will ascend to emptiness and void.

Such is the way of studying immortality.

15.15　殊途一會歸要終
If you lose the path even in one instance, your return will end.

Merging the three into one, spreading the one into three, such is the core of Dao. The *Xuanmiao neipian* 玄妙內篇 (Inner Record of Mystery and Won-

---

[8] Same citation as in 7.11 above.

der) says, "If you desire to attain long life, the three and one must all be bright."[9]

15.16 閉塞三關握固停
Close and block the three passes, clench your fists quite tight.

The *Scripture* says, "The mouth is the Pass of Heaven, the pivot of essence and spirit. The hands are the Pass of Humanity, the control of flourishing and decline. The feet are the Pass of Earth, the gate where destiny arises."[10] There is also a pass of primordial *qi* located three inches below the navel, which is sometimes called the three passes. It is in charge of keeping essence steady and preserving *qi*. Do not spread or leak it recklessly.

15.17 含漱金醴吞玉英
Contain and rinse with golden spring and swallow jade glow.

Golden spring and jade glow are liquids in the mouth. The *Dadong jing* says, "To practice the method of absorbing the mysterious root, in your mind visualize the entrance of the stomach, seeing there a female with the physical form of a baby but without any clothes or garb. Standing right at the stomach duct, she opens her mouth and issues cloud-spirit fluid. Looking up, she exhales the five *qi* which then collect and fill the mouth, inside and out, with liquids and fluids. Once they fill your mouth, swallow them, and send them directly into the mouth of the mysterious female. Do this five times. Once complete, click the teeth five times and swallow the saliva seven times."[11]

15.18 遂至不饑三蟲亡
Continue this until you are no longer hungry and the three worms perish.

The *Dongshen jue* 洞神訣 (Instructions of Cavern Spirit) says, "The upper worm is white and green; the middle worm is white and yellow; the lower worm is white and black. When people die, these three worms emerge and

---

[9] The *Xuanmiao neipian* is an early hagiography of Laozi that survives in citations. See Kohn 1995, 223. The citation is from the *Xuanmiao yunü zichuan xiandao* 玄妙玉女資傳仙道 (The Way of Immortality Transmitted by the Jade Maiden of Mystery and Wonder, DZ 868, SV 359-60), 6b. The text is a Tang record of practice instructions Laozi received from his mother after her canonization in 666.
[10] *Neijing* 18.3-5. For a discussion of these passes, see Cai 2006, 137-41.
[11] This cites the same passage as in 3.1 above. Citation unclear.

become corpse ghosts. They transform into living entities and bring calamity to people's physical forms, striking at them and pushing to destroy them.

Beyond this, there is also a host of worms that pursue people, causing them to perish. For this reason, students of immortality remain clear [YQ: focused] and diligent, preparing the five clear *qi*. After that, they take herbal remedies to expel the three worms."

It also says, "The upper deathbringer is called Peng San 彭珊 [YQ: Ju 琚]; he causes people to relish excitement and nice flavors, to engage in passions and desires, foolishness and obstructions. The middle deathbringer is Peng Zhi 彭質; he causes people to accumulate treasures and relish joy and anger. The lower deathbringer is Peng Qiao 彭矯; he causes people to relish robes and garb, to pursue sensuality and female entertainment."[12] Such are the names of the three worms.

15.19   心意常和致欣昌
If your heart and intention are always in harmony, you can attain delight and brilliance.

When connected to Dao, you are free from obstructions.

15.20   五岳之雲氣彭亨
With the clouds of the five sacred peaks, your *qi* is strong and proud.

The *qi* of the five organs are the clouds of the five sacred peaks, "Strong and proud" is an expression for flowing connection and freedom from obstruction.

15.21   保灌玉廬以自償 [= 1/24]
Protect and moisten the Jade Hut, and you will naturally be fulfilled.

The Jade Hut is the nose. Once the three worms have perished, perfect *qi* merges in harmony. It issues from and enters through the mysterious female

---

[12] *Dongshen jue* is a generic name for instructions contained in Daoist scriptures. A detailed description of the worms and deathbringers appears in the late-Tang *Chu sanshi jiuchong baosheng jing* 除三尸九蟲保生經 (Scripture on Preserving Life by Removing the Nine Worms and Three Deathbringers, DZ 871, SV 364-65; Kohn 1995), 7a-9a. For their evolution and visual representation, see Huang 2011, 33-42; 2012, 52-64.

continuously without interruption.¹³ Hence the text says, "naturally be fulfilled."

15.22   五形完堅無災殃
The five-part physical form whole and stable, you will be free from disasters and calamities.

This refers to the five limbs and the physical form of the five organs. Visualize and refine them until Dao is complete and in an empty chamber you will bring forth whiteness. When the five organs are stable and whole, naturally disasters and diseases will not arise, but spirits and *qi* will naturally correspond with each other.

Sixteen

16.1   上睹三元如連珠
Above gaze at the Three Primes, lined up like a string of pearls.

The Three Primes are the primes of the three luminants: sun, moon, and stars. They do not refer to the Three Primes of upper, medium, and lower.

16.2   落落明景照九隅
Scattered widely like bright lights, they shine throughout the nine corners.

The three luminants rest above and illuminate downward throughout the nine corners. The nine corners are the nine directions. This says to always visualize the sun and the moon, to pervasively shine through the entire body.

16.3   五靈夜燭煥八區
The five numinous forces illuminate the night, flaming through all eight regions.

The five numinous forces are the five planets. Luminous and fiery, they are like a net through the entire body. If you can always visualize them, you will end together with heaven and earth.

---

¹³ Both the expression "mysterious female" (*xuanmu* 玄牝) and the term "continuously" (*mianmian* 綿綿) appear in *Daode jing* 6.

16.4　子存內皇與我游
You visualize the internal sovereigns and wander along with me.

The great Dao has no mind of its own: if there is an impulse, it will respond.

16.5　身披鳳衣銜虎符
Your body is covered by a phoenix robe; your rank marked by a tiger talisman.

Such are the clothes and ornaments of immortal officials.

16.6　一至不久升虛無
At one in attainment, not long and you ascend to emptiness and nonbeing.

One is an expression for not two. Studying Dao means focusing on oneness and joining one's organism with the numinous forces. Spirit immortals can achieve that. As the *Nanhua zhenjing* 南華真經 (Perfect Scripture of Southern Florescence) says: "If people can maintain the One, the myriad affairs are done!"[14]

16.7　方寸之中念深藏 [= 1/26]
In the center of the square inch, envision a deep storage.

The center of the square inch is the lower pass [YQ: prime], located three inches below the navel. Square and round, one inch in size, it is used to store essence [YQ: where males store essence]. Hence it speaks of "deep storage."

16.8　不方不圓閉牖窗
Neither square nor round, firmly close the orifices and windows.

"Square" means still, while "round" means active. Neither active nor still, just attend to shutting and sealing it, never letting it leak recklessly

16.9　三神還精老方壯 [= 1/27]
The three spirits revert essence: even if old, you recover vigor.

Revert spirit and essence to the three fields, and you can lengthen longevity and extend your years.

---

[14] *Zhuangzi* 12.

16.10 魂魄內守不爭競
The cloud and white spirit agents are firmly maintained within, never competing or fighting.

The cloud spirit agents are yang, while the white spirit agents are yin. The *Yijing* (Book of Changes) says, "One yang, one yin: that is called Dao."[15]

16.11 神生腹中銜玉璫
As the spirits arise in your belly, your rank is marked by a jade pendant.

Maintain all inside and do not let anything leak, then the spirits will arise and your rank is marked with a pendant.[16] Belly and heart bright from the inside, your mouth expels pearls and jade. The *Wuchen xingshi jue* says, "One inch straight up from between the eyebrows, enter in for one inch: this is the Purple Tower [YQ: pass] of jade pendants."[17] [YQ: I humbly observe that the meaning of the passage does not quite match the text.]

16.12 靈注幽闕那得喪 [= 1/28]
If numinous force soaks the Dark Towers, how will you ever be destroyed?

As the spirits arise in the belly, numinous *qi* flows and connects everywhere. Therefore, you do not perish. The towers of essence are located in the kidneys. The kidneys rule water, and their color is black. Their *qi* connects to the ears, which both stand tall. The towers are an image for something lofty and high.

* * *

Visualize the spirits and maintain the One, and you will be free from obstacles and early death.

16.13 琳條萬尋可蔭仗
Rather, jeweled branches, ten thousand yards tall, will shelter you completely.

When the body is in line with the host of numinous forces, like a forest they intermingle and radiate widely. Like jade trees, ten thousand yards tall, they

---

[15] *Yijing*, *Xici* 1.5 (Sung 1971, 280).
[16] This first sentence is not contained in YQ.
[17] YQ 52.15b, same as 6.5 above.

provide shade and shelter.[18] This is an external image. Jeweled branches indicated jade trees. Ten thousand yards is a way of expressing great height and long distance. When body and physical form join perfection, they are being shaded and sheltered by the spirits in their brightness.

16.14   三魂自寧帝書命
The three cloud spirit agents naturally calm, the emperor writes you a new destiny.

When you cultivate the body and the spirits are at peace, the emperor will write an edict. Once the Dao of perfection is complete, your name will be written in the imperial registers, and you enjoy eternal vision.

* * *

Once the Dao of perfection is complete, your name will be written in the imperial registers.

Seventeen

17.1   靈臺鬱藹望黃野 [= 1/31]
The Numinous Terrace grows thickly and luxuriant, looking at Yellow Wilderness.

The heart is the Numinous Terrace. The spleen is Yellow Wilderness. Always focus on the One and you can visualize and see the Yellow Court.

* * *

The Numinous Terrace is the heart. It says that if in your heart you focus on the One and visualize to see the Yellow Court, then this is Yellow Wilderness.

17.2   三寸異室有上下 [= 1/32]
The separate chambers of the three inch-size [spaces] are upper and lower.

The three elixir fields—upper, middle, and lower—have three locations that are each different. Each chamber is one inch square and round, thus the text says "three inch-size [spaces]." Today, when people talk specifically about the heart as the square inch, they refer to this [YQ: one] location.

---

[18] This first part of the commentary appears only in the *Xiuzhen shishu* version.

17.3   間關營衛高玄受

Between them, at the passes, nutritive and protective [*qi*] are received, lofty and mysterious.

Between the three fields, in each case there are spaces and passes, where nutritive and protective *qi* divide, going high and going low. The heart can receive them when you visualize and envision this.

17.4   洞房紫極靈門戶 [= 1/33]

In the Grotto Chamber with its purple beams are the gates and doors of the numinous forces.

The *Dadong jing* says, "Moving in between the eyebrows for three *fen* there is the double elixir field; moving into the bone segment for three *fen* there is the terrace pass. Straight in deeper for seven *fen*, on the left there is the hearth chamber, on the right there is the purple door.

"Moving in for one inch, there is the palace of the Hall of Light. On the left is the Lord Bright Lad; on the right is the Honorable Bright Lady. Moving in for two inches, there is the Grotto Chamber. On the left is Lord Blossomless; on the right is Lord White Prime; in the center is the Yellow Lord Lao.

"Moving in for three inches, there is the Palace of the Elixir Field, also known as the Niwan Palace. The Lord Infant of the Upper Prime resides there; on the right is the Lord Imperial Minister. Moving in for four inches, there is the Palace of Flowing Pearls. The Perfected Lord of Flowing Pearls resides there. Moving in for five inches, there is the Palace of the Jade Emperor. The Perfected Mother of Jade Clarity resides there.

"One inch straight above the Hall of Light, there is the Palace of the Heavenly Court. The Perfected Lady of Highest Clarity resides there. One inch straight above the Grotto Chamber, there is the Palace of Ultimate Perfection. The Imperial Lord of Great Ultimate resides there. One inch straight above the Elixir Field is the Palace of Cinnabar Mystery. The Lord of the Great One and Central Yellow resides there. Two inches straight above the [Palace of] Flowing Pearls is the Palace of the Great Sovereign. The Most High Lord resides there."[19]

This is what the text means when it says, "the gates and doors of the numinous forces."

---

[19] Same as above, in the commentary to *Neijing* 2.9.

17.5 是昔太上告我者 [= 1/34]
This is what the Most High told me that night!

"Me" is how the Great Emperor of Fusang refers to himself. He says that "once my Dao was complete," at night, the Lord of the Dao gave him the *Yellow Court* timing [YQ: arts]. The text here says that the Dao is never far off, but always rests in the Elixir Field. Hence it uses the words "that night."

17.6 左神公子發神語
The spirit on the left, the Prince, issues spirit speech.

The *Dadong jing* says, "On the left is Blossomless."[20] Here he is called "the Prince." It is just another way of referring to him. "Issue spirit speech" means that, if you focus on the One in your heart, the spirits will teach about Dao.

17.7 右有白元並立處
On the right is White Prime, standing right alongside.

To the right and left are those who support the students of Dao.

17.8 明堂金匱玉房間
The Hall of Light, the golden casket, is the Jade Chamber.

These all refer to the palace of highest prime, as explained above.

17.9 上清真人當吾前 [= 1/36]
The Perfected of Highest Clarity appears before me.

The spirit of the section of highest prime is always in the area of the Heavenly Court.

17.10 黃裳子丹氣頻煩
The Yellow-Garbed [Master], Child Cinnabar, helps when *qi* is distressed and troubled.

This speaks of the lad of the central prime who resides in the Red City. When distressed and troubled, his *qi* arises and there is neither decline nor exhaustion.

---

[20] Part of the above citation, 2.9 and 17.4.

17.11　借問何在兩眉端
Maybe to ask what is at the tip of the two eyebrows.

This refers to the location of the Hall of Light.

17.12　內俠日月列宿陳
Internally I clasp the sun and the moon, line up the constellations.

The *Wuchen xingshi jue* says,[21]

The Most High Perfected summoned the five planets in the Grotto Chamber following the transmission he had received from the Lady of the Southern Ultimate. According to this,

Every day at midnight sit or recline, and in your heart visualize the great white star of the west [Venus] between your eyebrows, straight up and in one inch, at the golden tower with jade pendants, where the sun is on the left and the moon on the right.

Next, see the chronogram star of the north [Mercury] in the dark palace of the imperial domain, located one inch in at five *fen* from the hairline.

Now, visualize the year star of the east [Jupiter], in the vermilion terrace of the grotto tower, located one inch in behind they eyes.

From here, envision the fiery star of the south [Mars] in the flowery chamber with its jade gates, located five *fen* in about five fen from the corner area of the eyes.

Finally, see the guardian star of the center [Saturn], in a long valley of yellow chambers, located two *fen* straight in from the human center [nose].

"In addition, visualize them all connected and hanging down from above. Once complete, click your teeth five times, swallow the saliva for five rounds, and softly intone this incantation:

Purple Tower of lofty prime:
Within you hold five spirits.
Precious and brilliant, they spread their splendor,
Issuing radiance that penetrates all gates.

Let your essence and *qi* accumulate and rise,
Then transform into five old men.
With plain kerchiefs on your heads,
You wear green cloaks over scarlet skirts.

---

[21] YQ 52.15b-16a, all except the first paragraph.

On the right you have the flowing bell on your belt,
On the left you carry the pendant of the tiger perfected.
In your hand you hold the heavenly vajra,
As you spread scarlet flying mist.
Your feet tread on the Flowery Canopy,
And you issue rays of light that refine my body.

The three luminants come to protect and maintain me
And get me to attain perfection.
Nurturing my cloud spirit agents and controlling my white spirit agents,
I ride the whirlwind and fly up as an immortal.

This is what the text intends. It is full of internal imagery.

17.13   七曜九元冠生門
The seven brilliant ones and nine primes crown your Gate of Life.

The seven brilliant ones are the seven stars; they match the seven orifices in human beings. The nine primes are the nine chronograms; they match the nine orifices in human beings. You cannot lose even one of them, thus the texts speaks of the "Gate of Life."

Eighteen

18.1   三關之中精氣深 [= 1/37]
In all three passes, essence and *qi* are deep.

This says that the Pass Primordial is where males store their essence. It also refers to the text below which points to the mouth, hands, and feet as the three passes. Yuanyangzi identifies the Hall of Light, Grotto Chamber, and Elixir Field as the three passes. Any of these interpretations can be used as the basis for visualization.

18.2   九微之內幽且陰
In the Nine Tenuities, all is dark and shady.

The *Dadong jing* says, "The Three Primes transform in secrecy and turn into the three bureaus."[22] Then they are called Great Clarity, Great Simplicity,

---

[22] Same citation as in 7.11 above.

and Great Harmony. Three times three make nine. Therefore, there are three elixir fields and also three grotto chambers. The upper Three Primes are the Nine Palaces. Inside each palace, essence is subtle. Hence the text speaks of the Nine Tenuities. When it uses the work "dark," it means they are mysterious and cannot be seen.

18.3　口為心關精神機
The mouth is the Pass of the Heart [Heaven], the core mechanism of essence and spirit.

This says that here issues the emotions; it is like a pivoting mechanism.

18.4　足為地關生命棐
The feet are the Pass of Earth, the yew of life and destiny.

This says that evolving destiny uses the self and body to manifest life. Yew makes up its half-door.

18.5　手為人關把盛衰
The hands are the Pass of Humanity, the handle of flourishing and decline.

Looseness and holding on [YQ: containment] come from the self.

Nineteen

19.1 若得三宮存玄丹
If you want to attain the Three Palaces, visualize mysterious cinnabar.

The three elixir fields are palaces, thus it speaks of "Three Palaces." Mysterious cinnabar is Cinnabar Prime, that is, the heart. Visualize and think of the heart. Hence, the text points only to one place here.

19.2 太一流珠安昆侖
The Great One and Flowing Pearls are at peace in Kunlun.

The Great One and [Palace of] Flowing Pearls refer to the pupils [YQ: essence] of the eyes. The *Dongshen jing* 洞神經 (Cavern Spirit Scripture) says, "The head is the Lord of the Three Terraces, also described as Kunlun." This indicates the upper Elixir Field. It also says, "The navel is the Lord of the Great One, also described as Kunlun."[1] This refers to the lower Elixir Field. It says, in the heart visualize the three elixir fields. Then spirit will gleam before the eyes. This is just what the original text means when it says, "If you want to avoid death, cultivate Kunlun."[2] [YQ: Kunlun is a famous mountain.]

19.3 重重樓閣十二環 [= 1/39]
The Multi-storied Tower or Pavilion has twelve rings.

This says that the esophagus has twelve rings that are stacked one upon the other, resting right above the heart. The heart is the Scarlet Palace, it looks like a building or pavilion. That's why the text uses these words.

19.4 自高自下皆真人
Both high above and down below, it is occupied by perfected.

Above and below, in the elixir fields as much as in the Twelve-storied Tower, there are perfected [YQ: and spirits]. The explanation [YQ: text] is as noted above.

---

[1] Dongshen is the bibliographic classification of texts of the Three Sovereigns lineage (see Steavu 2019). Mount Kunlun as the navel is found in *Laozi zhongjing* 1.14; as the head it is noted in *Neiguan jing* (Scripture of Inner Observation, DZ 641, SV 500; YQ 17; Kohn 1989; 2010, 179-87), 3b.

[2] W*aijing* 1/38.

19.5　玉堂絳宇盡玄宮
The jade hall with scarlet eaves covers the mysterious palace.

The Scarlet Palace and Hall of Light correspond to each other above and below. Both are palaces and chambers.

19.6　璇璣玉衡色蘭玕
Jasper Sphere and Jade Scale [Dipper stars] in color are like orchids and gems.

This is an image of the rotating motion of the bony rings of the esophagus. Orchids and gems indicate their color.

19.7　瞻望童子坐盤桓
Look up and regard the lad sitting quite relaxed.

Visualize and see the lad in the Red City, the perfected [YQ: sovereign] Child Cinnabar. 'Sit' here means that the spirit is at peace and in stillness.

19.8　問誰家子在我身
Ask what kind of person resides in my body?

This means that he is already there.

19.9　此人何去入泥丸
And how does this person leave and enter the Niwan?

He corresponds to all the spirits of the upper prime, as above so below. The *Dongshen jing* says, "The brain is the Niwan Palace."[3]

19.10　千千百百自相連
Thousands upon thousands, hundreds upon hundreds—they are naturally linked together.

The spirits originally emerge from the One. "The One generates the two; the two generate the three; the three generate the myriad beings."[4] They change and transform and never leave our body and mind.

---

[3] Citation unclear.
[4] Citation from *Daode jing* 42, where the One emerges from Dao to begin the sequence.

152 / INNER SCRIPTURE

19.11   一一十十似重山
One by one, ten by ten, they look like layered mountains.

Visualize and see the myriad beings; layer upon layer, they sit peacefully. "Mountains" here serves as an image on the way they sit.

19.12   雲儀玉華俠耳門
Like Cloud Presence (Yunyi) and Jade Florescence (Yuhua) crowd at the ears' gate.

Cloud Presence and Jade Florescence are names of [spirits of] hairs and whiskers. It says that they reside in the area of the ears. The *Dadong jing* says, "The spirit of the hair is called Verdant Florescence."[5] Generally, anything with the word "florescence" in it [YQ: indicates something flourishing in great numbers], like the blossoms of grasses and trees.

19.13   赤帝黃老與我[己]魂
The Red Emperor and Yellow Lord Lao join my cloud spirit agents.

The Red Emperor is the imperial lord of the south. The Yellow Lord Lao is the lord of the center. The cloud spirit agents are yang deities, while the white spirit agents are yin spirits. Yin and yang correspond to each other, thus the text says "join my cloud spirit agents." The *Taiwei lingshu* says, "Human beings have three cloud spirit agents. The first is called Womb Radiance, the second is Vibrant Numen, and the third is Dark Essence."[6] Always call out and chant their names, then the three will never leave your body.

19.14   三真扶胥共房津
The three perfected together support and nurture my chambers and liquids.

The cloud spirit agents plus the Red Emperor and the Yellow Lord Lao are the three perfected. This says that they mutually correspond with each other to support and nurture liquids and *qi*.[7]

19.15   五斗煥明是七元
The five dippers, brilliant and bright: here are the seven primes.

---

[5] Citation unclear.
[6] The same text including these three names is also cited above in *Neijing* 11.10.
[7] The YQ edition does not have any commentary to this line.

The five dippers are the five planets. The seven primes are the stars of the Northern Dipper. [YQ: According to the *Lingbao jing* 靈寶經 (Scripture of Numinous Treasure), there are five dipper constellations in the five directions, also called the five dippers.[8]] The *Dongfang jue* 洞房訣 (Instructions on the Grotto Chamber) says, "Visualize the stars known as the [YQ nine or] seven primes either when rising from sleep or when just about going to bed, but after finishing a meal. Softly intone the following incantation:

> The five stars are open and connected.
> The six harmonies are in the Purple Chamber.
> Revolve to the prime, be secret in Dao
> Vastly spread the seven chronograms.
>
> Generating the cloud spirit agents is the Mysterious Father.
> Generating the white spirit agents is the Mysterious Mother.
> Transforming both, they complete my body.
> Assisting my tendons and bones is the Prince [Blossomless].
> Managing my essence and *qi* is White Prime.
>
> May I gain long life and eternal vision[9]
> As a flying immortal in the ten heavens![10]

19.16   日月飛行六合間
The sun and moon fly about between the six harmonies.

---

[8] Ge Hong's *Baopuzi* (ch. 19) mentions a work called *Lingbao jing* (Ware 1966, 209), which comprises three sections, known as *Zhengji* 正機 (Proper Mechanism), *Pingheng* 平衡 (Equalizer), and *Feigui shou* 飛龜授 (Flying Turtle Transmission). What these terms refer to is not clear, but it may have had to do with worship of the Northern Dipper (Yamada 2000, 228; Chen 1975, 62). While Highest Clarity recognizes a pair of dippers in the north and south (Robinet 1993; Noguchi et al. 1994, 548), dipper constellations in all five directions do not become prominent until in the 10th century. A set of six new texts (DZ 622-27) present talismans and invocations as well as devotional measures of protection involving scriptural recitation and formal rites for the dippers, preferably undertaken on one's birthday, at new moon, or on generally auspicious days (Kohn 2000, 160; Yusa 1983, 334).
[9] This expression goes back to *Daode jing* 59,
[10] *Dongfang shangjing* 洞房上經 (Highest Scripture of the Grotto Chamber, DZ 405, SV 147-48), 19ab.

The area between heaven and earth is known as the six harmonies. Visualize and envision the sun and the moon, planets and stars inside the body. Ten thousand images like a forest or network, they are all around the sky, clear and distinct [YQ: they are all at once like doorways of heaven and earth, clear and distinct].

19.17   帝鄉天中地戶端
Imperial homestead, heavenly center, plus the tip of the earth door.

Enter in one inch above the eyebrows, about five *fen* from the hairline is the imperial homestead. One inch above the Hall of Light is the Heavenly Court, also known as the heavenly center. The nose is the earth door of the upper section of the body. In your mind, visualize all the various spirits of the sun and the moon, planets and stars, and more. Always keep them at the "tip," that is, above the nose and below the hairline.

19.18   面部魂神皆相存
The cloud spirit agents and spirits of the face are all visualized together.

Inside and outside, heart [YQ: stars] and spirits naturally are in full accord.

Twenty

20.1   呼吸元氣以求仙
Inhale and exhale primordial *qi* in order to pursue immortality.

Search out [the elixir] Flying Root, gather mysterious brilliance, swallow the five sprouts, obtain the nine mists, absorb nourishment, engage in embryo respiration—all these methods are ways to work with the *qi* of heaven and earth, yin and yang, the four seasons and the five phases.

20.2   仙公公子似 [已] 在 [可] 前
The Immortal Master and the Prince seem to [YQ: already] come [YQ: be] before you.

This refers to the *Dongfang jue*.[11] The palace of the Grotto Chamber on the left houses [YQ: Lord] Blossomless, also known as the Prince. The Immortal Master indicates a student of the *Yellow Court* [methods], that is, the immor-

---

[11] See 9.7 above.

tal master of the *Yellow Court*. Practicing according to the "Instructions on the Grotto Chamber," one visualizes the Prince. Hence it says, "come before you."

20.3   朱鳥吐縮白石源
The red bird issues a continuous thread, the spring of the white stones.

The red bird is an image of the tongue. The white stones stand for the teeth. Issuing a continuous thread refers to guiding and pulling the fluids and liquids of the body. This emphasizes that the *qi* of yin and yang flows without every stopping. Hence the text speaks of "the spring."

20.4   結精育胞化生身
Combine essence and set up the womb, then transform it to generate a new body.

The place of the original self is where all arises from.

20.5   留胎止精可長生
Stick with the womb and stop [the outflow of] essence, and you attain long life.

The *Zhen'gao* says, "The Perfected of Highest Clarity issued the following oral instructions: 'Anyone studying Dao should keep the mind at peace and nourish the spirit, absorb nourishment, and heal all diseases. Keep the brain palace firm and full, never letting mysterious essence pour out. After that, you can visualize spirit and absorb *qi* by inhaling and exhaling with the three luminants.' If you engage in intercourse repeatedly and let essence leak out, your *qi* will be destroyed and spirit will perish, your essence will wither and your numinous force will be exhausted. Even if you repeatedly put yourself forward in the jade registers, the golden books, and the great ultimate, how could you ever be released from non-life [death]?

In the old days, the former masters always warned against these things saying, 'Those engaged in the study of life: one bout of intercourse will cause the loss of one year's worth of medicinal potential; two bouts of intercourse will cause the loss of two years' worth of medicinal potential; if you keep on going like that, then all the unstopped healing potential will pour out of your body.' For this reason, perfected and immortals are always very careful about this. They consider it a great taboo in the pursuit of life."[12]

20.6   三氣右回九道明
The three *qi* revolve to the right, the nine pathways are bright.

The three qi are the energies of the three elixir fields. Revolving to the right means that they flow in an ongoing, continuous circuit. Balancing and harmonizing yin and yang, the four passes and nine orifices are all connected and flowing, bright and radiant, free from ailments.

20.7   正一含華乃充盈
Properly match the One, contain florescence, and fill to overflowing.

Contain [YQ: Visualize] and match properly by maintaining the One, and spirit and *qi* will blossom and flourish. Then you can extend to and fill the six harmonies, stride on beings and change along with all.

20.8   遙望一心如羅星
Gaze far off with your unified mind, all seems like a network of stars.

Visualize and see the lad of the Red City residing in his castle, and it will seem like a brightly lit network of stars.

20.9   金室之下可不傾
Below the metal chamber, nothing can pour out.

This says that the heart resides below the lungs, which rule the phase metal and have the color white. This is what the text refers to when it speaks of the metal chamber. If one always visualizes it, one attains long life and is free from death.

20.10   延我白首反孩嬰
Delay me getting a head of white and let me recover youth.

This refers to internal affairs. It says one gains a youthful complexion and does not die.

---

[12] The *Zhen'gao* does not contain this exact passage, but it refers variously to methods of supplementing the brain and fortifying essence. See Smith 2013, 91, 135-37, 212; 2020, 98, 101.

Twenty-One

21.1 瓊室之中八素集 [= 1/40]
In the jasper chamber, the eight simplicities come together.

This refers to the clear and perfect jasper chamber of the upper prime. It is an image for the bones of the organism.

21.2 泥丸夫人當中立
The lady of the Niwan always stands within.

The *Scripture* says, "In the Grotto Chamber there are father and mother." The mother is the lady mentioned here, also known as the Mother of the Dao. The Niwan and Grotto Chamber were explained earlier.

21.3 長谷玄鄉繞郊邑
The long valley and mysterious homestead encircle towns and open spaces.

The long valley is the nose. The mysterious homestead is the kidneys. The towns and open spaces are the five organs and six viscera. It means that *qi* enters and leaves through the nose, then moves down and connects with the kidneys, and from there revolves to encircle the organs and viscera, then comes to reside in the Red City. Visualize and imagine them as city quarters on the inside and open spaces on the outside. They serve as internal images or metaphors.

21.4 六龍散飛難分別
The six dragons spread out and fly off, hard to distinguish and pin down.

This says that the *qi* of the six viscera are subtle and wondrous, mysterious and pervasive, but hard to distinguish and pin down. Still, one must strive to visualize them.

21.5 長生至慎房中急 [= 1/43]
To attain long life, be extremely careful with the urges of the bedchamber.

Qi perishes as fluids leak out, bone marrow withers and essence dries up. Even though it may overflow by a small drop [YQ: into the conduits], yet it will leak out through the Tail Gate. You cannot be careful enough about it!

158 / Inner Scripture

21.6 何為死作令神泣
How much will it get death activated and cause the spirits to weep!

If you are not careful about the bedchamber, you will hurt essence and lose brightness. That is why the spirits will weep.

21.7 忽之禍鄉三靈歿
Sudden you find yourself in the country of misfortune and the three numinous forces decease.

The country of misfortune is the realm of death. The three numinous forces are the three cloud spirit agents. They are called Vibrant Numen, Womb Radiance, and Dark Essence. They all decease and perish.

21.8 但當吸氣鍊子精
You just need to inhale *qi* and organize your essence.

Inhale and exhale, expel and take in, close the chamber and stop [the outflow of] essence.

21.9 寸田尺宅可治生 [= 1/45]
The inch-size fields and the foot-square residence: here you can regulate life.

This says that the residences of the three elixir fields are about one inch in size. That's why it speaks of "inch-seize fields." Work with the methods of visualizing the elixir fields and thereby regulate them toward life. The *Scripture* says, "The inch-size fields and foot-square residence. The foot-square residence is the face."[13]

21.10 若當決海百瀆傾
But if you burst open the ocean, the hundred rivers all pour out.

This says that once there is lascivious leakage in the bedchamber, you will now know how to close and stop it.

---

[13] This cites the YQ commentary to *Waijing* 1/45.

21.11   葉去樹枯失青青
All released and gone, the tree withers and loses all its greenery.

This is an image for the death of the person, when there is no more *qi* of life.

21.12   氣亡液漏非己形
Qi perishes, fluids leak: no more self or physical form.

The *Xianjing* says, "Close the chamber and refine the fluids. Don't talk much, don't spit far."[14] This is just it.

21.13   專閉禦景乃長寧
Focus on closing, invoke the lights, and you can be forever calm.

To focus on closing off all emotions and desires, best visualize and absorb the radiance of the sun. The *Laozi* says, "A door well shut needs no bolts, and yet cannot be opened."[15] The *Shangqing ziwen lingshu* 上清紫文靈書 (Highest Clarity Numinous Book in Purple Characters) describes a method of extracting [the lixir] Flying Root. "Always when the sun first rises, face east, click your teeth nine times. Once done, quietly intone the following incantation that contains the names of the three cloud spirit agents and the five emperors of the sun:

> Sun Cloud-Spirit, Vermilion Light, Radiating Scabbard, Green Luster, Revolving Mist, Red Lad, Mysterious Flame, Whirlwind Sign.[16]

Once you complete chanting and calling these sixteen words, close your eyes, make your hands into fists, and visualize a five-colored mist rising from the center of the sun and coming to encircle your entire body. Next, see the rays of the sun as a flowing mist joining together to enter your mouth. This is called the Flying Root of Solar Florescence, Jade Womb, and Water Mother. Still facing the sun, swallow this mist in forty-five gulps. Once complete, swallow the saliva for nine rounds."[17]

---

[14] Unclear. See 2.6 above.
[15] *Daode jing* 27.
[16] Rihun 日魂, Zhujing 珠景, Zhaotao 照韜, Lüying 綠映, Huixia 回霞, Chitong 赤童, Xuanyan 玄炎, Biaoxiang 飆象.
[17] DZ 639, 4b; also translated in Bokenkamp 1997, 314-15.

21.14   保我泥丸三奇靈 [= 1/47]
Protect my Niwan and the three marvelous numinous forces.

The Niwan is the upper Elixir Field. The *Dadong jing* says, "The Three Primes transform secretly and constitute the Three Palaces."[18] The first contains the three lords of Great Clarity; the second has the spirits of the three elixir fields; and the third houses the deities in charge of talismans and ledgers. Hence the text speaks of the "three marvelous numinous forces."

21.15   恬淡閉視內自明
Quiet and bland, close off all vision and inside will be naturally bright.

This refers to methods of visualizing the three elixir fields, just as explained above.

21.16   物物不干泰而平 [= 1/48]
Being after being will not act out, there will be cosmic peace and balanced life.

Practice the Dao in perfect uprightness and wayward energies will not act out.

21.17   憨矣匪事老復丁
Completely guileless, free from affairs—even if old, you recover vigor.

Wild beasts will not attack you; raptor birds will not grapple with you. Even if old, you recover youthful vigor; even if sick, you are always strong. Completely guileless: that's inevitable.

21.18   思詠玉書入上清
Just think of and keep on reciting the *Jade Book* and you will enter Highest Clarity.

Study the *Inner Lights* [*Scripture*] with concentration and you cannot but obtain the way of the immortals.

---

[18] Same as in 7.11 above.

Twenty-Two

22.1   常念三房相通達 [= 1/49]
Always envision the three chambers, mutually connected and linked

The three chambers are the Hall of Light, the Grotto Chamber, and the Elixir Field. Together with the palaces of Flowing Pearls, the Five Emperors, the Heavenly Court, the Ultimate Perfected, the Mysterious Cinnabar, the Niwan, the Great Sovereign, and so on, they sit to the left and right, above and below, all mutually connected.

22.2   洞得視見無內外
Pervade them all in perfect vision, and there is no more inside or out.

Visualize and imagine them [YQ: the three elixir fields], three times three making nine, then merge the nine and make them into one. Brightly penetrating heaven above [YQ: bright and mysterious, pervasive and penetrating], there is no more inside or out.

22.3   存漱五牙不饑渴 [= 1/50]
Visualize further rinsing with the five sprouts: no longer feel hunger or thirst.

The *Lingbao jing* describes a method of absorbing and ingesting the five sprouts.[19] The five sprouts are the living *qi* of the five phases; they match the primordial essence of the five organs. The *Yuanjing jing* 元精經 (Scripture of Primordial Essence) says, "Always on the day of Spring Beginning, at cock crow enter the chamber and face east. Bow nine times, then sit up straight and click the teeth nine times. Imagine and visualize the Lord Lao of [Primordial] Beginning in charge of the green numinous force, ruler over the peaceful gem and flowery forest of the eastern direction, together with ninety million followers descend into your chamber. Densely packed like clouds, they envelope and cover your entire body. Allow them to enter through your

---

[19] This refers to the *Lingbao wufuxu* (3.21a), which outlines the method five sprouts, that is, the visualization and ingestion of the pure *qi* of the five directions. See Lagerwey 2004, 143; Robinet 1989, 165; 1993, 75; Despeux 2006, 56-57

162 / INNER SCRIPTURE

mouth and directly them to your liver. Then intone the following incantation:

> Green Heaven of Nine *Qi*,
> Highest Essence of Primordial Beginning,
> Sovereign Elder and Venerable Deity:
>
> Your robe and garb of feathery green,
> Control and manage the celestial bureaus!
> Year Star of flaming brightness,
> Spread your brilliance and float your fragrance!
> Mold and irrigate my physical body
> So above I can sup on bright mist
> As below I absorb and pull in the essence of wood!
>
> Steadily let me nourish the green sprout
> To protect and shield me against decay and annihilation!
> With my liver full to overflowing,
> Let jade mushrooms grow naturally within.
>
> Extend my years and preserve my longevity,
> Let me complexion recover youthfulness.
> As my five *qi* mingle and merge in harmony,
> Let me live as long as heaven and earth!

Once complete, pull in the green *qi* and swallow it nine times, then stop. In this manner you absorb the [*qi* of the] eastern direction, utilizing the twelve words of the *Chishu yuwen* 赤書玉文 (Jade Text Written in Red)."[20]

22.4   神華執巾六丁謁 [= 1/51]
Spirit Florescence holding her headdress, the Six Ding come to present themselves.

As regards Spirit Forescence, the *Yuli jing* says, "The Jade Maiden of the Mysterious Radiance of Great Yin is the Mother of the Dao. She wears a robe studded with five-colored pearls and resides above the spleen and below the

---

[20] *Chishu yujue* 赤書玉訣 (Jade Instructions Written in Red, DZ 352, SV 216-17), 2.4b-5a. The twelve words refer to the title of the deity at the start of the incantation.

Flowery Canopy, consisting of yellow clouds."[21] The Six Ding are jade maidens and yin deities associated with the six *ding* [earthly branches].

The *Laojun liujia futu* 老君六甲符圖 (Lord Lao's Talismans and Charts of the Six Jia) says, "[YQ: The Six Ding each have their own deity.] The deity of *dingmao* is the jade maiden Sima Qing, in charge of living in sufficiency; the deity of *dingchou* is the jade maiden Zhao Ziyu, in charge of moving along with *qi*; the deity of *dinghai* is the jade maiden Zhang Wentong, in charge of floating adrift; the deity of *dingyou* is the jade maiden Zang Wengong, in charge of attaining joy; the deity of *dingwei* is the jade maiden Shi Shutong, in charge of warding off obstacles; the deity of *dingsi* is the jade maiden Cui Juqing, in charge of opening the heart."[22] It says that, if you absorb and refine yourself with [the elixir] Flying Root and complete the Dao of visualizing and rinsing with the five sprouts, you will be able to command these deities of the Six Ding.

22.5　　急守精室勿妄洩
Urgently maintain the chambers of essence, never letting it leak out recklessly.

The chambers of essence are the three elixir fields. Keep them connected above and below without any interruption. Control them from the heart, which is in fact the middle Elixir Field. It is where all tardiness and urgency arise, the root and base of all perfected and reckless [behavior].

22.6　　閉而寶之可長活 [= 1/52]
Close and treasure it, and you can live forever.

---

[21] *Laozi zhongjing* 1.5.

[22] A complete list of jade maidens associated with the sexagenary cycle appears in *Lingfei liujia shangfu* 靈飛六甲上符 (Highest Talismans of the Maidens of the Six Jia, DZ 84, SV 174-75). A set of deities of the Six Ding and Six Jia is also found in the ritual manual, *Shangqing liujia qidao bifa* 上清六甲祈禱祕法 (DZ 584, SV 1241). The Six Ding are further associated with a liturgical tradition connected to the Yellow Emperor and documented in the *Huangdi Taiyi bamen rushi jue* 黃帝太一八門入式訣 (Instructions Transmitted by the Yellow Emperor for Penetrating the Order of the Eight Gates of the Great One, DZ 586, SV 760). However, the names given here are different. They appear as cited from the same source in the late Ming collection *Sancai tuhui* 三才圖會 (Illustrated Compendium of the Three Powers) and in the Qing encyclopedia *Gujin tushu jicheng* 古今圖書集成 (Complete Collection of Charts and Books, Old and New), *Shenyi dian* 神異典 32. Martial in nature, they are today presented in colorful images, e.g., http://3zn.org/list.asp?unid=4288.

Keep the gathering places of your essence well together.

22.7 起自形中初不闊
Let it arise from within the physical form, initially not ample.

Balance the heart and control the *qi:* it is subtle and wondrous, quite formless.

22.8 三官近在易隱括
The three bureaus are immediately present, easy to seclude and enclose.

This says that the palaces [YQ: bureaus] of the perfected in the three elixir fields are immediately present in the human body. They hide and enclose essence and *qi*, so always activate the heart as their lord and ruler.

22.9 虛無寂寂空中素
In emptiness and nonbeing, serene and calm, rest simply in the void.

This refers to external affairs. "Rest simply" has two meanings.

22.10 使形如是不當污 [= 1/54]
Get the physical form to be like this and you should be free from defilements.

Get the physical form to be light and pure like undyed gauze strands fluttering in the void [open air]. Also, within the body all should be void and simple. Get it to be like a vessel, always light and simple, empty and still. "Defilement" refers to being involved in external affairs.

22.11 九室正虛神明舍
When the nine chambers are properly empty, the spirits in their brightness will stay.

The nine chambers are the Nine Palaces in the head as well as the nine orifices of the human body. Get the Palaces above to be glowing and flowery and the nine orifices to be perfectly proper, and the host of spirits will remain in place. The *Dongshen jing* says, "Heaven has nine stars, [YQ: two of which are hidden]: thus, we speak of nine heavens. Earth has nine palaces: thus, we speak nine earth [regions]. Human beings have nine orifices: thus, we speak of nine lives."²³ It indicates the location from where humans arise and come to life.

22.12   存思百念視節度 [= 1/55]
Visualize and think of the many hundreds, see them with their sections and measures.

Visualize and envision that there are hundreds of spirits in the body, moving up and down as you inhale and exhale, always in accordance with the codes and methods. It also says, "Thousands upon thousands, hundreds upon hundreds—they are like layered mountains."²⁴ [YQ: This is an image of the many spirits.]

22.13   六府修治勿令故 [= 1/56]
The six viscera cultivated and regulated, there is no need for further orders.

The *Dongshen jing* says, "Among the six viscera, the lungs are the Palace of the Jade Hall, the office of the Secretary. The heart is the Scarlet Palace, the office of Primordial Yang. The liver is the Palace of Green Solitude, the office of the Orchid Terrace. The gall bladder is the Palace of Purple Tenuity, the office of the Non-Ultimate. The kidneys are the Palace of Dark Glory, the office of Great Harmony. The spleen is the Palace of Central Yellow, the office of Great Simplicity."²⁵ This is different from the common definition of the six viscera.

22.14   行自翱翔入天路
Practice this and you naturally soar up and enter the road to heaven.

This means you ascend as an immortal and undergo physical transformation.

Twenty-Three

23.1   治生之道了不煩 [= 1/58]
The Dao of regulating life frees you from all troubles.

Nonaction, clarity, and simplicity come together to maintain the will.

---

²³ Citation unclear.
²⁴ This combines two earlier lines: 19.10-11.
²⁵ *Lingbao wufuxu* 1.20ab.

23.2　但修洞玄與玉篇
Merely cultivate according to the *Dongxuan* (Mystery Cavern) and the *Yupian* (Jade Chapters).

Dongxuan refers to the *Lingbao Dongxuan* (Mystery Cavern of Numinous Treasure). The perfected text here called *Yupian* is the *Huangting* [*jing*].

23.3　兼行形中八景神
Equally practice the [activation of the] eight lights or spirits in the physical form.

The *Yupian* [YQ: *wei jing* 玉篇 [緯]經 (Scripture of the Jade Chapters [YQ: Weft]) says: "The five organs contain the lodges of the celestial spirits of the eight trigrams. The [YQ: eight] emissaries of the Great One are the rulers of the [YQ: days of the eight] divisions [of the year]. The eight trigrams together with the Great One constitute the Nine Palaces. Outside of the eight trigrams is the Twelve-storied Tower."[26] This tower is the breath pipe [YQ: esophagus]. "In the navel is the Lord of the Great One who rules people's destiny. He is also called [YQ: Central Ultimate,] Great Abyss, Chaos, and Great Ultimate [YQ: Eminent Pivot]."[27] He is in charge of the 13,000 radiances of essence [YQ: 12,000 spirits] in the human body.

23.4　二十四真出自然
The twenty-four perfected emerge from naturalness.

Heaven has twenty-four perfected forms of *qi*, which are also present in the human body. It also has the locations of the three elixir fields. Three times eight makes twenty-four: these perfected are nothing but the Dao-*qi* of pure naturalness.

23.5　高拱無為魂魄安　[= 1/59]
Lofty and reverent, in deep nonaction, cloud and white spirit agents are at peace.

Practice forgetting and sit in oblivion, cast off form and do away with understanding.[28]

---

[26] *Laozi zhongjing* 1.14, 17, 13. Its alternative title is *Yuli jing*.
[27] *Laozi zhongjing* 1.17. The number 12,000 appears in 1.13.
[28] This refers to *Zhuangzi* 6, as already cited in the commentary to *Neijing* 1.4 above.

23.6   清淨［静］神見與我言
In clarity and purity [YQ: stillness], the spirit appears and speaks to me.

Rest in clarity and stillness and the spirit of the heart will naturally appear. Keeping the gaze centered, never reaching outside, he is just like I say. He is called the Perfected of the Yellow Court.

23.7   安在紫房幃幕間   [= 1/60]
At peace in the Purple Chamber, between its screens and curtains.

The Purple Chamber with screens and curtains is also called the Scarlet Palace. It is where the Lad of the Red City rests peacefully. To visualize and think of the spirit of the heart, imagine his shape in this setting.

23.8   立坐室外三五玄
Even standing or sitting beyond the parlor, the three and five in mystery.

This says that as long as the eight lights, that is, the twenty-four perfected spirits, nurture and protect the human body, the perfect *qi* of the three elixir fields and five organs are balanced and soft and you are free from disaster and disease.

23.9   燒香接手玉華前
Burn incense and fold your hands before Jade Florescence.

Jade Florescence is the area in front of the Flowery Canopy, that is the Heavenly Court between the eyebrows. It is also called the ancestral prime of the spirits, the cavern residence of the perfected. Best visualize it by moving from the face.

23.10   共入太室璇璣門
Jointly enter the great chamber and the gate to the Jasper Sphere.

The *Dongfang jing* 洞房經 (Scripture of the Grotto Chamber) says, "In heaven, there are the Great Chamber, the Jade Chamber, and the Cloud Court."[29] They are places where the Yellow Lord Lao of the Center resides. The jade chamber is also called the Purple Chamber or the Scarlet Palace. It connects to the Hall of Light. Above it is the Flowery Canopy, which pervasively con-

---

[29] Citation unclear.

nects to the palaces in the east and west as well as to the Yellow Court on the right and left. All people's bodies contain these, as explained above. Jasper Sphere is the name of its central pivot.

23.11   高研恬淡道之園 [= 1/62]
Lofty and sublime, quiet and bland: the garden of pure Dao.

Examine essence in serenity and blandness, and perfect *qi* comes wandering.

23.12   內神 [視] 密盼盡睹真
Closely look at the spirits within [YQ: In inner vision regarding closely], fully gaze at the perfected.

Enter stillness in meditation and visualization, and the hundred spirits will appear like a forest.

23.13   真人在己莫問鄰
The perfected are in your very own self: no question they come close.

The *Yutai jing* [YQ: *Yuli jing*] says, "Laozi is the cloud spirit agent of heaven, the lord of naturalness; he is always attended to by the lords of Dao on the right and left."[30] The human body contains all of them.

23.14   何處遠索求因緣
Which place would be too far or isolated when pursuing karmic affiliations?

The *Daojing* says, "All-pervading is the great Dao: it can be found on the right and left."[31] The text means that it is not far.

Twenty-Four

24.1   隱形 [影] 滅 [藏] 形與世殊
Seclude the physical form [shadow] and destroy [hide] the physical form: be different from the ordinary world.

Those studying immortality should contain their brightness and hide their brilliance, destroy their traces and conceal their all clues.

---

[30] *Laozi zhongjing* 1.6.
[31] *Daode jing* 34.

24.2   含氣養精口如朱
Contain *qi* and nourish essence, the mouth like a pearl.

Flesh and skin like ice and snow [YQ; water and emptiness], meek and modest like a young girl.

24.3   帶執性命守虛無 [= 2/2]
Support inner nature and attend to destiny, maintain emptiness and nonbeing.

Rest in emptiness and stillness, serenity and blandness, obscurity and nonaction.

24.4   名入上清死錄除
Then your name will be entered in Highest Clarity and taken out from the registers of death.

Attaining registration as an immortal, you will be ranked above with a mystery name.

24.5   三神之樂由隱居
The joy of the three spirits comes from secluded living.

Regulating the body in nonaction, the spirits are joyful. Regulating the state without engaging in affairs, people are at peace. The three spirits are the deities of the three elixir fields.

24.6   倏欻游遨無遺憂
Suddenly, abruptly you are wandering and roaming, free from loss and distress.

Suddenly, abruptly means something emerges quickly. The text below says, "You ride up suddenly, embracing life, and come to feast at the eastern mound."[32] According to another explanation, "suddenly, abruptly is the name of a dragon. "Free from loss and distress" means separate and free.

24.7   羽服一整八風驅 [= 2/4]
Once the feathery garb is all set, the eight winds drive.

---

[32] *Neijing* 26.7

The eight winds are the winds of the eight directions. "Drive ahead" means sweep the road. The feathery garb is the garb of immortals. According to the precious texts of Highest Clarity, immortals wear feathery robes of five colors, while the Perfected of the Great One is clad in a robe of nine colors. It says, "Robes and seals of flying feathers indicate the garb of the immortals." Hence this description.

* * *

. . . robes of five colors. The *Feixingyu jing* 飛行羽經 (Scripture of Winged Flight) says, "The Perfected of the Great One is clad in a robe of nine colors."[33] Flying clouds and feathery seals indicate the garb of the immortals.

24.8　　控駕三素乘晨霞
Guiding and steering the three simplicities. you ride on auroral mists.

This refers to external affairs. The three indicates nine mists, that is, the conveyance of spirits and immortals.

24.9　　金輦正立從玉輿
The golden flower properly established, you ride in a jade chariot.

The *Yuanlu jing* 元錄經 (Scripture of Primordial Registration) says, "The mysterious spirits and eight sages of the nine heavens of Highest Clarity ride in carriages drawn by nine phoenixes or dragons."[34] Jade chariots and golden carriages indicate the equipment and utensils of immortals.

24.10　　何不登山誦我書
How could you not climb into the mountains and chant my book?

The book is the *Huangting* [*jing*].

24.11　　鬱鬱窈窕真人墟
Thick and dense, secluded and withdrawn: the waste land of the perfected.

In the mountains, all is dark and desolate.

24.12　　入山何難故躊躇

---

[33] A text of this title appears in DZ 428, SV 170. This citation is unclear.
[34] Citation unclear.

Entering the mountains, what difficulty could make you irresolute and undecided?

Your emotions and [YQ: collected] will are not firm.

24.13　人間紛紛臭如帛

Ordinary people, in contrast, are confused and disorderly: their stench is like soiled rags.

Diseased and polluted, ordinary people are not lovable. "Soiled rags" indicates something extremely stinky.

*　*　*

In the ordinary world, one cannot be a lord. "Soiled rags" means a lowly, nasty fabric.

Twenty-Five

25.1　五行相推反歸一 [= 2/6]
The five phases promote each other, then they come back and return to the One.

The five phases are metal, wood, water, fire, and earth [YQ: water, fire, metal, wood, earth]. When they promote each other, metal generates water, water generates wood, wood generates fire, fire generates earth, and earth generates metal.[1] They complete a circuit and start again. [YQ add: They also overcome each other: water overcomes fire, fire overcomes metal, metal overcomes wood, wood overcomes earth, earth overcomes water, and water again overcomes fire. They complete a circuit and start again.]

　　The way they promote each other, is that they come back and return to the One. One here is the number of water, the head of the five phases, and the ancestral origin of the myriad beings. Laozi says: "Dao generates the One, the One generates the two, the two generate the three, and the three generate the myriad beings."[2] The again, the "[*Book of*] *Changes* has the Great Ultimate, which generated the two forces."[3] The Great Ultimate is the One. The two forces are heaven and earth. Heaven and earth generate the myriad beings. And the myriad beings all come back [YQ: end] and return to the One. The One is another word for nonbeing. It marks the completion of beings. Hence the text says, "they come back and return to the One.

25.2　三五合氣九九節 [= 2/7]
The three and five merge their *qi* in nine times nine sections.

The *Miaozhen jing* 妙真經 (Scripture of Wondrous Perfection) [YQ: *Xuanmiao jing*] says: "The three in heaven are the sun, moon, and stars—they are called the three luminants. On earth, they are pearls, jade, and gold—they are called the three treasures. In the human body, they are ears, mouth, and nose—they are called the three life senses."[4]

---

[1] The YQ begins this sequence with "water generates wood" and ends it with "metal generates water."
[2] *Daode jing* 42.
[3] *Yijing, Xici* 1.11 (Sung 1971, 299).
[4] The *Miaozhen jing*, a medieval text associated with Laozi, survives in fragments, collected in Maeda 1987, 27-32 (Kohn 1995, 207-08). This citation is not among them. It is not found in the *Xuanmiao* text cited in 15.15 above, either.

Heaven, earth, and humanity are the three powers: they each contain the five phases. The five are imperial essences, thus the text says, "The three and five merge their *qi*." Three times three makes nine. [YQ: Therefore, the text speaks of "the three and five." Their essence is constant and as they merge with the three, the nine palaces emerge.]

Now, as the three all contain the five, they produce a host of different species, harmonize and balance the myriad beings, regulate and transform yin and yang, cover and support heaven and earth. Due to them, radiance illuminates all throughout the four seas and there are wind and rain, thunder and lightning, spring and summer, fall and winter, cold and heat, dampness and dryness, as well as clear and turbid forms of *qi*. All the various forms of living beings, if they did not obtain the merged *qi* of the three and five, they would never come to exist. Hence it says, "The way of heaven is not far away." The three and five all return to the origin. The three and five and the pivotal stem of heaven and earth; they form the central core of the six harmonies, the *qi* divisions of the Nine Palaces. Nine times nine is eight-one and that makes one section.

25.3   可用隱地回八術
Make sure to utilize the eight arts of revolving and hiding in the earth.

The Nine Palaces contain arts [YQ: methods] of hiding and invisibility, of change and transformation. The *Taishang basu benchen yinshu* 太上八素奔晨隱書 (Most High Secluded Book of the Eight Simplicities on Traveling across the Planets) mentions these "eight arts."[5] Also, the *Taiwei balu shu* 太微八錄術 (Arts of the Eight Registers of Great Tenuity) has, "Great Tenuity has three lords. The first is called Lord Great Sovereign; the second is called Lord Heavenly Sovereign; and the third is called Yellow Lord Lao. Representing the *qi* of the Three Primes, they mingle and merge their essence and enter and leave the palace of Great Emptiness [YQ: Simplicity] in Highest Clarity."[6] Being hidden, invisible, and formless, [YQ: If you can visualize and think of them], you will attain long life.

---

[5] The *Basu jing* indeed speaks of eight arts of hiding in the earth ((DZ 426, 5b).
[6] This refers to the *Taiwei huangshu jiutian balu zhenwen* 太微黃書九天八錄真文 (Perfect Writ of the Eight Registers of the Nine Heavens from the Yellow Book of Great Tenuity, DZ 257, SV 192), 1a.

25.4   伏牛幽闕羅品列
Reclining Ox and Dark Towers are all set out in order.

Reclining Ox is an image for the kidneys. The kidneys are the Dark Towers. The *Zhonghuang jing* says, "The left kidney is the Lord of Mystery Wonder; the right kidney is the Lord of Mystery Prime."[7] "All set out in order" means that you can see them as you [YQ: visualize and] think of them.

25.5   三明出華生死際
The three bright ones emerge in full flower: life and death have their rhythm.

The three bright ones in heaven are the sun, moon, and stars; on earth, they are texts, seals, and florescences; in human beings, they are ears, nose, and mouth. They mark the rhythm of life and death. [YQ add: "Rhythm means the divisions of sound."]

25.6   洞房靈象斗日月 [= 2/8]
The numinous constellations of the Grotto Chamber: Dipper, sun, and moon.

Visualize the Three Primes [YQ: luminants] in the Grotto Chamber. The Grotto Chamber and Hall of Light were already explained above.

25.7 父曰泥丸母雌一
The father is called Niwan; the mother is the Female One.

In the Hall of Light reside lord and minister; in the Grotto Chamber reside husband and wife; in the Elixir Field reside father and mother. Niwan is the name of the spirit of the brain. The *Daojing* says, "Know the male and maintain the female."[8] "Male" here means the One in nonaction.

25.8   三光煥照入子室 [= 2/9]
The three luminants shine forth like flames and enter into your parlor.

They brightly illuminate all four directions.

---

[7] The text appears in YQ 13. It has an extensive discussion of the left and right kidneys but does not mention the names of the resident spirits.
[8] *Daode jing* 28.

25.9   能存玄真萬事畢 [= 2/10]
Visualize the mysterious perfected and the myriad affairs are done.

Zhuangzi says, "If one can maintain the One, the myriad affairs are done."[9]

25.10   一身精神不可失 [= 2/11]
You must never lose essence or spirit in the entire body.

Always visualize and envision them, never pausing even for an instant.

Twenty-Six

26.1   高奔日月吾上道 [= 2/13]
Rising up and traveling to the sun and the moon: this my highest Dao.

"My" refers to the Lord of the Dao. It is about *qi* methods of swallowing the sun as documented in the *Lingshu ziwen,* also known as the course of red and cinnabar, metal essences, mineral lights, water mother, and the jade embryo. According to this, "Always when the sun first rises, face east and click your teeth nine times. In your heart, softly intone the following incantation that contains the names of the three cloud spirit agents and the five emperors of the sun. It runs:

> Sun Cloud-Spirit, Vermilion Light, Radiating Scabbard, Green Luster, Revolving Mist, Red Lad, Mysterious Flame, Whirlwind Sign.

Once you exhaling with these sixteen words, close your eyes, make your hands into fists, and visualize a five-colored flowing mist entering your mouth."[10]

The *Shangqing lingshu* 上清靈書 [YQ: *zishu* 紫書] also describes a method of swallowing lunar essence. "As the moon rises, face west, click your teeth ten times, and in your heart softly intone the names the five cloud spirit agents of the moon and the appellations of the five lunar ladies. The incantation goes:

---

[9] *Zhuangzi* 12.
[10] The same citation also appears in the commentary to *Neijing* 21.13. The passage is discussed in detail in Wang 2010, 172-74.

Moon Cloud-Spirit, Loving and Sad, Fragrant Glamour,
Screened Solitude, Elegant Emptiness, Numinous Orchid,
Dense Flower, Combined Excellence, Pure Gold,
Clear Luster, Glowing Countenance, Simple Sign.[11]

Once you complete the recitation of these twenty-four characters, make your hands into fists and close your eyes. Visualize a concentrated radiance of five colors in the moon and make it enter your mouth. There may also be a yellow *qi* in the lunar radiance, about the size of an eye's pupil. Its name is Flying Yellow. Lunar florescence is the essence of the jade embryo." If you cultivate in this way, you can travel to the sun and the moon and become a spirit immortal.[12]

26.2　鬱儀結璘善相保
Dense Regalia and Knotted Spangles kindly provide mutual protection.[13]

Dense Regalia (Yuyi) is the immortal who travels to the sun. Knotted Spangles (Jielin) is the immortal who travels to the moon. Their sounds accord with each other and their *qi* seek each other out, thus the two immortals come to provide mutual protection and support

26.3　乃見玉清虛無老
And in due course you see the Elders of Emptiness and Nonbeing in Jade Clarity.

Ascending to the Three Clarities above, you merge and join with Dao.

26.4　可以回顏填血腦
You can recover your complexion and fill both blood and brain.

The cloud and white spirit agents recover youth: you attain completion as a perfected.

---

[11] Yuehun 月魂, Aixiao 曖蕭, Fangyan 芳艷, Yiliao 翳寥, Wanxu 婉虛, Linglan 靈蘭, Yuhua 鬱華, Jieqiao 結翹, Chunjin 淳金, Qingying 清瑩, Jiongrong 炅容, Subiao 素標.
[12] *Taiji zhenren shenxian jing* 太極真人神仙經 (Scripture of Perfected and Spirit Immortals of the Great Ultimate, DZ 1404, SV 612), 13ab, under the heading "Methods of Picking and Absorbing Lunar Essence according to the *Lingshu ziwen*."
[13] This passage is also translated in Esposito 2004, 369. For more on lunar absorption and travel, see Wang 2010.

26.5   口銜靈芒攜五皇
In your mouth you hold numinous rays as you carry along with the five sovereigns.

Your mouth emits numinous [YQ: cloud] *qi* in five colors, like radiant plants shining in all four directions. Together with the five sovereigns and Lord Lao you wander about the six harmonies.

26.6   腰帶虎籙佩金璫
At your waist and belt the tiger register, suspended the gold pendant.

This refers to the garb of the immortals. The *Jiuzhen jing* says, "The Yellow Lord Lao of the Center wears a mysterious dragon and divine tiger talisman at his waist and a bell of flowing gold on his belt. He has a staff with purple hair in his hands."[14] The word "register" here means talisman.

26.7   駕欻接生宴東蒙
You ride up suddenly, embracing life, and come to feast at the eastern mound.

Suddenly or abruptly refers to riding wind-*qi*, which arrives without warning. [YQ add: Some also say that "abruptly" is the name of a dragon.] The eastern mound is a mountain in the immortal realm in the eastern sea. Embracing life is an expression for long life. It means embracing and linking with the *qi* of life. Once you do that, you suddenly take off and wander to these places.

Twenty-Seven

27.1   玄元上一魂魄煉 [= 2/30]
Mystery Prime and Highest One—that's how the cloud and white spirit agents are refined.

Treasure the One to refine the spirit. Once spirit is refined, you can merge with the One.

27.2   一之為物頗 [叵] 卒見
The One is a being, yet you have little chance to [YQ: cannot] ever see it.

---

[14] Same as 5.2 above.

The One is another appellation for nonbeing. The heart serene and bland, you can attain it. You can [YQ add: know it but] not see it.

27.3   須得至真始顧盼 [眄]
You must attain foremost perfection, then you can begin and hope to see [YQ: glimpse] it.

Maintain perfection and keep your will full, and the One naturally returns to you.

27.4   至忌死氣諸穢賤
Be careful foremost with the *qi* of death and all sorts of defilement and lowliness.

For all undertakings relating to flying elixirs, refined medicines, absorption of *qi*, swallowing of mist, and so on, be careful about seeing the *qi* [YQ: affairs] of suffering [YQ: death] and corpses, sickness and defilement. They are called the combined troubles for all areas of life. [YQ: These are things all practitioners of guarding life collectively know about.] This being so, the foremost Dao thrusts into emptiness but is fundamentally free from purity and defilement. For people to take hold of perfection properly, however, there is a distinct difference between purity and defilement. Since they are different and not equal, right and wrong arise within while life and death appear without. Thus, clarity and purity are the foot-soldiers of life while turbidity and defilement are the foot-soldiers of death. For this reason, when nourishing life, one must be careful about them.

27.5   六神合集虛中宴
The six spirits merge and assemble to feast in emptiness.

The various spirits of the Six Jia, Six Ding, six viscera, and so on all reside in the body. When all [YQ in the body] is empty and void, they feast and are [YQ add: happy and] at peace. [YQ add: If not, they are sad and cry.]

27.6   結珠固精養神根 [= 3/1]
By stringing pearls and steadying essence, one nourishes the spirit root.

Stringing pearls is an expression for swallowing the saliva: front and back should be in mutually interchange like pearls. Steadying essence means not letting it leak out recklessly. The spirit root is the physical form and bodily frame. Now the way the spirit is in the body is like a country having a lord and the lord governing the people. The people use the lord to get orders, while the lord uses the people as his foundation. The two are mutually bound in both matter and organization. Therefore, to keep alive [YQ: become a ruler of life], balance and nourish them.

27.7   玉笈金籥常完堅 [= 3/2]
Keep the jade bolt and golden lock always closed and firm.

Laozi [YQ: The *Daojing*] says, "A door well shut needs no bolts, and yet cannot be opened."[15] A lock is closing mechanism. A bolt is a key.

27.8   閉口屈舌食胎津
Close the mouth and curl the tongue to ingest embryonic liquid.

Curling the tongue to connect the flow of [YQ: guide] liquids and fluids. By ingesting liquid, one grows the immortal embryo, thus the text speaks of "embryonic liquid."

27.9   使我遂煉獲飛仙
This causes me to keep on refining and become a flying immortal.

This will be achieved through concentrated effort and diligent sincerity.

Twenty-Eight[16]

28.1   仙人道士非有神 [= 3/12]
Immortals and Daoists do not have inherent divinity.

They cultivate and study to accumulate essence [YQ: to attain it].

28.2   積精累氣以為真 [= 3/13]
But they accumulate essence and gather *qi* and thus become perfected.

---

[15] *Daode jing* 27, also cited in the YQ commentary to *Neijing* 4.5.
[16] DZ 403 (SV 348), reprinted in Zhou and Sheng 2015, 111-16, contains a commentary to verses 28 through 30 by Jiang Shenxiu 蔣慎修, the only surviving fragment of the commentary by an otherwise unknown figure of the late Tang or early Song. It is translated here, in each case introduced with "Jiang."

They steady essence and maintain *qi*, accumulate and refine them in order to complete their path to perfection. They cultivate and study to attain it.

* * *

Some editions do not have this line; therefore, I omit my commentary.

* * *

Jiang: "Divinity" is spaceless; "perfected" means existing beings. In the spaceless, the way of immortality has no way to be present; in a state of existing beings, one can accumulate and bind [*qi*] and reach completion.

28.3   黃童妙[內]音難可聞
The wondrous [Jiang: esoteric] sounds of the Yellow Lad are hard to hear.

The Yellow Lad is the Perfected of the Yellow Court, also known as the Lad of the Red City. Wondrous sounds are the wondrous words of the way of the Yellow Court.

28.4   玉書絳簡赤丹文
The *Yushu jiangjian* (Jade Book in Scarlet Tablets), the *Chidan wen* (Text in Red Cinnabar).

This refers to the *Huangting jing*, also called the *Taidi jinshu* 太帝金書 (Golden Book of the Great Emperor) and the *Donghua yupian* 東華玉篇 (Jade Chapters of Eastern Florescence).

* * *

Jiang: In the office of the spleen section, there is a bright lad; the text calls him the Yellow Lad. The *Huangting* [*jing*] comes in three parts that should all be chanted and experienced, yet without engaging the five organs with outside entities; therefore, the text speaks of "esoteric sounds." What is known as the hidden stanzas of all the heavens, I think, applies to this.

Now, utmost ones do not engage with [these stanzas] upon hearing them, while ordinary people hear them but cannot comprehend them. That is, not engaging upon hearing and hearing but being unable to comprehend both is what the text means when it says "hard to hear." Those desiring to hear and also comprehend are primordial and different from this: they merely search out core intention.

The path to immortality comes with many methods, all centered on matching yang and reaching ascension. By cultivating and refining essence, one can reach pure yang. For this reason, books and entities related to the quest are spoken about in terms of "jade." Jade as an entity represents the essence of pure yang.

The *qi* of Highest Clarity descends and links up with beings. Therefore, the text appears in "tablets" which come in "scarlet" color. Scarlet as a color is descended from the Dao of heaven. When we speak of "pure yang," that means basically one yin and one yang that are cultivated and refined to perfection. The fundamental interaction of yin and yang is that they intermingle and in due course create a text, which is both "red" and "cinnabar." Red matches fire and is yang; cinnabar matches two [water] and is yin. Searching out the core intention of Dao and virtue and looking at the color of beings—that is just like this.

The book contains Dao; the tablets contain text. Containing Dao means holding the essence of pure yang; containing text means manifesting the Dao of heaven. This marks the difference between images and entities. The text here divides into yin and yang, alternatingly applies soft and hard, creates complex interweaving of the three and five—all in order to produce structure and integration. Among things, it represents flowering; among seasons, it matches the summer. Through it, the Dao of heaven descends in plenty, undergoing myriad transformations to spread pure dew into the age. It is analytical and organized, concentrated and subtle, embracing and illuminating the wonders of Dao: thus is the extended meaning of "red cinnabar."

28.5   字曰真人巾金巾 [= 3/8]
He is also known as the Perfected; he wears a metal-colored kerchief.

The Perfected is the Yellow Lad. The color of metal is white, which belongs to the west and rules the lungs. The white of the lungs rests above the heart, hence it says, "he wears a golden kerchief." The *Jiuzhen jing* says, "The Green Emperor of the East wears a robe and cape of green jade brocade, a flying skirt of verdant floresence, and a cinnabar hibiscus headdress. He also wears a golden kerchief."[17] Yuanyangzi says, "The Perfected leans on *wu* [south], steps on *zi* [north], walks on *mao* [east], and carries *you* [west]. *You* is metal/gold.

*   *   *

Jiang: To understand the meaning of this title [Perfected], we must realize that by accumulating essence and binding *qi*, one completes perfection. This appellation, therefore, indicates that the person has completed Dao and is now venerable. Thus, he can take on this name. As Laozi says, "To call it something, I speak of Dao."[18] This is the same idea. "He wears a metal-

---

[17] Same as 12.5 above.
[18] *Daode jing* 25.

colored kerchief" means that when essence and *qi* germinate, they begin in the lungs. For this reason, he is adorned like this.

28.6   負甲持符開七門 [= 3/9]
Clad in armor and holding talismans, he opens the seven gates.

The *Laojun liujia sanbu fu* 老君六甲三部符 (Lord Lao's Talisman of the Six Jia and Three Sections) says,[19]

> The spirit of Jiazi is called Wang Wenqing 王文卿
> The spirit of Jiaxu is called Zhan Zijiang 展子江
> The spirit of Jiashen is called Hu Wenchang 扈文長
> The spirit of Jiawu is called Wei Shangqing 衛上卿
> The spirit of Jiachen is called Meng Feiqing 孟非卿
> The spirit of Jiayin is called Ming Wenzhang 明文章

When you visualize these six spirits and call out their names, the seven orifices will be open and connected. Then you will be free from all sickness and disease.

28.7   火兵符圖備靈關
With fire soldiers, talismans, and charts, he orders the numinous passes.

The red seal and register for beheading the various forms of wayward *qi* serve to deploy the fire soldiers of the three and five. The *Weiling shenzhou* 衛靈神咒 (Divine Incantation to Guard Numen) says,[20]

> Oh, cinnabar heaven of the south:
> Let the three *qi* flow in radiance,
> Let the martial planet [Mars] revolve to illuminate
> And pervasively shine throughout greater yang.
>
> Above there is red essence—
> A numinous lad who opens brightness
> And comprehensively commands the fire soldiers

---

[19] These deities are divine generals in charge of time, quite like the jade maidens of the Six Ding, mentioned in 22.4 above. The names similarly appear in later encyclopedias and the figures are presented in colorful images (see e.g., http://www.tongfoxiang.net/p/260.html; https://www.fjfoxiang.com/p/2921.html).
[20] YQ 47.3a.

Who in turn defend and guard the Three Palaces.

This refers to the fire soldiers as related to the three and five.

The talismans are those of the eight simplicities and six spirits, yang essence and the jade embryo, refining immortality and harboring essence, flying lights and yellow florescence, mineral [YQ: central] lights and inner transformation, pervading spirit and mirroring Qian [trigram Heaven], and so on.

The charts include the Great One's Chart of the Three and Five Merged in Chaos, the Six Jia's Chart of Up and Down and Yin and Yang, the Chart of Six Jade Maidens of the Six Jia Connecting to the Numinous Forces, the Chart of the Perfected of the Great One, the Chart of Cleansing and Bathing in the Eastern Well, Lord Lao's Chart of Inner Vision, the Charts of the Western Ascension of the Eight Scribes, the Chart of Harboring the Lights of Ninefold Change, the Chart of the Red World, and many more. With them you can guard and defend the numinous passes, that is, the three passes, the four passes, and so on. They are all present in the body.

* * *

Jiang: "Clad in armor" relates to the turtle and snake of the north; it means standing with one's back to yin to defend oneself. "Fire soldiers" relate to the vermilion bird of the south; it means facing yang to subdue the enemy. The "seven gates" are the ears, eyes, nostrils, and mouth—commonly called the gates of life. The gates of life connect to the outside, while consciousness and inner nature harmonize within. Therefore, Zhuangzi says, "Listening stops with the ears; the mind stops with the talismans."[21] Seen from this angle one can understand the function of the six entries [senses], that is, they all work with talismans to link [inner] heaters and [external] doors.

This means that to open the seven gates, one must first "hold the talismans." Only by holding the talismans can the gates be opened. Then there is no chance of being punished for doing it recklessly. Now, in holding the talismans and opening the gate, one must first be "clad in armor." This means that, once the gates of life have been opened, the six robbers [of the senses] start to push in. Therefore, one must urgently defend oneself. If one's defenses are steady, then one can deal with any issues that come up from behind. This is why the text says, "Clad in armor and holding talismans, he opens the seven gates."

"Talismans and charts" [in the next line] refer to the *River Chart* with its nine squares that all need to be aligned within oneself: three on the left,

---

[21] *Zhuangzi* 4.

seven on the right, nine on the head, one beneath the step, two and four mark the flanks, while six and eight are the feet. In this manner the entire body, above and below, is fully covered and one can "defend the numinous passes."

The "numinous passes" are the three passes within. The three forces all manifest Dao, and humanity closely matches heaven and earth: thus, they are numinous. Essence and spirit rise and decline, forming the foundation of life and destiny: within, they harmonize with the numbers [of the *River Chart*]; on the outside, they match cosmic principle. In this manner, there is no chance to incur blame for recklessly activating them.

Similarly, in ruling the country, one uses talismans and tokens for identification at the gates and passes. Before they are opened to allow entering and leaving, one must have the right talisman. Gates are close to the central city; passes are far away. When those close by are properly opened, then those far off cannot be in disorder. For this reason, the texts says, "Fire soldiers, talismans, and charts order the numinous passes."

28.8 前昂後卑高下陳 [= 3/5]
Raised in front, low behind: they line up top to bottom.

This is a physical image of how they are arranged and positioned.

* * *

Jiang: "Raised in front" connects to the vermilion bird, that is, above the step. "Low behind" connects to the turtle and snake, that is, below the step. First the text speaks of "raised" and "low," then it says "top to bottom;" this indicates the relative positions of raised and low. In other words, raised is top and low is bottom. People need to be aligned correctly and distribute these areas well: such is their activity.

28.9 執劍百丈舞錦幡
Holding swords of a hundred fathoms, they dance with brocade banners.

This shows the physical shape of the divine soldiers with their banners and swords.

* * *

Jiang: "Holding swords of a hundred fathoms" is an expression for being majestic and strong. "Dance with brocade banners" is a literary way to express intense vibration. All these are tools used by the fire soldiers. "Banners" indicate a large multitude [of troops] that get people to follow along with music.

Dancing with swords is done to vanquish the enemy: it gets people to cower in fear. For this reason, they hold them.

28.10   十絕盤空扇紛紜
Ten strands of broken weave, they coil in empty air—fanning out, confused and numerous.

In empty air, they produce *qi*; glowing and blazing, they move like lightning flashes.

* * *

Jiang: Nine strands in ten colors: closely connected, they turn into brocade; separated, they become broken weave. Broken weave is a name for colors not closely connected in a fabric; here it refers to the banners. The idea is the same as in the *Duren jing*, when it speaks of "numinous banners made from ten strands of broken weave."[22]

In the section on the gall bladder, the text says, "He wears a robe of nine-colored brocade and a skirt of green florescence."[23] There are five primary colors. Added into patterned fabric, ordered and scattered, they become nine key strands. Just as wood emerges from earth [in the five phases], so green and yellow merge into one organism and change to become green: thus, the ten colors come about.

This particular verse discusses the Dao of the perfected. The key is to eradicate and eliminate all forms of wayward *qi* and falsehood, to keep the spirit whole and well maintained. One must match the numbers of talismans and charts, closely align and harmonize them, so that when outside entities come close, one can resist them even without flags. The ten colors, therefore, swirl and circulate in intricate and esoteric patterns, none arising as predominant at any time. Then, even if there should be some form of wayward *qi* and falsehood, one can wave the banners. Who then would ever invade one's shelter?

Still, before one has mastered the art of eradication and elimination, there may be a situation that can be described as impossible to win, which means one gets ready for the enemy to be victorious. In such a situation where it is impossible to win, there are no other arts: one must rely on the majestic spirits in their brightness. This is why, when all ten colors are well

---

[22] The expression appears in the *Duren jing jizhu* 度人經集註 (Collected Commentaries to the Scripture of Universal Salvation), attributed to the early Tang Daoist Cheng Xuanying 成玄英.
[23] *Neijing* 14.8.

ordered, they fully correspond to the gall bladder. The gall bladder, moreover, belons to lesser yang, thunder and lightning, and the eight kinds of tremor. Dragon flags streak across the sky, coiling worms wake and rise up: above and below intermingle greatly, they match each other in all respects and create a gorgeous web of brocade.

The perfected join the multitude of humanity on the outside; they are complete with heaven on the inside. They stand solitary and never waiver; they circulate about and never perish. Like this, they are far away from beings; their internal structure is separate, like broken weave. Therefore, the text above speaks of "brocade banners," and further down uses the expression "ten strands of broken weave." It focuses on the core of the matter.

28.11   火鈴冠霄隊[墜]落煙
[Holding] fire bell, capped with clear mist, he chases [Jiang: drops] and scatters the smoke.

Holding a fire bell of golden essence is a person wearing a cap of penetrating mist. The troops and regiments in their shape look like scattering mist and dense clouds.

* * *

Jiang: "Fire bell" indicates the majestic sound of the gall bladder. In this context, it refers to the support of Majestic Brightness. Now, various forms of wayward *qi* and falsehood cause people to drop into darkness [hell]—representing the inferior way; fire bell flies up into the void—standing for the superior way. The majestic sound of the gall bladder rises up and does not drop; therefore, all things that drop into darkness are subject to its control.

For this reason, the methods of fire bell, even though it tends to fly up into the void and is "capped with clear mist," can work to "drop and scatter" [bad things]. The earlier section on the gall bladder says that one "wields" [the fire bell],[24] but here the text says that one "drops" it. The two actions of wielding and dropping complete each other.

"Smoke" as an entity cannot be dropped. When the text says, "He drops and scatters the smoke," it refers to an action of throwing it down and suppressing it. Now, fire is an entity of yang, while bells are classified as yin. A fire bell is therefore yin within yang, corresponding to the trigram Li [fire]. Li corresponds to profit above and utility below, expressing the principles of inner nature and destiny.

---

[24] *Neijing* 14.4.

28.12　安在黃闕兩眉間
Then rests peacefully in the Yellow Tower between the two eyebrows.

Visualize and think of the fire soldiers, their *qi* and forms assembling in the Heavenly Court. The Heavenly Court is also called the Yellow Tower. It is located between the two eyebrows.

28.13　此非枝葉實是根 [= 3/10]
He is neither branch nor leaf: he is indeed the root.

This is the very foundation of studying immortality.

* * *

Jiang: The Heavenly Court occupies the position of heaven; the Yellow Court matches the way of earth. The way of earth rules all within; its area of activation is below. Because it is both within and below, when it moves outward and connects above there must be a tower—a tower being something that presides high over the path. The area between the two eyebrows is indeed the Heavenly Court. The tower of the Yellow Court is also in this area, and so the text uses the name "Yellow Tower."

The Yellow Tower marks the great path that links heaven and earth, coming and going, rising and descending. When heaven and earth are in good harmony, they generate myriad transformations. The Dao of the perfected lies most centrally and wondrously in this. Because the two match and harmonize above and below, they function as the two powers.

As the position of the Yellow Court is below and that of the Yellow Tower is above, the text speaks of "resting peacefully." Resting peacefully indicates the appearance of presence. The appearance of presence is there because there is no place where Dao is not. Since there is no place where Dao is not, there is the appearance of presence; this is the reason why it is present.

"Branches and leaves" both issue from the root but are not themselves the root. Because they are not themselves the root, they can flourish and wither, renew and decay as the sun revolves and the moon transforms: yet the root does not go along with them. Perfected people return to the root and recover life; solitary, they complete their heavenly nature. In contrast, thieving and boasting fellows engage in literary pursuits and business, taking advantage of all situations, enjoying food and drink, goods and material wealth, accumulating and showing them off, always running after and pursuing more. All those of this ilk clearly are part of "branches and leaves."

For this reason, the perfected are "clad in armor and hold talismans" to "open the gates" and "order the passes." They cut off all connections to outside entities, reverse their radiance, and turn back their shine onto themselves. We can accordingly say that in them all movement and stillness issue from the root and there is no chance of them being vain or reckless. As the text says, "He is indeed the root."

Twenty-Nine

29.1　紫清上皇太道君
The Highest Sovereign of Purple Clarity, the Lord of the Great Dao,

He is also called the Lord of Jade Morning Light (Yuchen jun 玉晨君).

* * *

Jiang: This gives the comprehensive names of all the sovereigns of nonaction and lords of creative doing in the figure of a single emperor. Earlier verses divide him into two, but this combines him into one. Matching the earlier section which spoke about the Dao of the perfected, how they cut off all connections to outside entities, reverse their radiance, and turn back their shine onto themselves, and so on, there really is no division or distinction. They recognize cosmic truth and complete Dao: accordingly, they are called perfected. Now, all the sovereigns of nonaction and lords of creative doing comprehensively are integrated in this Emperor of the One, jointly issuing and functioning in mutuality. This Dao is subtle and wondrous: it cannot be grasped by thought or measured, be comprehended by division or analysis. Only the perfected truly know.

29.2　太玄太和俠侍端
Great Mystery and Great Harmony accompany and attend to all.

Great Mystery and Great Harmony are auspicious names of perfected immortals.

29.3　化生萬物使我仙
They transform and generate the myriad beings, causing me to be immortal.

This indicates the successful effort of Dao and *qi*.

* * *

Jiang: Great Mystery is the mysterious heaven of the north, which engenders and sprouts all beings in their transformations, the place to steady the Numinous Root. Great Harmony is the azure heaven of the east, which entrusts and harmonizes all beings in their lives, the place to attain the numinous rays.

The two spirits accompany and attend to all; venerable in nature, they return to the Emperor of Oneness as the Dao of immortality is complete.

Now, even though the Dao of immortality is vast, its core lies in continued existence and lasting life. Therefore, moving from north to east, I move toward the center of yang, embracing the principle of transformation and life as it is well ordered. As the four seasons complete their annual cycle, and as my heavenly Dao is complete, I stop at the center of yang, attending to all

29.4　飛升十天駕玉輪
In flight I ascend to the ten heavens, riding a jade-wheeled [carriage].

I take off suddenly and leave.

29.5　晝夜七日思勿眠
Day and night for seven days, I think of them and never sleep.

I have foremost sincerity and extreme dedication.

* * *

Jiang: The number of heavens is usually nine, but the text here speaks of "ten heavens," adding an empty one. This is just like the Great Expansion [of *Yijing* divination], where one begins with an empty one to mark the wondrous origin.

The perfected of old recognized cosmic truth and completed Dao, wondrously comprehending the instructions of the Emperor of the One. For this reason, they can transcend and go beyond even the nine heavens, solitarily wandering about the realm of emptiness and oneness. This is what the text means when it says, "In flight I ascend to the ten heavens." Ascending in flight means joining the waves of yang, expressed in the text as "jade [wheeled] carriage." Jade is the symbol of pure yang; carriage stands for Dao below. In other words, one strides on the *qi* of pure yang and ascends from below.

Now, yang moves from below; such is the season of return. "In seven days, he comes and returns."[25] Thus, seven is the number of return. Thinking of this constantly is how one reaches above. Striding on pure yang and reaching above is not something one can attain when enjoying sleep. The people of old heard of Dao and continuously thought of it for seven days, getting to the point where they got to it bone-deep. Once they got to it, there was no more need for sleep. This is the effort needed in the practice of cultivation, to at-

---

[25] *Yijing*, Hexagram 24. See 11.8 above.

tain the Dao of the perfected, always related to talk of the source and beginning of all.

29.6   子能行此可長存
If you can practice this, you can live forever.

Extending years is the way of spirit immortality.

29.7   積功成煉非自然
Accumulating merit, completing the refinement: this is not part of naturalness.

Study and attain this Dao.

* * *

Jiang: The transformations generating the myriad beings cause me to be immortal, but the emperor determines actual immortality. The emperor determining immortality happens naturally. For this reason, what happens to me subjectively is the interior way. "If you can cultivate this, you can remain forever" means that you have to study to reach completion. Studying to reach completion is not something that happens naturally. For this reason, what happens to you as an object is the inferior way. Now Dao is not the same as naturalness, but that does not mean it is not natural. The text says that "this is not part of naturalness," meaning it serves to establish the teaching. Once the teaching is established properly, study and naturalness can merge into one.

29.8   是由精誠亦守一［由專］
All comes from concentrated sincerity and maintaining the One [YQ: and from single focus].

Maintain the One as initially, then you can complete the Dao and more.

* * *

Jiang: "Concentrated sincerity and single focus" are things necessary to "accumulate merit and complete refinement." Sincerity means being free from doubt. Focus means there is no duality. Free from doubt about things means that things correspond just fine. No duality in the heart means that the spirit is intensely centered.

Shangqiu Kai believed an untruth to be real and duly dived into the river and found a pearl: he was free from doubt and things corresponded well to him.[26] The old hunchback was aware of nothing but cicada wings and thus never failed to catch them: there was no duality and his spirit was intensely centered.[27]

As students of Dao visualize and imagine the Three Palaces, the myriad spirits correspond to their vision and concentrated sincerity is achieved. Should any outside entity come to question them, they remain clear and do not lose or drop [their concentration]. For this reason, they must eliminate and destroy all karmic causes and connections, do away and eradicate all fame and profit, unify their mind and set their will fully on Dao: then Dao can be attained.

29.9   內守堅固真之真
Maintaining all within to be firm and steady: perfected and again perfected.

This comes from giving up all ranks. [YQ: Never lose order and regularity.]

29.10   虛中恬淡自致神
In emptiness, quiet and bland, you naturally attain spirit.

This is because spirit lives on emptiness.

* * *

Jiang: "Maintaining all within to be all firm and steady" is another way of expressing "concentrated sincerity and single focus." "Maintaining all within" means that there is no other pursuit: with nothing else going on, there is full focus. "Firm and steady" means holding on without solidity, and holding on without solidity means sincerity.

As one is in full focus with nothing else going on, it is impossible to lose perfection. If one then adds holding on without solidity, one reaches being "perfected and again perfected." That is, being in full focus with nothing else going on and holding on without solidity, nothing however concealed is not pervaded. Then one is "in emptiness, quiet and bland," opening all that is concealed. "Emptiness" means that there is no more need to focus on maintaining all within. "Quiet and bland" means there is no need to focus on keeping all firm and steady. In other words, all the various methods of maintaining all within to be firm and steady, once in emptiness, quiet and bland,

---

[26] This refers to the story of the simpleton who was fearless and could accomplish all manner of things told in the *Liezi* 列子 (Book of Master Lie), ch. 2 (Graham 1960, 40).
[27] This relates to the story of the hunchback catching cicadas in *Zhuangzi* 19. Watson 1968, 199.

become extraneous. These various methods are not in themselves sufficient to enter Dao. If they were not extraneous and insufficient to attain Dao, this attainment could not be pursued through the spirit. Rather spirit naturally arrives there.

Thirty

30.1   百穀之實土地精
The kernels of the hundred grains are the essence of earth and soil.

Stalks and kernels are collectively called "grains." They are classified as yin.

30.2   五味外美邪魔猩 [= 3/14]
The five flavors may be beautiful on the outside, but they are wayward demons causing stinky rot.

They are not the perfect *qi* of clarity and emptiness.

* * *

Jiang: "The essence of earth and soil" is not sufficient to nourish spirit; it can only nourish the physical form. "Wayward demons causing stinky rot" are not sufficient to nourish the physical form; they can only issue odors and increase decay. Increasing decay and calling it "beautiful" is a way to beautify evil. Not sufficient to nourish spirit and calling it "essence" is to say that it might be used to supplement perfection. Remaining attached to earth and soil, one stays closely related to the lower principles and can never say that "in flight one ascends to the ten heavens."

30.3   臭亂神明胎氣零
Their stench disturbs the spirits in their brightness and causes embryonic *qi* to fragment.

Embryonic *qi* means the flavor of no flavor; it is the proper *qi* of naturalness. In absorbing *qi,* there are methods of proper embryo respiration. "Fragment" is like "lose."

30.4   那從反老得還嬰
How would you ever reverse aging and recover youth?

[YQ add: This says you cannot attain it.] White hair turns black again, lost teeth regrow. This sentence should be placed right after "you naturally achieve spirit existence" (29.10). Placed here it is not of the same kind.

30.5   三魂忽忽魄糜傾

The three cloud spirit agents are careless and indifferent; the white spirit agents are wasted and collapsed.

"Careless and indifferent" means not serene and bland. "Wasted and collapsed" means withered and destroyed.

* * *

Jiang: The "spirits in their brightness" are set up to create goodness on the basis of clarity and emptiness, order and attainment. On the other hand, food and drink, disgust and greed weaken inherent *qi* and cause a loss of clarity and emptiness. This will result in "stench that disturbs."

"Embryonic *qi*" is what people receive from heaven. In a state of chaos, it merges in harmony: vital principle emerges from within this, naturally steady and solid. Then, however, seeing and listening, eating and breathing push toward the outside: they bore another opening each day, and embryonic *qi* "fragments."[28]

The spirits in their brightness, being disturbed by stench, each day come closer to destruction until there is none left to "reverse aging." Embryonic *qi* scatters and perishes until there is none left to "recover youth." The cloud spirit agents are essentially numinous, but as the spirits in their brightness are disturbed by stench, they can no longer be numinous as long as one lives. Thus, "the three cloud spirit agents are careless and indifferent." The white spirit agents are closely bound to the physical form. When embryonic *qi* scatters and perishes, the physical form and bodily organism are ruined and destroyed. That is, "the white spirit agents are wasted and collapsed."

30.6   何不食氣太和精 [= 3/15]

How can you not ingest pure *qi* and the essence of Great Harmony?

This pushes for the Dao of absorption and refinement.

---

[28] This refers to the Hundun story in *Zhuangzi* 2, where the emperors of the north and south bore a new hole into the formless emperor of the center to afford him sense orifices.

30.7   故能不死入黃寧 [= 3/16]
Then you can reach no-death and enter yellow calm.

Yellow calm means completing the Dao of the *Yellow Court*.

* * *

Jiang: "Human life is a coming-together of *qi*. If it comes together, there is life; if it scatters, there is death."[29] This means that by "ingesting pure *qi*," one can get it to come together and not scatter. "Great Harmony" signals the *qi* of lesser yang. It depends on harmony for its generation and the mouth is the official in charge of it. Rinsing and swallowing the numinous fluid, one can generate a radiant florescence. This supports the root of the vital principle. There is no need to rely on artificial outside entities; it is sufficient in itself to afford nourishing [life]. "Then you can be free from death."

"Yellow calm" is the state of health created by Chaos Vigor, the divine official who governs the spleen section. Digesting grain and scattering *qi*, he is in charge of the hundred diseases. For this reason, he is always active and never calm. Now, if one uses perfect *qi* to nourish naturally and does not rely on artificial outside entities, the official has nothing to rule or govern. Then he can be calm and support health.

To discuss this further, the text previously said, "Maintaining all to be firm and steady: perfected and again perfected. In emptiness, quiet and bland, you naturally attain spirit."[30] Doing so, one gets to "accumulate merit and complete refinement,"[31] becoming a perfected. Based on this, the text here insists that one should abandon and do away with all outside entities, so that perfect *qi* can nourish naturally and on this basis one can be free from death.

However, in adepts who have just started to study, heavenly perfection is not yet whole; they cannot maintain the spirits in a steady state at all times. Therefore, they have to resort to various means to supplement the vital principle. Also, generally they do not have ways to keep from being disordered. Thus, they nourish inner steadiness with the help of outside entities: they cannot quite yet abandon and do away with them.

Now, heaven produces the means of nourishing essence, so that spirit and *qi* can attain a state of cosmic peace. Earth produces the means of nourishing the physical form, so that skin and epidermis can be full and plenteous. One can rely on these to harmonize potency and create proper order in the spleen and stomach, bringing forth fragrant richness and luscious glory, supplementing them greatly. Then the bright lad in the Great Storehouse will

---

[29] *Zhuangzi* 22.
[30] *Neijing* 29.9-10.
[31] *Neijing* 29.7.

rule well to harmonize the hundred grains and properly apply the five flavors, extracting and refining them to a state of newness, circulating and moving them everywhere.

The palace where he resides is called the Yellow Court. A court is a place of distribution and government; the central section is where Lord Lao is active. When one accumulates merit and completes refinement, maintains all within to be firm and steady, then the hundred grains and five flavors are all abandoned and done away with, and one abides in emptiness, quiet and bland. At this point, the officials of the spleen and stomach rest in the chamber of emptiness and enters a state called "yellow calm." In yellow calm, even though one has not yet separated from the physical body and sensory experiences, one is yet close to being serene and unmoving. The nonaction and naturalness of the perfected of the ten heavens have their foundation in this.

Thirty-One

31.1   心典一體五藏王 [= 3/18]
The heart is in charge of the entire organism, the king of the five organs.

The heart receives all in emptiness, it is the residence where the spirits sojourn. For this reason, it is called the king.

31.2   動靜念之道德行 [= 3/19]
In activity and stillness, envision it: Dao and potency functioning together.

This says to envision the lad called Cinnabar Prime. As long as you envision him, he is present; as soon as you forget him, he is no longer there. Envisioning him, he eases the heart and soon will start talking to you; forgetting him, he rejects the heart and wholly enters spirit. Hence the text says, "Dao and potency functioning together."

31.3   清潔喜氣自明光 [= 3/20]
Clear and pure, joyful in *qi*: naturally bright and radiant.

That is because you always envision him.

31.4   坐起吾俱共棟梁
Rising and sitting I am always with you, joined like pillars and beams.

The spirit uses the body for its parlor and residence, thus it says "together like pillars and beams." "I" here is the lad Cinnabar Prime.

31.5   晝日曜景暮閉藏 [= 3/21]
At sunrise, shining brilliant lights; at sunset, closes organs.

Zhuangzi says, "In waking hours, men's bodies hustle; in sleep, their cloud spirit agents go off visiting."[1]

31.6   通利華精調陰陽
Connecting to and utilize flowery essence as you balance yin and yang.

---

[1] *Zhuangzi* 2.

This says that heart and spirit in their working and lodging closely match the eyes. Flowery essence is the essence of the eyes. When the heart opens, so do the eyes. Sunrise is yang; sunset is yin. Hence it says, "balance yin and yang."

Thirty-Two

32.1   經歷六合隱卯酉 [= 3/23]
Passing through all six harmonies, seclude yourself in *mao* [east] and *you* [west].

The working and lodging of the elevated heart come from the ongoing rhythm of yin and yang. During the day it passes along; at night, it goes into hiding. The six harmonies are heaven and earth, above and below, plus the four directions. *You* and *mao* indicate sunrise and sunset. Darkness and hiding go together.

32.2   兩腎之神主延壽
The spirit of the two kidneys rules extended longevity.

The spirit of the kidneys is Mysterious Gloom, also known as Raising Offspring. He belongs to the direction of the north and presides over sunset and night. If people can concentrate their heart-mind [YQ: stop their essence], they can extend their longevity. Heshang gong says, "The kidneys store essence."[2]

32.3   轉降適斗藏初九 [= 3/24]
Revolving and descending, going with the Dipper, he stores it first at nine.

Nine is the number of yang. Dipper here indicates the North Culmen. It rules over the descent of yang, commonly described as yang *qi* sinking down in order to merge with yin. The *Yijing* says, "Qian represents the primordial. [All nines: we see the host of dragons] without beginning. [Good fortune]."[3] "Without head" means storing.

32.4   知雄守雌可無老
Know the male and maintain the female, and you can be free from old age.

---

[2] *Heshang gong zhangju* 河上公章句 (Verses and Sayings of the Master on the River, DZ 682, SV 72-74), commentary to ch. 6.
[3] Hexagram 1, judgment and summary of lines (Song 1971, 1-2).

"Maintain" the female is an expression for storing the nine.

32.5   知白見黑急坐守
Know the bright and see the dark: urgently sit down to practice.

The *Daojing* says, "Know the male and maintain the female; know the bright and maintain the dark."[4] Both refer to storing the nine.

Thirty-Three

33.1   肝氣鬱勃清且長 [= 3/26]
Liver-*qi* is dense and changeable, clear and long.

The liver is in the position of the east and phase wood; it rules the spring and serves as the foundation of all living *qi*. "Clear and long" are expressions for the color and appearance of its *qi*.

33.2   羅列六府生三光 [= 3/27]
Move through the six viscera in the right order: generate the three luminants within.

Visualize and imaging living *qi* as it shines everywhere through the five organs and six viscera, like the sun and moon, the stars and chronograms radiate their brilliance and brightness.

33.3   心精意專內不傾
The heart-mind concentrated and intention focused, it will not collapse within.

This means being able to know the One. Just like rain moistens the myriad beings, so jade nectar moistens the hundred limbs.

33.4   上合三焦下玉漿 [= 3/28]
Above merge with the Triple Heater, below the jade nectar.[5]

This says that liver-*qi* rises up and merges with the *qi* of the Triple Heater; it sinks down and forms liquid in the mouth. This is like yin-*qi* rising up to

---

[4] *Daode jing* 28.
[5] This line appears only in the YQ version.

form clouds and sinking down to create rain. Just like rain moistens the myriad beings, so jade nectar moistens the hundred limbs and nine orifices.

33.5   玄液雲行去臭香 [= 3/31]
Mysterious fluids flow like clouds, removing all stench and fragrance.

If perfect *qi* circulates and flows, you will be free from disaster and disease.

33.6   治蕩髮齒煉五方
Regulate and cleanse hair and teeth, refine the five directions.

Like clouds move about and rain spreads, there is no place that is not connected. The five directions here are the five organs.

33.7   取津玄膺大 [入] 明堂 [= 3/32]
Gather liquids in the Mysterious Sphincter: great [enter] the Hall of Light.

To work with the way of swallowing saliva, by all means move it down through the Mysterious Sphincter and let it enter the esophagus. The esophagus is also called the Multi-storied Tower. Below it is the Hall of Light, beneath which is the Grotto Chamber, and yet further down is the Elixir Field. This is the central section.

33.8   下溉喉嚨神明通 [= 3/40]
Moving down and moistening the esophagus, the spirits in their brightness connect.

Body and destiny are ruled by liquids and *qi*.

33.9   坐侍華蓋游貴京
Sitting and attending to the Flowery Canopy, float to the Noble Capital.

The Flowery Canopy is the lungs. The liver sits below the lungs. The Noble Capital is the Elixir Field.

33.10   飄飄三帝席清涼
Airy and wispy are the three emperors, their seats clear and fresh.

The three emperors are the Dao lords of the three elixir fields. They are also called perfected. This says that liver-*qi* as pure *qi* is airy and wispy, circulating and flowing through the locations of the three elixir fields. Liver-*qi* is the essence of the eyes. Hence it says, "their seats clear and fresh."

33.11   五色雲氣紛青蔥
Cloud *qi* of five colors is as prolific as green onions.

Liver-*qi* intermingles with the *qi* of the five organs, looking like clouds [YQ: it rises and turns into five-colored clouds].

33.12   閉目內眄自相望
Closer your eyes and look within: you will naturally spot it.

Always practice visualization and envisioning, and the five organs will naturally appear.

33.13   使心諸神還相崇
This will cause the heart and the numerous spirits to revert and offer homage.

The Lad of the Red City is the perfected of the heart organ. The spirits merge and align in the same office and jointly come to venerate and pay their respects.

* * *

The Lad of the Red City meets the perfected of the five organs. They merge and align their talismans, then jointly come to venerate and pay their respects.

33.14   七玄英華開命門
The seven mysterious ones, glowing and florescent, open the Gate of Destiny.

The seven orifices are flowing and connected, entirely free from restraint and obstruction.

33.15   通利天道存玄根 [= 3/47]
Connecting to and engaging with heaven's Dao, visualize the mysterious root.

The body is root and foundation.

33.16   百二十年猶可還
By reverting you can still reach 120 years.

Urgently cultivate and practice: time must not be lost.

33.17   過此守道誠甚 [獨] 難
Miss this chance to maintain Dao, and sincerity gets very [YQ: singularly] difficult!

Demise and death are drawing close.

33.18   唯待九轉八瓊丹
Just rely on the ninefold reverted elixir of the eight kinds of jasper.

The divine elixir of ninefold reversion is the means to ascend into heaven in broad daylight. The *Jiudan lun* 九丹論 (Discourse on the Nine Elixirs) by Baopuzi 抱樸子 (Master Who Embraces Simplicity) says, "Having examined and read many books on nourishing life, collected and gathered numerous recipes on attaining eternal vision, I have unrolled and studied thousands of schemes. Among all of them, none comes close to the great essential teaching of the reverted elixir of the golden fluid."[6]

The *Huangdi jiuding shendan jing* 黃帝九鼎神丹經 (Yellow Emperor's Scripture of the Divine Elixir of the Nine Tripods) says, "The emperor took it and ascended as an immortal to live as long as heaven and earth. Riding the clouds and steering dragons, he enters and leaves Great Clarity."[7]

The eight kinds of jasper are: cinnabar, realgar, copper, sulfur, mica, salpeter, slake, orpiment—things like that.

33.19   要復精思存七元
Then again concentrate on visualizing the seven primes.

Even though you take the divine elixir, you still must also practice the way of the *Yellow Court*. The seven primes are the perfect spirits of the seven stars and also of the seven orifices. Then again, the prime lords known as the five emperors plus the lords White Prime and Blossomless are also described as Dao lords of the seven primes. The *Dongfang jue* says, "Visualize the seven

---

[6] *Baopuzi* 4.1a, "Gold and Cinnabar" (*Jindan* 金丹); Ware 1966, 68.
[7] A text of this title appears in DZ 885, SV 378-79. A similar characterization appears in the biography of Liu An 劉安 in the *Shenxian zhuan* 神仙傳 (Biographies of Spirit Immortals). Campany 2002, 234.

primes, then intone the incantation: 'Revolving primes, hidden and invisible; vastly scattered, the seven chronograms.'"[8] This refers to the seven primes.

33.20   日月之華救老殘
The flowery [shine] of the sun and the moon saves from old age and decline.

The left eye rules [YQ: is] the sun; the right eye rules [YQ: is] the moon. The eyes rule the liver and match the direction of the east and the phase wood. The position of wood is spring, and spring is living *qi*. Hence it says it "saves from old age and decline."

33.21   肝氣周流絡無端 [= 3/49]
Liver-*qi* flows in circles, without end or beginning.

Zhuangzi says, "Though the grease burns out of the torch, the fire passes on."[9] In the same way, as long as life gets intake and nourishment, destiny continues.

Thirty-Four

34.1   肺之為氣三焦起 [= 3/50]
The active *qi* of the lungs rises from the Triple Heater.

The *Zhonghuang jing* says, "The head of the lungs is the Triple Heater."[10] The active *qi* of the lungs is called dense *qi*.[11] Dense *qi* rises from the Triple Heater. Hence it says, "Rises from the Triple Heater." Another explanation states that the Triple Heater for the most part does not have a purpose of its own but in fact signifies the upper portion of the three [YQ: five] organs, forming three heaters. The world "heater" means hot. The meaning of the phrase is that the top of the liver, heart, and lungs is hot.

---

[8] The last line appears in the title of the *Huoluo qiyuan fu* 豁落七元符 (Talismans of the Vastly Scattered Seven Primes, DZ 392, SV 604), which presents fourteen relevant talismans but no incantation.
[9] *Zhuangzi* 3.
[10] YQ 13.33a, same as above, 8.8.
[11] "Dense *qi*" translates *qisou* 氣嗽, which literally means "cough" or maybe "phlegm."

34.2　視聽幽冥候童子
Look and listen in the dark and gloom, thus waiting for the lad.

The lad here is the spirit of the heart who resides in the Red City. Yuanyang-zi says, "Watch downward [YQ: the world] from a distance and visualize the lads. The lads are the pupils of the eyes." This says that, if people want to know about life and death, they should place the fingers of their hands at the corners of their eyes and wait for radiance to arise in the eyes. If there is radiance, it means life; if there is no radiance, it means death.

34.3　調理五華精髮齒
Balance and regulate the five florescences, sublimate hair and teeth.

The five florescences are the *qi* of the five organs. The *Xianjing* says, "The hair you want to comb multiple times; the teeth you want to click a lot."[12]

34.4　三十六咽玉池里
Thirty-six times swallow the content of the Jade Pond.

The mouth is the Jade Pond, also called the Flowery Pond. Swallow the saliva and guide it into the Elixir Field. This is what we call watering and moistening the Numinous Root.

34.5　開通百脈血液始
Open and connect the hundred conduits, so blood and fluids can start out.

The blood and fluids in the body use the mouth as their original starting point.

34.6　顏色生光金玉澤　[= 3/56]
Color fresh, complexion radiant: glossy like gold and jade.

All hundred conduits are open and connected.

34.7　齒堅髮黑不知白　[= 3/55]
Teeth firm, hair black, never turning white.

Reverse aging and recover youth.

---

[12] Unclear. See 2.6 above.

34.8　　存此真神勿落落 [= 3/57]
Visualize these perfected and spirits, never let them be scattered.

Focus on the spirits, never being lazy.

34.9　　當憶紫 [此] 宮有座席
Keep your intention on the Purple [YQ: this] Palace with its seats and thrones.

The Purple [YQ: This] Palace is the palace of the lungs. "Seats and thrones" are where the spirits are at peace. The *Zhonghuang jing* says, "At the top of the lungs sits the Triple Heater."[13] It is where the Mystery Dragon Lord (Xuanlong jun 玄龍君) [YQ: Mystery Lord Lao (Xuanlao jun 玄老君)] resides.

34.10　　眾神合會轉相索 [= 3/58]
The numerous spirits assemble jointly, they turn about so you can gain close linkage.

With the numerous spirits all gathered together, how can there be wayward forms of essence?

Thirty-Five

35.1　　隱藏羽蓋看天舍 [= 3/60]
The secluded storehouse has a feathery canopy: see the heavenly shelter.

This explains what's going on with the spleen palace. The spleen palace holds the Elixir Field and the Yellow Court. Located in the center and the position *wuji*, it belongs to the phase earth. Looking up from there, one sees the liver and the lungs, like a canopy or a shelter.

35.2　　朝拜太陽樂相呼 [= 3/61]
Pay homage and bow to great yang, rejoice with every exhalation.

The numerous spirits come together in the spleen palace to pay their respects to the highest spirit immortals. They rejoice and are happy to be summoned. The text here says that the cloud spirit agents and the numerous immortals assemble jointly. [YQ: This says that cloud spirit agents, the spirits, and the

---

[13] YQ 13.33a, same as 8.8. above.

many deities jointly assemble here.] The *Suling jing* says, "The highest spirit immortals include the Lord of Greater Yang (Taiyang jun 太陽君), [YQ add: the Lord of Lesser Yang (Shaoyang jun 少陽君),] the Lord of Great Emptiness (Taixu jun 太虛君), and the Lord of Dazzling [YQ: Magnificent] Simplicity (Haosu jun 皓[浩]素君). The host of immortals and patriarchs of Dao wander there and delight in them."[14]

35.3   明神八威正闢邪 [= 3/62]
The spirits in their brightness and Eight Daunters properly close off all forms of wayward *qi*.

The eight numinous spirits are full of bright potency; they represent the proper methods and expulsion of all forms of wayward *qi*. They protect and guard the spleen palace.[15] The Eight Daunters are the eight numinous spirits. The *Zhen'gao* says, The *Beidi shagui zhou* 北帝殺鬼咒 (Incantation of the Northern Emperor Slaying Demons) runs:

> Oh, seven upright [stars] and eight numinous [spirits]:
> Most high, dazzling in your fierceness!
> Huge beasts with long foreheads,
> Your hands hold the imperial gong.
> Simple and spooky [lit. "owl"], you ride a triple carriage
>   [YQ: control the three spirits]
> And majestically stride upon coiling dragons!
>   [YQ: A divine king with a majestic sword.][16]

This is a method of maintaining and protecting yourself, destroying all wayward energies and eliminating all misfortune. Chant as appropriate. [YQ: This is a method of protection, a way to close off all wayward energies.]

35.4   脾神還歸是胃家 [= 3/63]
The spirit of the spleen reverts and returns: such is the stomach homestead.

The spleen is a function of the stomach, thus its spirit returns there.[17] The spirit of the spleen is called Always Present, also known as Cloud Spirit Pa-

---

[14] The *Suling jing* is found in DZ 1314, SV 187-88. Citation unclear.
[15] This first part does not appear in the YQ edition.
[16] *Zhen'gao* 10.10b.
[17] In this and the following three lines (35.4-35.7) of commentary, the first sentence does not appear in the YQ.

vilion. The spleen grinds up food and dissolves it, which is also the job of the stomach homestead. The *Zhonghuang jing* says, "The stomach is the Great Storehouse."[18] The Great Storehouse is the spleen and the belly.

35.5   耽養靈根不復枯 [= 3/64]
Indulge and nourish the Numinous Root, never again allow it to wither.

Cultivate the spirits of the Yellow Court, love and nourish inner nature and destiny, never again allowing them to wither and decay. The spleen is the Yellow Court, the root and foundation of human destiny. Nourish it with concentrated heart and you extend your years and become a spirit immortal.

35.6   閉塞命門保玉都 [= 3/66]
Close and seal the Gate of Destiny, protect the Jade Capital.

The body is the Jade Capital. Closing the Elixir Field and the Gate of Destiny is to protect essence. Yuanyangzi says, "The Gate of Life is the lower Elixir Field, the place of the spirits where essence and *qi* enter and leave. [YQ add: "Nourish the lad and close the lower lock, always protecting the ruler. The ruler is the body.] The body is the Jade Capital, the location where the spirits assemble." It is like a capital city.

35.7   萬神方胙壽有餘 [= 3/67]
The myriad spirits rightly worshiped: your longevity will be extensive.

As the host of numinous forces descend and bless you, you can extend your years. "Worship" means honor. Because the myriad spirits are nourished and properly honored, your longevity will be excessive.

35.8   是謂脾建在中宮 [= 3/68]
This is called the establishment of the spleen, located in the Central Palace.

The spleen rules the Central Palace, the position of the potency of earth

35.9   五藏六府神明主 [= 3/69]
The five organs and six viscera are all ruled by spirits in their brightness.

This refers to the ruler of the spleen.

---

[18] Text in YQ 13. Citation unclear, same as 15.1 above.

35.10　上合天門入明堂 [= 3/70]
Above they merge at heaven's gate and enter the Hall of Light.

Visualize the *qi* of the five organs and six viscera merging above at heaven's gate. Heaven's gate is between the two eyebrows, also known as the Heavenly Court. One inch in between the eyebrows is the Hall of Light.

35.11　守雌存雄頂三光
Maintain the female and visualize the male: be crowned by the three luminants.

Laozi's *Scripture* [YQ: The *Daojing*] says, "Know the male and maintain the female."[19] Female or the feminine stands for being weak and soft. The three luminants are the sun, moon, and stars.

35.12　外方內圓神在中
Square on the outside, round within: the spirits reside right there.

Square on the outside, round within is an image for the Hall of Light. The spirit of the spleen and the Perfect One reside there.[20]

35.13　通利血脈五藏豐 [= 3/73]
Connecting with and engaging blood vessels and [*qi*] conduits, the five organs are abundant

Spirit is serene, the heart is clear [YQ: still].

35.14　骨青筋赤髓如霜
Bones green, muscles red, marrow is like hard frost.

The hundred bones and nine orifices are all perfect and proper.

35.15　脾救七竅去不祥 [= 3/76]
The spleen aids the seven orifices, eliminating all that's inauspicious.

---

[19] *Daode jing* 28.
[20] This second sentence does not appear in the YQ.

The spleen connects to stomach *qi* to match an outside orifice. It controls all forms of wayward *qi* and repels all evil.²¹ As the spleen grinds up food and dissolves it, the ears are keen and the eyes perceptive.

35.16   日月列布設陰陽 [= 3/77]
The sun and moon align and spread, extending yin and yang.

Qi divides and spreads between the eyebrows: the left is yang; the right is yin. The sun is yang and rules over men; the moon is yin and rules over women. [YQ: The sun and yang; the moon is yin. The sun is for men; the moon is for women.]

35.17   兩神相會化玉漿 [英]
The two spirits meet each other and transform into jade nectar [YQ: glow].

Yin and yang meet and generate essence, transforming into men and women. [YQ: Men and women, yin and yang are expressions for natural liquids and fluids.]

35.18   淡然無味天人糧
Bland and without flavor, it is a key staple of the celestials.

As the spirits merge and meet, there is flavor and there is not.

35.19   子丹進饌肴正黃
Child Cinnabar brings delicacies to nurture proper yellow.

The lad uses yellow *qi* as food to nourish himself. Delicacies are *qi*. Child Cinnabar is a perfected. He brings about the perfect *qi* of the Elixir Field. The spleen is Central Yellow; it grinds up food and dissolves it.

35.20   乃曰瑯膏及玉霜
Then it is called cornelian salve and jade frost.

Liquids and fluids are a visual image of essence and *qi*.

---

²¹ In many verses from here on, the first sentence(s) of the commentary does not appear in the YQ. The end of the separate part is marked with an asterisk.

35.21　太上隱環八素瓊
The highest secluded rings contain eight simple kinds of jasper.

The esophagus is called the Multi-storied Tower and also known as the highest secret rings. Inside are simple fluids like the eight kinds of jasper, that is, it contains fluids like the eight simple kinds of jasper. The Scarlet Palace is next to the Multi-storied Tower of twelve rings. [YQ add: This is the esophagus.] Inside are simple liquids like the eight kinds of jasper.

35.22　溉益八液腎受精
Moisten and enhance these eight liquids, and the kidneys receive essence.

Enrich the eight liquids and enter them into the kidneys, where they become jade essence. Swallow the liquids and let them flow down into the palace of the kidneys, where they become [YQ: transform into] jade essence.

35.23　伏於太陰見我形 [= 3/78]
Yield to great yin to see my physical form.

The kidneys are between great yin and yielding yang: this is the beginning of the physical form. Great yin is the Grotto Chamber. This presents a physical image of envisioning the jasper fluids.

35.24　揚風三玄出始青
Raise the wind, and the three mysteries emerge and begin in green.

The kidneys match the three months of winter, their color is mysterious [dark]. When yin reaches its ultimate, it turns into yang and generates spring, which emerges as green *qi*. Raising the wind means to stimulate transformation. The two *qi* of yin and yang plus kidney [YQ: harmonized] *qi* make three, and the three generate the myriad beings—[YQ add: generating beings is] subtle and wondrous. Therefore, it says, "the three mysteries emerge and begin." "Green" means that when the myriad beings first emerge, their color is green. The *Taiping jing* says, "Accumulated clarity forms essence."[22]

35.25　恍惚之間至清靈 [= 3/83]
In the midst of the vague and obscure, reach clarity and numinosity.

---

[22] Same as 14.1 above.

The three mysteries emerge in their inner nature, their *qi* subtle and wondrous. You cannot pursue them with physical form or material substance, thus you are "in the midst of the vague and obscure." Only from here can you reach the realm of clarity and emptiness. The [YQ: living] *qi* of yin and yang is most subtle and most wondrous.

35.26   坐於飆臺見赤生
Sit on Whirlwind Terrace and see the Infant being born.

Frolicking above Whirlwind Terrace, see the perfected Infant. This refers to balanced and luxuriant *qi* transforming into the Infant. The Infant is the perfected. Whirlwind Terrace [YQ add: is a vast and windy space. It] is where spirit immortals frolic and assemble.

35.27   逸域熙真養華榮
In the realm of leisure, glorious and perfected, nourish flowery prosperity.

Proudly frolicking on Whirldwind Terrace is looking up at the perfected in the realm of leisure. Sagely and joyful in flowery prosperity, the perfect *qi* beyond all beings naturally nourishes life.

35.28   內盼沉默煉五形 [= 3/81]
Gazing within and deeply silent, refine the five-part physical form.

Gently gaze at the perfected and feight s [within], revert your gaze and practice inner vision. Cultivate and refine [YQ: internally observe] physical form and organism, and spirit and *qi* will remain forever.

35.29   三氣徘徊得神明
The three *qi* flutter to and fro, and attain the spirits in their brightness.

As you gaze within and refine the physical form, the *qi* of the three fields is activated and you are connected with the spirits and numinous forces. This refers to the *qi* of the three elixir fields.

35.30   隱龍遁芝云 [雲] 瑯英
Secluded dragon and invisible mushrooms are called [YQ: clouds of] cornelian glow.

The liver and gall bladder form the hidden dragon, while the orifices and conduits are inner mushrooms. Spleen-*qi* transforms the host of fluids, thereby producing cornelian glow. The *Xianjing* says, "The liver and gall bladder are linked with the green dragon."[23] Hence the text speaks of "invisible mushrooms" [lYQ: "hidden dragon."] [YQ add: The five organs and nine orifices relate to the eight extraordinary vessels. As regards the eight extraordinary vessels, traditional physicians speak of twelve conduits within the human body plus eight extraordinary vessels, which include the yang activation, yin activation, yang maintenance, and yin maintenance as well as the Penetrating, Governing, Conception, and Belt Vessels.] "Clouds of cornelian glow" refers to the liquids and fluids generated from spleen-*qi*.

35.31   可以充饑使萬靈
Then you can always satisfy hunger and command the myriad numinous forces.

Mushrooms that glow cause people to not feel hungry and easily command the host of the numinous forces. Absorbing *qi*, Dao is complete and you can direct and command ghosts and spirits.

35.32   上蓋玄玄下虎章
Above a canopy of dark mystery, below the tiger seal.

Absorbing and refining, Dao is complete, and heaven will bring you jade seals of divine tigers. This refers to the garb and ornaments of the spirit immortals. The *Yuanlu jing* says, "The immortals have a canopy of mysterious feathers and a [YQ add: jade] seal of divine tigers."[24]

Thirty-Six

36.1   沐浴盛潔棄肥薰
Bathing and cleansing overflow with purity, do away with all fats and smells.

This is an afterword, explaining the methods of entering stillness and holding on to essence. The word "overflow" is the old form of the word "clean." Fats stand for fish and meat; {YQ add: smells indicate] the five pungent vegetables.

---

[23] Unclear. See 2.6 above.

[24] Citation unclear. The text is also cited in 24.9 above.

36.2　　入室東向誦玉篇
Enter the oratory, face east, and chant the *Jade Chapters*.

Face the Great Emperor. The Great Emperor is in the east.[25]

36.3　　約得萬遍義自鮮
When you have completed ten thousand repetitions, the meaning is naturally obvious.

When the number of repetitions is sufficient and your merits are numerous, the meaning is naturally clear. Never leaves the center of the body.

36.4　　散髮無欲以長存　[= 3/98]
Spread the hair, stay free from desires, and you can remain forever.

Be still like an abyss and free from all desires, and you can attain long years. The *Xianjing* says, "To absorb the nine auroras, you must first spread the hair."[25] The method of embryo respiration similarly says, "Lie down face up and spread the hair." Another source has, "First put all emotions outside, then spread the hair."[27]

　　"Make sure the pillow is 1.2 inches high. Curl both hands into fists around the thumb and close your eyes. Stretch the arms at five inches from the body, Rinse and fill the mouth with liquids and fluids, then swallow them three times. Softly and subtly pull in *qi* through the nose for five or six breaths, then expel it. One inhalation and one exhalation make one breath. Once you reach ten expulsions, you can let the *qi* get longer. Once it has reached its full length, start over again. Complete forty-nine [YQ: four times nine] repetitions: this makes one round."

　　Examining the meaning of the text, it becomes clear that this spreading of the hair is not unique to this path. Generally, spreading the hair means resting in nonaction and natural attainment. [YQ add: One is free from external emotions and desires.]

36.5　　五味皆至正氣還　[= 3/96]
The five flavors all attained, proper *qi* reverts.

---

[25] Both text and commentary also appear in *Dengzhen yinjue* 3.1a.
[26] Unclear. See 2.6 above.
[27] This additional source is not mentioned in the YQ.

Spirit coagulated and fluids flowing, proper *qi* enters the organs It completes the five flavors and lets them reach fullness. The five them merge into one: the Dao of naturalness.

36.6   夷心寂悶勿煩冤
Easy at heart, quiet and dull, you are free from trouble and oppression.

If you don't even see there is a heart, you are naturally free from dullness. Quiet means still. In a state of quietude, there are clarity and stillness. Laozi [YQ: The *Daojing*] says, "When the government is sad and dull, the people are contented and generous."[28]

36.7   過數已畢體神精
Numerous rounds already complete, both organism and spirit are sublime.

Numerous rounds already complete, the body enters emptiness and wonder. Focus and concentration are achieved.

36.8   黃華玉女告子情
The Jade Maiden of Yellow Florescence comes to tell you secrets.

The spirit of the Elixir Field will explain the meaning of the scripture. The hidden deity of the Elixir Field comes to speak to you.

36.9   真人既至使六丁
Once the perfected has arrived, you can command the Six Ding.

Once the spirit of the Yellow Court has arrived, you can direct and command the Six Ding. The perfected is one who instructs students of Dao. The spirit has arrived means that essence is fully present. [YQ: The perfected is the entity in the body that instructs students. "Arrive" means that essence is fully present.] The Six Ding we already explained above.

36.10   即授隱芝大洞經
He soon hands over the hidden mushrooms of the *Dadong jing*.[29]

---

[28] *Daode jing* 58.

[29] This line does not appear in the *Xiuzhen shishu* edition.

"Hidden mushrooms" means secrets. This is a metaphor for the rare and glowing quality of immortals.

36.11 十讀四拜朝太上
Intone it ten times, give four bows, and pay homage to the Most High.

That is, bow to the Most High Lord Lao. The *Yujing zhenjue* 玉精真訣 (Perfected Instructions on Jade Essence) says, "As for reciting the *Donghua yupian* (Jade Chapters of Eastern Florescence), you must declaim it ten times and give four bows."[30] The *Yupian* (Jade Chapters) is this text.

36.12 先謁太帝後北向
First visit the Great Emperor, then face north.

The Great Emperor is in the east; the seven primes reside in the north.

36.13 黃庭內經玉書暢

The *Huangting neijing* (Inner Scripture of the Yellow Court), the *Yushu* (Jade Book), is luxuriant.

As described above, cultivate it by paying homage and bowing. In this manner you can complete the Dao of the *Huangting* [*jing*] and connect to the power of the *Yushu* (Jade Scripture).

* * *

The Dao of immortality is complete.

36.14 授者曰師受者盟
The one who bestows it is the teacher; the receiver swears the vow.

This says that obtaining the scripture requires merit and dedication, which means only an appointed teacher can bestow it on others. This text is worthy and weighty. [YQ: This text can be considered weighty; thus, it is subject to swearing a vow.]

---

[30] A text of this title, an apocryphal work of Highest Clarity, appears in DZ 1327, SV 156. It describes the proper ways of addressing the deities and reciting sacred scriptures; it also mentions the Lord of Eastern Florescence. But it does not contain this citation.

36.15   雲錦鳳羅金鈕纏
Cloud-like brocade, phoenix gauze, golden buttons and wraps

These things tokens required when swearing the vow.

36.16   以代割髮肌膚全
Represent cutting the hair while keeping flesh and skin whole.

In the old days, when people swore vows, they had to pledge not to transmit anything recklessly and demonstrate this by cutting their hair and drinking blood. Today, this is represented by cloud-like brocade, thus keeping flesh and skin whole.

* * *

For the contract to be sincere and not fake, blood must flow and hair be cut.

36.17   攜手登山歃液丹
Holding hands, you climb the mountain and smear your mouth with the cinnabar fluid.

As transmitted in the elixir scriptures, smearing the mouth with blood sets up the vow. Anyone studying the divine elixir and golden fluid must first swear a vow and only then can receive transmission.

* * *

Anyone receiving and practicing the way of the *Yellow Court*, must first swear a vow and then can receive transmission.

36.18   金書玉景乃可宣
The golden book and jade lights then can be explained.

Once the vow is sworn, one can explain and transmit the methods of the spirit immortals. The tokens must be in place when the text is bestowed.

* * *

The tokens must be in harmony, only then can there be bestowal.

36.19   傳得審 [可] 授若 [告] 三官
Once transmission is achieved, you examine and [YQ: can] bestow the text, as if [YQ: and declare it] to the three bureaus.

The three bureaus are those of heaven, earth, and water.

36.20　勿令七祖受冥患

Do not let your ancestors of seven generations suffer from underworld afflictions.

If you bestow [YQ: transmit] the text to the wrong person, your ancestors of seven generations will suffer calamities [YQ: calamities will extend to previous generations.] [YQ add: "Afflictions" can be read to mean repeated stays.]

36.21　太上微言致神仙

These subtle words of the Most High express spirit immortality.

They must be venerated and honored.

36.22　不死之道此真文

The way of no-death is right in this perfect text.

This scripture contains the Dao of eternal life: receive it with your whole heart and practice it with worship.

Recitation Ritual

Methods of Honoring and Reciting the *Inner Light Scripture of the Yellow Court*[1]

When you are about to enter the hall of purification, first halt outside the door and click your teeth three times. Close your eyes and imagine that inside the chamber there is the *qi* of purple clouds. Dense and vibrant, it comes to cover and envelope your entire body. Jade lads attend you on the left; jade maidens attend you on the right. The three luminants and various precious mushrooms glitter widely, both inside and out. Intone the following incantation:

> Heaven is bright, *qi* is clear;
> The three luminants shine widely.
> In my golden chamber, home of jade;
> Five mushrooms grow like gems.
>
> Mysterious clouds and purple canopies
> Come to illuminate my form.
> Jade lads and attendant maidens
> Provide me with extensive numinosity.
>
> The nine emperors, all purified,
> Lighten the space.
> The three luminants, all together,
> Arrange themselves above.
> I get to ride on a flying canopy
> And ascend to the Purple Court.

Now pull in the *qi* thirty-nine times and swallow it.

---

[1] *Tuisong Huangting neijing jing fa* 推誦黃庭內景經法 at the end of YQ 12 (Zhou and Sheng 2015, 20-21).

Once this is complete, you may enter the door. Face north and perform four bows. Kneel upright and click your teeth twenty-four times. Offer the following petition:

> To the all-highest heavenly perfected, Jade Star, Highest Lord of the Dao:
> I, so-and-so, today am entering the chamber to recite and chant the *Jade Scripture*, refine my spirit and treasure my organs. I beg you, as you reside in my stomach palace, to brightly illuminate my entire body and let me ride on emptiness, so I can rise up and pay homage to the imperial court.

Once this is complete, turn to face east and pay your respects to the Great Emperor. Click your teeth once more, twelve times, and offer this petition:

> Great Emperor of Fusang, Divine King of the Valley of the Rising Sun:
> I, so-and-so, today endeavor to chant the *Jade Scripture*. I beg you to order the divine mushrooms of this oratory to grow naturally, the jade florescence to glitter like gems, the three luminants to shine widely, and the ten thousand forms of good fortune to bless my womb immortal, so that I can attain the same numinosity as the emperor.

After concluding this, continue to face east and recite the *Scripture* ten times, that is, for one round. At the end, face north and bow four times, then again pay your respects to the east. This time there is no need to repeat the petition, just bow as prescribed and recite the *Scripture* more or less often, but in rounds of ten times.

If you receive the *Scripture* without following this method, thus failing to perform the proper sequence of bending down and looking up, you will labor your spirit in vain and make no progress whatsoever in your quest for immortality.

If you breach the instructions five times, all your effort will be wasted and your life will be cut short. If you breach them ten times, your body will die violently by wind or sword. After death you will become a lowly ghost, forced to shoulder heavy rocks. Beyond that, you will suffer rebirth for ten thousand kalpas, yet never in the human realm.

Also, on the festival days of the eight seasonal markers [equinoxes, solstices, and seasons' beginnings], send gold bracelets and nine feet of undyed silk as an offering to the master who has the scripture. When the master receives these tokens, he immediately will record your data as a disciple of high learning—the county, district, village, and hamlet or your residence, your last and first names, the year, month, day, and hour of your birth—onto those nine feet of undyed silk. Then, on top of a local mountain or hill, ideally on the side of a sheer cliff, he will face north and send a memorial with your name to the Palace of the Green Emperor. Clicking his teeth twenty-four times, he softly intones the following incantation:

> As heaven circulates along its path of *qi*,
> The eight pathways revolve their essence.
> As the three and five accord with proper timing,
> Ninefold blessings extend in turn.
>
> I command the perfected, in mystery and serenity,
> To support this quest for imperial numinosity.
>
> My jade sword well raised,
> I today submit a memorial with a clear name
> To be diligently recorded in the five sacred peaks
> By the numinous directors of the nine administrations.
>
> May they record what I am presenting,
> So it will be heard in Jade Clarity above.
> After three years, may they come
> And receive so-and-so in his physical form,
> Letting him ride on the eight lights
> And ascend to the Purple Court.

When done with this, bury the undyed silk below the steep cliff. Do this for three years in a row and the perfected will descend.

If you miss one festival day, your effort will be wasted, your life will be cut short, and you cannot attain immortality. If you fail to honor the covenant for three festival days, you will be reported to the three lower offices and receive judgments without end.[2]

The Perfected of Clarity and Emptiness says: "Anyone cultivating the *Huangting neijing jing* must follow the way of chaos transformation as outlined by the imperial lords and powerful spirits."

After completing the reading, again pay your respects with an incantation. When all this is done, kneel upright facing east. Close your eyes and

---

[2] From here to the end, the text matches *Dengzhen yinjue* 3.2b-5a.

internally imagine your body spirits in form and complexion, long and short, big and small. Call out their names and appellations and have each return to their original palace.

If you do not practice according to this method, even if you chant the text many tens of thousands of times, the perfected spirits will not stay. To the end, your toils will without response; on the contrary you will diminish *qi* and tire the spirits, having no effect on extending your destiny.

From here, I will list the central protagonists of the *Scripture* in clear presentation:

The spirit of the hair is Verdant Florescence (Canghua), also known as Great Prime (Taiyuan). His form is 2.1 inches tall.

The spirit of the brain is Root of Essence (Jinggen), also known as Niwan. His form is 1.1 inches tall.

The spirit of the eyes is Brightness Above (Mingshang), also known as Glowing and Mysterious (Yingxuan). His form is 3 inches tall.

The spirit of the nose is Jade Mound (Yulong), also known as Numinous Firmness (Lingjian). His form is 2.5 inches tall.

The spirit of the ears is Open Leisure (Kongxian), also known as Dark Field (Youtian). His form is 3.1 inches tall.

The spirit of the tongue is Connecting Destiny (Tongming), also known as Proper Cord (Zhenglun). His form is 7 inches tall.

The spirit of the teeth is Edge Point (Efeng), also known as Network Thousand (Luoqian). His form is 1.5 inches tall.

The seven deities of the face listed above all wear purple robes and skirts of flying brocade. They also all have the form of infants. Think of them as sitting upright, aligned straight across the face, each in his own palace. Once done with this, again click your teeth twenty-four times, swallow the *qi* twelve times, and intone the following incantation:

> The numinous source scatters its *qi*,
> It coagulates and forms you, my spirits.
> Spread out and line up front and back,
> All controlled and governed by Niwan.
>
> Above and below supporting each other,
> All seven arrange yourselves in order.
> As your flowing form continues to change,
> Love and nourish my flowery prime.

Pulling in the eight numinous forces,
Help me to penetrate the grotto gates above.
Guarding and harnessing the inner lights,
Let me ascend to the imperial stars.

After finishing this, think of the following deities.

The spirit of the heart is Cinnabar Prime (Danyuan), also known as Maintaining Numen (Shouling). His form is 9 inches tall and he wears a flying skirt of cinnabar brocade.

The spirit of the lungs is Dazzling Florescence (Haohua), also known as Emptiness Complete (Xucheng). His form is 8 inches tall and he wears a robe of undyed brocade and a yellow sash.

The spirit of the liver is Dragon Smoke (Longyan), also known as Containing Brightness (Hanming). His form is 6 inches tall and he wears a cape of green brocade.

The spirit of the kidneys is Mysterious Gloom (Xuanming), also known as Raising Offspring (Yuying). His form is 3.6 inches tall and he wears a robe of verdant brocade.

The spirit of the spleen is Always Present (Changzai), also known as Cloud Spirit Pavilion (Hunting). His form is 7.3 inches tall and he wears a robe of yellow brocade.

The spirit of the gall bladder is Dragon Brilliance (Longyao), also known as Majestic Brightness (Weiming). His form is 3.6 inches tall and he wears a robe of nine-colored brocade and a green, florescent skirt.

The six perfected listed here reside within the five organs and have palaces in the six viscera. Their form is that of small infants, their complexion that of glowing lads. Think of them as sitting upright, aligned straight across the body. Click your teeth twenty-four times, swallow the *qi* twelve times, and intone the following incantation:

Five organs and six viscera:
May your perfect spirits all stay in place.
Summarily controlled by the Scarlet Palace,
Succeed each other in good order above and below!

As the Infant in the golden chamber
Resides in the place with the four half doors [heart],
Your various dark chambers, mysterious towers,
And divine homes connect in one mechanism.

> Now merge and transform to bring forth pure spirit,
> To let my *qi* be perfect and my essence subtle.
> Guard and integrate it in my Elixir Field,
> So I can shine equally with the sun
> And attain the company of the eight lights,
> Harmonize my physical form, and fly off in ascension.

The Perfected of Purple Tenuity says: "In the old days, Master Meng recited the *Huangting* [*jing*]. He cultivated it according to this way for eight years, and the Perfected of the Yellow Court descended to receive him. How amazing it that?"

The secret formulas of the *Huangting* [*jing*] are all covered here. Activate the spirits in the physical form from morning to night: remember them constantly without ever forgetting, and you won't even have to recite the *Huangting* [*jing*].

Appendix

Texts Cited in *Neijing* Commentaries[1]

Loc	Title	Edition	Citation
33.18	*Baopuzi*	DZ 1185	4.1a
25.3	*Basu benchen yinshu*	DZ 426	5b
7.16	*Basu jing*	DZ 426	unclear
4.9	*Benjing*	generic	unclear
6.9		generic	unclear
1.2	*Benxing jing*	DZ 345	unclear
1.3	*Biyao jing*	DZ 1363	unclear
2.9	*Dadong jing*	DZ 6	*Jiugong zifang tu*, DZ 156
3.1		DZ 6	unclear
6.2		DZ 6	YQ 51
7.11		DZ 6	*Taidan yinshu*, DZ 1330
1.7		DZ 6	similar statement in ch. 9
9.7		DZ 6	*Dongfang neijing zhu*, DZ 133
15.11*		DZ 6	*Taidan yinshu*, DZ 1330
15.17		DZ 6	Unclear, same as 3.1
17.4		DZ 6	*Jiugong zifang tu*, DZ 156
17.6		DZ 6	*Jiugong zifang tu*, DZ 156
18.2		DZ 6	*Taidan yinshu*, DZ 1330
19.12		DZ 6	Unclear
21.14		DZ 6	*Taidan yinshu*, DZ 1330
5.1	*Danbu zhang*	not found	Unclear
1.13*	*Daode jing*	DZ 664	ch. 50
4.5		DZ 664	ch. 27
10.3		DZ 664	ch. 45
19.10		DZ 664	ch. 42
19.15		DZ 664	ch. 59
21.13		DZ 664	ch. 27
23.14		DZ 664	ch. 34

---

[1] Another list, compiled by Mehdi Arronis, appears in Lai 2021, 485. Items marked with an asterisk are cited in the Wuchengzi commentary.

25.1		DZ 664	ch. 42
25.7		DZ 664	ch. 28
27.7		DZ 663	ch. 27
32.5		DZ 664	ch. 28
35.11		DZ 664	ch. 28
36.6		DZ 664	ch. 58
4.7	*Daoji jing*	not found	*Sanyuan zhenyi jing*, DZ 253
23.10	*Dongfang jing*	not found	Unclear
19.15	*Dongfang jue*	DZ 405	*Dongfang shangjing*
20.2		DZ 405	*Dongfang neijing zhu*, DZ 133
33.19		DZ 405	*Huoluo qiyuan fu*, DZ 392
19.2	*Dongshen jing*	generic	*Laozi zhongjing* 1.14
19.9		generic	unclear
22.11		generic	unclear
22.13		generic	*Lingbao wufuxu*, DZ 388, 1.20ab
15.18	*Dongshen jue*	generic	*Baosheng jing*, DZ 871
3.5*	*Dongzhen jing*	generic	*Sandao shunxing jing*, DZ 33
24.7*	*Feixing yujing*	DZ 428	unclear
32.2	*Heshang gong*	DZ 682	ch. 6
33.18	*Jiuding shendan jing*	DZ 885	*Shenxian zhuan*
1.7*	*Jiutian shengshen jing*	DZ 318	*Shangqing jing bijue*, DZ 1291
5.2	*Jiuzhen jing*	DZ 908	*Zhen'gao* 9, *Wushang biyao* 17
10.5		DZ 908	*Zhen'gao* 9, *Wushang biyao* 17
12.5		DZ 908	*Zhen'gao* 9, *Wushang biyao* 17
26.6		DZ 908	*Zhen'gao* 9, *Wushang biyao* 17
28.5		DZ 908	*Zhen'gao* 9, *Wushang biyao* 17
2.4*	*Jiuzhen zhongjing*	DZ 908	*Yunji qiqian* 1, DZ 1032
22.4	*Laojun liujia futu*	not found	various related documents
28.6	*Laojun liujia sanbu fu*	not found	various related documents
19.15	*Lingbao jing*	generic	unclear
22.3		DZ 388	*Lingbao wufuxu* 3.21a
26.1	*Lingshu ziwen*	DZ 639	4b
25.2	*Miaozhen jing*	not found	unclear
16.6	*Nanhua zhenjing*	DZ 670	*Zhuangzi* 12
5.4	*Neiwai shenzhi jijue*	not found	unclear
26.1	*Shangqing lingshu*	DZ 1404	13ab
11.4	*Shengxuan jing*	DZ 1122	unclear
4.2	*Shifang jing*		*Wushang biyao* 17

APPENDIX / 225

	= Qishisi fang jing	in DZ 446	Taiping yulan 675
11.4	Suling jing	DZ 1314	unclear
35.2		DZ 1314	unclear
14.1	Taiping jing	DZ 1101	Wang 1979, 190
35.24			Wang 1979, 190
6.3	Taisu danjing jing	DZ 1245	Shixing biyao jing, DZ 1363
25.3	Taiwei balu shu	DZ 257	1a
11.10	Taiwei lingshu	DZ 639	9b-12a
19.13		DZ 639	9b-12a
28.7	Weiling shenzhou	YQ 47	3a
6.5	Wuchen xingshi jue	YQ 52	15b
16.11		YQ 52	15b
17.12		YQ 52	15b-16a
2.6	Xianjing	generic	unclear
8.10		generic	unclear
15.10*		generic	unclear
21.12		generic	unclear
34.3		generic	unclear
35.30		generic	unclear
36.4		generic	unclear
6.1	Xiaomo jing	DZ 1344	Zhen'gao 9
15.15	Xuanmiao neipian	fragments	Xuanmiao yunü zichuan xiandao, DZ 868
11.8	Yijing		Hexagram 24
16.10			Xici 1.5
25.1			Xici 1.11
32.3			Hexagram 1
22.3	Yuanjing jing	not found	Chishu yuejue, DZ 352
24.9	Yuanlu jing	not found	unclear
35.32		not found	unclear
36.11	Yujing zhenjue	DZ 1327	unclear
6.5	Yuli jing = Laozi zhongjing	DZ 1168 YQ 18-19	1.5
15.9		DZ 1168	1.17
22.4		DZ 1168	1.5
23.3		DZ 1168	1.14, 1.17
23.13		DZ 1168	1.6
13.11	Yuqing jinshu	DZ 1355	in parts
1.1	Yutai jing	not found	Miaomen youqi 2, DZ 1123

4.8	Zhen'gao	DZ 1016	Shangqing wozhong jue, DZ 140
20.5		DZ 1016	unclear
35.3		DZ 1016	10.10b
8.8	Zhonghuang jing	YQ 13	33a
15.1		YQ 13	unclear
25.4		YQ 13	unclear
34.1		YQ 13	p. 33a
34.9		YQ 13	p. 33a
35.4		YQ 13	unclear
25.9	Zhuangzi	DZ 670	ch. 12
31.5		DZ 670	ch. 2
33.21		DZ 670	ch. 3
21.13	Ziwen lingshu	DZ 639	4b

Bibliography

Andersen, Poul. 1994. "Talking to the Gods: Visionary Divination in Early Taoism." *Taoist Resources* 5.1:1-24.

Archangelis, Imios, and Miaoyu Lanying. 2010. *Jade Writings—Yellow Court Classic: Individual Phase Space User Manual*. Lake Mary, Fla.: Avatar Solutions.

Arthur, Shawn. 2013. *Early Daoist Dietary Practices: Examining Ways to Health and Longevity*. New York: Lexington Books.

Baldrian-Hussein, Farzeen. 2004. "The *Book of the Yellow Court*: A Lost Song Commentary of the 12th Century." *Cahiers d'Extrême-Asie* 14:187-226.

Bokenkamp, Stephen R. 1993. "Traces of Early Celestial Master Physiological Practice in the *Xiang'er* Commentary." *Taoist Resources* 4.2:37-52.

_____. 1997. *Early Daoist Scriptures*. With a contribution by Peter Nickerson. Berkeley: University of California Press.

_____. 2020. *A Fourth-Century Daoist Family: A New Translation and Study of the Zhen'gao or Declarations of the Perfected, Volume 1*. Berkeley: University of California Press.

Boltz, Judith M. 1987. *A Survey of Taoist Literature: Tenth to Seventeenth Centuries*. Berkeley: University of California, China Research Monograph 32.

Boltz, William G. 1982. "The Religious and Philosophical Significance of the 'Hsiang-erh Lao-tzu' in the Light of the Ma-wang-tui Silk Manuscripts." *Bulletin of the School for Oriental and African Studies* 45:95-117.

Bumbacher, Stephan Peter. 2001. "Zu den Körpergottheiten im chinesischen Taoismus." In *Noch eine Chance für die Religionsphäno-menologie?*, edited by D. Peoli-Olgiati, A. Michaels, and F. Stolz, 151-72. Frankfurt: Peter Lang.

_____. 2102. *Empowered Writing: Exorcistic and Apotropaic Rituals in Medieval China*. St. Petersburg, Fla.: Three Pines Press.

Cai Biming 蔡璧名. 2006. "Shen wai zhi shen: *Huangting neijing jing zhu* zhongde liangzhong zhenshen tuxiang" 身外之身: 黃庭內景經註中的兩種真身圖像. *Si yu yan* 思與言 44:131-96.

Campany, Robert Ford. 2002. *To Live as Long as Heaven and Earth: A Translation and Study of Ge Hong's Traditions of Divine Transcendents*. Berkeley: University of California Press.

_____. *Dreaming and Self-Cultivation in China, 300 BCE – 800 CE*. Cambridge, Mass.: Harvard University Asia Center.

Cao Jingnian 曹景年. 2009. "*Huangting jing* shenzhong you shen sixiang tanyuan" 黃庭經身中有神思想探源. *Zongjiao xue yanjiu* 宗教學研究 2009.3:184-86.

Carré, Patrik. 1999. *Le livre de la Cour Jaune: Classique taoïste des IV-V siècles*. Paris: Éditions du Seuil.

Chen Guofu 陳國符. 1975. *Daozang yuanliu kao* 道藏源流考. Taipei: Guting.

Chen Yingning 陳攖寧. 1980 [1933]. "*Huangting jing* jiangyi" 黃庭經講義, edited by Wang Weiye 王偉業. http://www.ifuun.com/a20181106169 37803/, pp. 24-38.

Despeux, Catherine. 2005. "Visual Representations of the Body in Chinese Medical and Daoist Texts from the Song to the Qing." *Asian Medicine: Tradition and Modernity* 1:10-52.

_____. 2006. "The Six Healing Breaths." In *Daoist Body Cultivation*, edited by Livia Kohn, 37-67. Magdalena, NM: Three Pines Press.

_____. 2019. *Taoism and Self-Knowledge: The Chart for the Cultivation of Perfection* (*Xiuzhen tu*), Translated by J. E. E. Pettit. Leiden: Brill.

Engelhardt, Ute. 1987. *Die klassische Tradition der Qi-Übungen. Eine Darstellung anhand des Tang-zeitlichen Textes Fuqi jingyi lun von Sima Chengzhen*. Wiesbaden: Franz Steiner.

Esposito, Monica. 2004. "Sun-Worship in China: The Roots of Shangqing Taoist Practices of Light. Part One—Yuyi and Jielin: The Taoist God of the Sun and the Goddess of the Moon." *Cahiers d'Extrême-Asie* 14:345-402.

Gai Jianmin 概健民. 1999. *Daojiao yixue daolun* 道教醫學導論. Taipei: Zhonghua daotong chubanshe.

Gao Zhenhong 高振宏. 2020. "Daocheng shenhua, mojie jiudu: Dunhuang ben *Laozi bianhua jing* yanjiu" 道成身化, 末劫救度: 敦煌本老子變化經研究. *Chutu wenxian yanjiu shiye yu fangfa* 出土文獻研究視野與方法 7:93-191.

Gong Pengcheng 龔鵬程. 1997. "*Huangting jing* lunyao" 黃庭經論要. *Shumu jikan* 書目季刊 31.1:66-81; 31.2:14-28; 31.3:54-66.

_____. 1998. *Daojiao xinlun erji* 道教新論二集. *Jiayi dalin: Nanhua guanli xueyuan*.

Graham, A. C. 1960. *The Book of Lieh-tzu*. London: A. Murray.

Harper, Donald. 1978. "The Han Cosmic Board." *Early China* 4:1-10.

_____. 1998. *Early Chinese Medical Manuscripts: The Mawangdui Medical Manuscripts*. London: Wellcome Asian Medical Monographs.

Hendrischke, Barbara. 2000. "Early Daoist Movements." In *Daoism Handbook*, edited by Livia Kohn, 134-64. Leiden: Brill.

_____. 2006. *The Scripture on Great Peace: The Taiping jing and the Beginnings of Daoism*. Berkeley: University of California Press.

Homann, Rolf. 1971. *Die wichtigsten Körpergottheiten im Huang-t'ing-ching*. Göppingen: Alfred Kümmerle.

Hwang, Shifu. 2015. *Hwang Tin Nei Jen Jing—The Interior Yellow Court Scriptures: The Internal Scenes of the Spirits of the Organs*. Bastrop, Texas: Shifu Hwang.

Jackowicz, Stephen. 2006. "Ingestion, Digestion, and Regestation: The Complexities of the Absorption of *Qi*." In *Daoist Body Cultivation*, edited by Livia Kohn, 68-90. Magdalena, NM: Three Pines Press.

Jia, Jinhua. 2018. *Gender, Power and Talent: The Journey of Daoist Priestesses in Tang China*. New York: Columbia University Press.

Kalinowski, Marc. 1983. "Les instruments astro-calendriques des Han et la méthode liu-jen." *Bulletin de l'École Française d'Extrême-Orient* 72:309-420.

_____. 1985. "La transmission du dispositif des Neuf Palais sous les Six-dynasties." In *Tantric and Taoist Studies*, edited by Michel Strickmann, 3:773-811. Brussels: Institut Belge des Hautes tudes Chinoises.

Kaltenmark, Max. 1967. "Au sujet du *Houang-t'ing king*." *Annuaire de l'École Pratique des Hautes Études* 75:117-18.

_____. 1974. "Miroirs magiques." In *Mélanges de Sinologie offerts à M. P. Demiéville*, 2:91-98. Brussels: Institut Belge des Hautes Études Chinoises.

_____. 1979. "The Ideology of the *T'ai-p'ing-ching*." In *Facets of Taoism*, edited by Holmes Welch and Anna Seidel, 19-52. New Haven: Yale University Press.

_____. 1988 [1953]. *Le Lie-sien tchouan*. Peking: Université de Paris Publications.

Kamitsuka Yoshiko 神塚淑子. 1990. "Hōsho seidōkun o megutte: Rikuchō jōseiha dōkyō no ichi kōsatsu" 放諸青童君めぐって：六朝上清道教の一考察. *Tōhō shūkyō* 東方宗教 76: 1-23.

Kim Sung-Hae 金勝惠. 1999. "*Huangting neijing jing* de shenzhi xiang yu qi: Shangqing pai chuantong zhong neizai chaoyue de tinei shen" 黃庭內景經的神之像與氣：上清派傳統中內在超越的體內神. *Daojia wenhua yanjiu* 道家文化研究 16:249-60.

Kleeman, Terry F. 1998. *Great Perfection: Religion and Ethnicity in a Chinese Millenarian Kingdom*. Honolulu: University of Hawaii Press.

_____. 2016. *Celestial Masters: History and Ritual in Early Daoist Communities*. Cambridge, Mass.: Harvard Yenching Institute.

Knoblock, John. 1988. *Xunzi: A Translation and Study of the Complete Works*. Vol. 1, Bks. 1-6. Stanford: Stanford University Press.

Kohn, Livia. 1991. "Taoist Visions of the Body." *Journal of Chinese Philosophy* 18:227-52.

_____. 1995. "Kōshin: A Taoist Cult in Japan. Part III: The Scripture." *Japanese Religions* 20.2:123-42.

_____. 1998a. *God of the Dao: Lord Lao in History and Myth*. University of Michigan, Center for Chinese Studies.

_____. 1998b. "The *Tao-te-ching* in Ritual." In *Lao-tzu and the Tao-te-ching*, edited by Livia Kohn and Michael LaFargue, 143-61. Albany: State University of New York Press.

_____. 2004. *The Daoist Monastic Manual: A Translation of the Fengdao kejie*. New York: Oxford University Press.

_____. 2008 [1995]. *Laughing at the Tao: Debates among Buddhists and Taoists in Medieval China*. Magdalena, NM: Three Pines Press.

_____. 2012. *A Source Book in Chinese Longevity*. St. Petersburg, Fla.: Three Pines Press.

_____. 2013. "The Daoist Body of *Qi*." In *Religion and the Subtle Body in Asia and the West: Between Mind and Body*, edited by Geoffrey Samuels and Jay Johnston, 16-32. London: Routledge.

_____. 2023. "The *Daodejing* in Daoist Practice." In *Dao Companion to the Philosophy of the Daodejing*, edited by Liu Xiaogan and Yuan Ai. New York: Springer.

Komjathy, Louis. 2002. *Title Index to Daoist Collections*. Cambridge, Mass.: Three Pines Press.

Kroll, Paul W. 1996. "Body Gods and Inner Vision: *The Scripture of the Yellow Court*." In *Religions of China in Practice*, edited by Donald S. Lopez Jr., 149-55. Princeton: Princeton University Press.

Kusuyama Haruki 楠山春樹. 1979. *Rōshi densetsu no kenkyū* 老子傳說の研究. Tokyo: Sōbunsha.

Lagerwey, John. 1981. *Wu-shang pi-yao: Somme taoïste du VIe siècle*. Paris: Publications de l'École Française d'Extrême-Orient.

_____. 2004. "Deux écrits taoïstes anciens." *Cahiers d'Extrême-Asie* 14:131-72.

Lai, Chi-tim. 2002. "The *Demon Statutes of Nüqing* and the Problem of the Bureaucratization of the Netherworld in Early Heavenly Master Daoism." *T'oung Pao* 88:251-81.

Ledderose, Lothar. 1984. "Some Taoist Elements in the Calligraphy of the Six Dynasties Period." *T'oung Pao* 70:246-66.

Levy, Howard S. 1956. "Yellow Turban Rebellion at the End of the Han." *Journal of the American Oriental Society* 76:214-27.

Li Gang 李剛. 2017. "Wei-Jin Nanchao Zhengyi dao shenxue sixiang poxi" 魏晉南朝正一道神學思想剖析. *Daojiao xue yanjiu* 道教學研究 2017/4:13-21.

Li Ping 李平. 2010a. "*Huangting jing* yu Tangdai daojiao xiudao zhuanxing" 黃庭經與唐代道教修道轉型. *Si yu yan* 思與言 48.4:109-55.

_____. 2010b. "*Huangting jing* yanjiu shi yu Tangdao xiudao zhuanxing" 黃庭經研究史與唐代修道轉型. In *Shehui, jingji, guannian shi shiye zhong de gudai Zhongguo* 社會經濟觀念史視野中的古代中國, 814-37.

Li Yangzheng 李養正. 1988. "Wei Huacun yu *Huangting jing*" 魏華存與黃庭經. *Zhongguo daojiao* 中國道教 1988/01:38-41.

_____. 1989. *Daojiao gaishuo* 道教概說. Beijing: Zhonghua shuju.

_____. 1995. *Daojiao jingshi lun'gao* 道教經史論稿. Bejing: Huaxia chubanshe.

Littlejohn, Ronnie. 2020. "The Walking Dead: Morality, Health, and Longevity in the *Xuanxue* Method of the *Xiang'er Commentary* on the *Laozi*." In *The Dao Companion to Xuanxue (Neo-Daoism)*, edited by David Chai, 129-48. New York: Springer.

Liu Yongxian 劉勇先. 2022. "Daojiao yishu wenji Shangqing *Huangting neijing jing*" 道教醫術文集上清黃庭內景經. *Dongfang shouzang* 東方收贜 2022/12:120-22.

Lu Di 芦笛. 2015. "Daojiao wenxian zhong zhi zhi hanyi kaolun" 道教文献中芝之涵義考論. *Shijie zongjiao yanjiu* 世界宗教研究 2015/3.

Ma Chengyu 馬承玉. 2005. "*Zhengyi fawen tianshi jiao jieke jing* de shidai ji Laozi Xiang'er zhu de guanxi" 正一法文天師教戒科經的时代及與老子想爾注的關係. *Zhongguo daojiao* 中國道教 2005/02:12-16.

Machle, E. J. 1992. "The Mind and the *Shen-ming* in the *Xunzi*." *Journal of Chinese Philosophy* 19:361-86.

Maeda Shigeki 前田繁樹. 1987. "*Rōshi myōshinkyō* shōkō" 老子妙真經小考. *Waseda daigaku daigakuin bungaku kenkyūka kiyō* 早稻田大學大學院文學研究科記要 14: 21-32.

Major, John S. 1986. "New Light on the Dark Warrior." *Journal of Chinese Religions* 13/14: 65-87.

Maspero, Henri. 1971. *Le taoïsme et les religions chinoises*. Paris: Gallimard.

_____. 1981. *Taoism and Chinese Religion*. Translated by Frank Kierman. Amherst: University of Massachusetts Press.

Mugitani Kunio 麥谷國雄. 1982. "*Kōtei naikeikyō* shiron" 黃庭內景經試論樣洋. *Tōyō bunka* 東洋文化 62:29-59.

Nakata Yūjirō 中田勇次郎. 1970. *Chūgoku shoron shū* 中國書論集. Tokyo: Nigensha.

Needham, Joseph, et al. 1983. *Science and Civilisation in China*, vol. V.5: *Spagyrical Discovery and Invention—Physiological Alchemy*. Cambridge: Cambridge University Press.

Neswald, Sara Elaine. 2009. "Internal Landscapes." In *Internal Alchemy: Self, Society, and the Quest for Immortality*, edited by Livia Kohn and Robin R. Wang, 27-53. Magdalena, NM: Three Pines Press.

Nickerson, Peter. 1994. "Shamans, Demons, Diviners, and Taoists: Conflict and Assimilation in Medieval Chinese Ritual Practice." *Taoist Resources* 5.1:41-66.

Noguchi Tetsurō 野口鐵朗, Sakade Yoshinobu 坂出祥伸, Fukui Fumimasa 福井文雅, and Yamada Toshiaki 山田利明, eds. 1994. *Dōkyō jiten* 道教事典. Tokyo: Hirakawa.

Olson, Stuart Alve. 2017. *Yellow Court: The Exalted One's Yellow Court External Scripture. Commentary by Wu Zhengzi*. Vol. 1. Phoenix: Valley Spirit Arts.

Pankenier, David W. 2013. *Astrology and Cosmology in Early China: Conforming Earth to Heaven*. Cambridge: Cambridge University Press.

Petersen, Jens O. 1989-90. "The Early Traditions Relating to the Han-dynasty Transmission of the *Taiping jing*." *Acta Orientalia* 50:133-71 and 51:165-216.

_____. 1990. "The Anti-Messianism of the *Taiping jing*." *Journal of the Seminar for Buddhist Studies* 3:1-36.

Pfister, Rudolf. 2006. "The Production of Special Mental States within the Framework of Sexual Body Techniques: As Seen in the Mawangdui Medical Corpus." In *Love, Hatred, and Other Passions: Questions and Themes on Emotions in Chinese Civilization*, edited by Paolo Santangelo with Donatella Guida, 180-94. Leiden: Brill.

Pregadio, Fabrizio. 2004. "The Notion of 'Form' and the Ways of Liberation in Daoism." *Cahiers d'Extrême-Asie* 14:95-130.

_____. 2006a. *Great Clarity: Daoism and Alchemy in Early Medieval China*. Stanford: Stanford University Press.

_____. 2006b. "Early Daoist Meditation and the Origins of Inner Alchemy." In *Daoism in History: Essays in Honour of Liu Ts'un-yan*, edited by Benjamin Penny, 121-58. London: Routledge.

_____, ed. 2008. *The Encyclopedia of Taoism*. 2 vols. London: Routledge.

_____. 2020. "Seeking Immortality in Ge Hong's *Baopuzi Neipian*." In *The Dao Companion to Xuanxue (Neo-Daoism)*, edited by David Chai, 427-56. New York: Springer.

_____. 2021. "The Alchemical Body in Daoism." *Journal of Daoist Studies* 14:99-127.

Puett, Michael. 2002. *To Become a God: Cosmology, Sacrifice, and Self-Divinization in Early China*. Cambridge, Mass.: Harvard University Press.

_____. 2005. "The Offering of Food and the Creation of Order: The Practice of Sacrifice in Early China." In *Of Tripod and Palate: Food, Politics and Religion in Traditional China*, edited by Roel Sterckx, 75-95. New York: Palgrave MacMillan.

_____. 2007. "Humans, Spirits, and Sages in Chinese Late Antiquity: Ge Hong's Master Who Embraces Simplicity." *Extrême-Orient, Extrême-Occident* 29:95-119.

_____. 2010a. "Becoming Laozi: Cultivating and Visualizing Spirits in Early-Medieval China." *Asia Major* (3rd s.) 23:223-52.

_____. 2010b. "Forming Spirits for the Way: The Cosmology of the *Xiang'er* Commentary to the *Laozi*." *Journal of Chinese Religions* 32:1-27.

Qing Xitai 卿希泰. 1988. *Zhongguo daojiao* 中國道教, vol. 1. Shanghai: Tongfang chuban chongxin.

_____. 1994. *Zhongguo daojiao* 中國道教, vol. 2. Shanghai: Tongfang chuban chongxin.

Rao Zongyi 饒宗頤. 1992 [1956]. *Laozi Xiang'er zhu jiaojian* 老子想爾注校箋. Shanghai: Wenyi.

Raz, Gil. 2007. "Imperial Efficacy: Debates on Imperial Ritual in Early Medieval China and the Emergence of Daoist Ritual Schemata." In *Purposes, Means and Convictions in Daoism: A Berlin Symposium*, edited by Florian C. Reiter, 83-109. Wiesbaden: Harrassowitz.

_____. 2008. "The Way of the Yellow and the Red: Re-examining the Sexual Initiation Rite of Celestial Master Daoism." *Nannü: Men, Women and Gender in China* 10:86-120.

Reiter, Florian C. 1990. *Der Perlenbeutel aus den drei Höhlen: Arbeitsmaterialien zum Taoismus der frühen T'ang-Zeit*. Asiatische Forschungen, vol. 12. Wiesbaden: Otto Harrassowitz.

Robinet, Isabelle. 1983. "Le *Ta-tung chen-ching*: Son authenticité et sa place dans les textes du Shang-ch'ing." In *Tantric and Taoist Studies*, edited by Michel Strickmann, 2:394-433. Brussels: Institut Belge des Hautes Etudes Chinoises.

_____. 1984. *La révélation du Shangqing dans l'histoire du taoïsme*. 2 vols. Paris: Publications de l'École Française d'Extrême-Orient.

_____. 1989. "Visualization and Ecstatic Flight in Shangqing Taoism." In *Taoist Meditation and Longevity Techniques*, edited by Livia Kohn, 159-91. Ann Arbor: University of Michigan, Center for Chinese Studies.

_____. 1993. *Taoist Meditation: The Mao-shan Tradition of Great Purity*. Translated by Norman Girardot and Julian Pas. Albany: State University of New York Press.

_____. 1997. *Taoism: Growth of a Religion*. Translated by Phyllis Brooks. Stanford: Stanford University Press.

Robson, James. 2009. *Power of Place: The Religious Landscape of the Southern Sacred Peak (Nanyue) in Medieval China*. Cambridge, Mass.: Harvard University Asia Center.

Saso, Michael. 1995. *The Gold Pavilion: Taoist Ways to Peace, Healing, and Long Life*. Boston: Charles E. Tuttle.

Schafer, Edward H. 1977. "The Restoration of the Shrine of Wei Hua-ts'un at Lin-ch'uan in the Eighth Century." *Journal of Oriental Studies* 15:124-38.

_____. 1980. *Mao-shan in T'ang Times*. Boulder, Col: Society for the Study of Chinese Religions Monograph 1.

_____. 1985. "The Eight Daunters." *Schafer Sinological Papers* 21.

Schipper, Kristofer M. 1975. *Concordance du Houang-t'ing king*. Paris: Publications de l'École Française d'Extrême-Orient.

_____. 1979. "Le Calendrier de Jade: Note sur le *Laozi zhongjing*." *Nachrichten der deutschen Gesellschaft für Natur- und Völkerkunde Ostasiens* 125:75-80.

_____. 1985. "Taoist Ritual and Local Cults of the T'ang Dynasty." In *Tantric and Taoist Studies*, edited by Michel Strickmann, 3:812-34. Brussels: Institut Belge des Hautes Etudes Chinoises.

_____. 1994. *The Taoist Body*. Translated by Karen C. Duval. Berkeley: University of California Press.

_____. 1995. "The Inner World of the *Lao-tzu chung-ching*." In *Time and Space in Chinese Culture*, editied by Chun-chieh Huang and Erik Zürcher, 114-31. Leiden: Brill.

_____, and Franciscus Verellen, eds. 2004. *The Taoist Canon: A Historical Companion to the Daozang*. 3 vols. Chicago: University of Chicago Press.

Seidel, Anna. 1969a. *La divinisation de Lao-tseu dans le taoïsme des Han*. Paris: École Française d'Extrême-Orient.

_____. "The Image of the Perfect Ruler in Early Taoist Messianism." *History of Religions* 9:216-47.

Small, Sharon. 2018. "A Daoist Exploration of *Shenming*." *Journal of Daoist Studies* 11:1-20.

Smith, Thomas E. 2013. *Declarations of the Perfected: Part One: Setting Scripts and Images into Motion*. St. Petersburg, Fla: Three Pines Press.

_____. 2017. "Xu Mi's Network: A Different Perspective on Higher Clarity Daoism." *Journal of Daoist Studies* 10:15-48.

_____. 2020. *Declarations of the Perfected, Part Two: Instructions on Shaping Destiny*. St. Petersburg, Fla.: Three Pines Press.

Staal, Julius. 1984. *Stars of Jade: Calendar Lore, Mythology, Legends and Star Stories of Ancient China.* Decatur: Writ Press.

Steavu, Dominic. 2019. *The Writ of the Three Sovereigns: From Local Lore to Institutional Daoism.* Hong Kong: Chinese University Press.

Strickmann, Michel. 1978. "The Mao-shan Revelations: Taoism and the Aristocracy." *T'oung Pao* 63:1-63.

_____. 1979. "On the Alchemy of T'ao Hung-ching." In *Facets of Taoism*, edited by Holmes Welch and Anna Seidel, 123-92. New Haven, Conn.: Yale University Press.

_____. 1981. *Le taoïsme du Mao chan: chronique d'une révélation.* Paris: Collège du France, Institut des Hautes Etudes Chinoises.

_____. 1996. *Mantras et mandarins: Le bouddhisme tantrique en Chine.* Paris: Gallimard.

Stuart, G. A. 1976. *Chinese Materia Medica: Vegetable Kingdom.* Taipei: Southern Materials Center.

Sung, Z. D. 1971. *The Text of Yi King.* Taipei: Chengwen.

Wachtel-Galor, S., John Yuen, John A. Buswell, and Iris F. F. Benzie. 2011. "Ganoderma Lucidum (Lingzhi or Reishi): A Medicinal Mushroom." In *Herbal Medicine: Biomolecular and Clinical Aspects*, edited by Iris F. F. Benzie and Sissi Wachtel-Galor, ch. 9. London: Taylor & Francis.

Wang Jian 汪剑 and He Zhongjun 和中浚. 2012. "Daojiao shangqing pai lianyang shu yu Zhongyi mingmen xueshuo liubian de guanxi" 道教上清派炼养术与中医命门学说流变的关系. *Nanjing zhongyi yao daxue xuebao* 南京中醫藥大學學報 13.4:201-04.

Wang Jiaxin 王家歆. 2010. "Jielin benyue yanjiu 結璘奔月研究". *Guoli Taizhong jishu xueyuan bao* 國立臺中技術學院報 14:163-84.

Wang Jing. 王璟. 2014. "*Zhengyi fawen tianshi jiaoke jing* chengshu niandai kaobian" 正一法文天師教戒科經成書年代考辨. *Chengda zhongwen xuebao* 成大中文學報 46:69-98.

Wang Ming 王明. 1979. *Taiping jing hejiao* 太平經合校. Beijing: Zhonghua.

_____. 1984 [1948]. "*Huangting jing* kao" 黃庭經考. In *Daojia he daojiao sixiang yanjiu* 道家和道教思想研究, by Wang Ming. Beijing: Zhongguo shehui kexue chubanshe.

Ware, James R. 1966. *Alchemy, Medicine and Religion in the China of AD 320.* Cambridge, Mass.: MIT Press.

Watson, Burton. 1968. *The Complete Works of Chuang-tzu.* New York: Columbia University Press.

Wilhelm, Richard. 1950. *The I Ching or Book of Changes*. Translated by Cary F. Baynes. Princeton: Princeton University Press, Bollingen Series XIX.

Xiao Dengfu 蕭登福. 2015. "Daojiao neidan zhuoyuan ji xiulian famen zhong de huangting shuo yu qihai shen'gui shuo" 道教內丹溯源及修煉法門中的黃庭說與氣海神龜說. *Hunan daxue xuebao—Shehui kexue ban* 湖南大學學報—社會科學版 2015.1:30-42.

Xu Kangsheng 許抗生. 1990. "*Huangting jing* qianxi" 黃庭經淺析. *Zhongguo daojiao* 中國道教 1990/03:21-26.

Xu Zhaoren 徐兆仁. 1998. "Daojiao de zhongyao jingdian: *Huangting jing*" 道教的重要經典: 黃庭經. *Wenshi zhishi* 文史知識 1998/12:98-102.

Yamada Takashi 山田俊. 1992. *Kohon Shōgenkyō* 古本昇玄經. Sendai: Tōhōku daigaku.

Yamada, Toshiaki. 1989. "Longevity Techniques and the Compilation of the *Lingbao wufuxu*." In *Taoist Meditation and Longevity Techniques*, edited by L. Kohn, 97-122. Ann Arbor: University of Michigan, Center for Chinese Studies.

_____. 2000. "The Lingbao School." In *Daoism Handbook*, edited by Livia Kohn, 225-55. Leiden: Brill.

Yang Fucheng 楊福程. 1995. "*Huangting neiwai erjing* kao" 黃庭內外二經考. *Shijie zongjiao yanjiu* 世界宗教研究 1995/3:68-76.

Yang Lihua 楊立華. 1999. "Huangting jing chongkao" 黃庭經重考. In *Daojia wenhua yanjiu* 道家文化研究, edited by Chen Guying 陳鼓應, 261-93. Beijing: Sanlian shudian.

Yoshioka Yoshitoyo 吉岡義豐. 1955. *Dōkyō kyōten shiron* 道教經典史論. Tokyo: Dōkyō kankōkai.

_____. 1959. *Dōkyō to bukkyō* 道教と佛教, vol. 1. Tokyo: Kokusho kankōkai.

Yu Wanli 虞萬里. 1991. "Wang Xizhi yu *Huanging jing* tie" 王羲之與黃庭經帖. *Shihui kexue zhanxian* 世界科學战线 1191/3:331-38.

_____. 1998. "*Huangting jing* xinzheng" 黃庭經新證. *Wenshi* 文史 29:385-408.

_____. 2001. "*Huangting jing* yongyun shidai xinkao" 黃庭經用韻時代新考. *Sheng-yun luncong* 聲韻論叢 10:209-41.

Yūsa Noboru 遊左昇. 1983. "Dōkyō to Chūgoku bungaku" 道教と中國文化. In *Dōkyō* 道教, edited by Fukui Kōjun 福井康順 et al., 2: 311-69. Tokyo: Hirakawa.

Zhan Shichuang 詹石窗. 2000. "*Huangting jing* de youlai ji qi yu Yixue de guanxi" 黃庭經的由來及其與易學的關係. *Guji zhengli yanjiu xuekan* 古籍整理研究學刊 2000.4:1-5.

Zhang Songhui. 張松輝. 1994. "*Zhengyi fawen tianshi jiao jieke jing* chengshu niandai kao" 正一法文天师教戒科经成書年代考. *Shijie zongjiao yanjiu* 世界宗教研究 1994/1:20-26.

Zheng Zhao 鄭昭. 2010. "Guanyu Huangting jingtu de niandai yu zuozhe" 關於黃庭經圖的年代與作者. *Yishu shi yanjiu* 藝術史研究 2010/01:81-84.

Zheng Zhiming 鄭志明. 2016. "*Huangting jing* yu caoqi Quanzhen dao de neidan sixiang" 黃庭經與草期全真道的內丹思想. *Quanzhen daoxue shu yanjiu baogao* 全真道學術研究報告 10.

_____. 2018. "*Huangting jing* de tianren ganying zhi dao" 黃庭經的天人感應之道. *Zongjiao zhexue* 宗教哲學 85:25-72.

Zhou Quanbin 周全彬 and Sheng Keqi 盛克琦, eds. 2015. *Huangting jing jizhu* 黃庭經集注. Beijing: Zongjiao wenhua chubanshe.

Zhu Yueli 朱越利. 1996. *Daozang fenlei tijie* 道藏分類題解. Beijing: Huaxia chubanshe.

Index

abyss, 67-68
aging, *see* youthfulness
alchemy, 175, 201
Always Present, 119, 221, 205
Armillary Sphere, 39, 43
armor, *see* weapons
ascension, 24, 177, 180, 189
Bai Lüzhong, 17
Baiyuan, 37
banners, 111, 134
Baopuzi neipian, 9-10, 19, 109, 153, 201
Basu benchen yinshu, 173
Basu jing, 117
bedchamber, 39-40, 157-59
Beidi shagui zhou, 205
bell: fire, 111, 134, 186; 186; golden, 124, 177; jade, 125
belly, 58, 71, 143, 178, 206
Benjing, 110, 114
Benxing jing, 95
Bian Shao, 2
Bianhua qishisi fangjing, 108
Biyao jing, 96
blood: in body 057, 76, 79, 88, 124, 176; at transmission, 89, 215
Blossoming Brightness, 27
Blossomless, 37, 126, 138, 146, 153-54, 201
body: as blessed, 34; explanation of, 26; halls and spirits in, 88; hiding of, 47; like ice, 106; as jade tree, 36, 144; lightness of, 48; at peace, 44-45
bones, 47, 76, 79, 94, 153, 157, 207
Boyang, 12
Bozhou, 2
brain: and blood, 176; and essence, 33, 35-36, 40, 52, 82, 98, 103, 155; gate, 36, 68, 70, 79; and hair, 134;

spirit of, 24, 115-16, 220; *see also* Nine Palaces; Niwan
breath pipe, 32, 166
breath, holding of, 33, 128
breathing, 11, 28, 34-35, 55, 58, 69, 72-73, 79-80, 83, 85, 100, 103, 112, 124, 127, 145, 154-55, 158-59, 214
Brightness Above, 115, 220
broken weave, 185
Cai Dan, 9-10
calligraphy, 12-13, 25
Canghua, 115, 220
Cao Cao, 7
Celestial Masters, 4, 6-9
Central Florescence, 88
Central Harmony, 31, 56
Central Palace, 75, 206
Central Peak, 121-22
Central Pond, 22, 31, 39, 111
central prime, 35, 146
Central Yellow, 165, 208
Changzai, 119, 221
chanting: of *Huangting jing*, 4, 6, 9-10, 015, 87-88, 91-92, 94, 217-22; from memory, 92; repetitions of, 212-14; ten thousand times, 40, 16, 87
chaos complete, 40, 48
Chaos Vigor, 131, 135-36, 194
charts, of gods, 183
Chen Baoguang, 20
Cheng Xuanying, 185
chicken egg, 37, 40, 65
Child Cinnabar, 22, 27, 38, 57, 73, 113, 146, 151, 208
Chishu yuwen, 162
Choufei, 128
Chuhui, 128
Chuxue ji, 19

Cinnabar Prime, 118, 221, 123, 124, 136, 150, 196
cinnabar, as water, 181
Clarity: and Emptiness, 219; and purity, 46, 66, 196; and stillness, 43, 167
cleansing, 35, 43-44, 82-83, 89-92, 94, 211
cloud and white spirit agents, 26, 40, 44, 54-55, 64, 93, 100, 126-27, 143-44, 148, 166, 176-77, 193, 204
cloud court, 167
Cloud Court, 167
Cloud Presence, 152
cloud residence, 112
cloud spirit agents: balancing of, 87; names of, 88, 127, 152, 158; nine, 117; visualization of, 154
Cloud Spirit Pavilion, 119, 221, 131, 136, 205
colors: 067, 80, 102; of spirits, 115; of worms, 139; *see also* five colors
commentators, 17-21
complexion, 52, 71, 87, 132, 169, 176, 203
Conception Vessel, 21-22
conduits, 76, 79, 129, 207, 210-11
Confucius, 99
Connecting Destiny, 116, 220
Containing Brightness, 118, 221
cornelian: glow, 210; salve, 208
Corpse Dog, 128
country: of misfortune, 158; ruling of, 22, 61, 73, 179, 184
covenant, 89-90, 215; *see also* transmission
crow, in sun, 55
Da daojia lingjie, 8-9
Dadi jinshu, 87
Dadong jing, 15, 19, 49, 97, 102-05, 112, 116-17, 122, 138-39, 145-46, 149, 152, 160, 213
Danbu zhang, 111
Danyuan, 118, 221

Dao: and creation, 151; and divinity, 59; and Laozi, 3; of perfection, 144; peace of, 35
Daode jing: 003-4, 7, 19, 99, 108, 123, 152, 154, 160, 168, 172, 174, 179, 198, 207; commentaries to, 18; primordial, 45; beyond purity, 178; recitation of, 16; like river, 83; ubiquitous, 187; of world, 85; values of, 23-24
Daoji jing, 109
Dark Essence, 127, 152, 158
Dark Field, 116, 220
Dark Parlor, 104-05
Dark Towers, 5, 22, 27-28, 30, 35, 50, 108-09, 174
Dark Warrior, 78, 121
day and night, 29, 32, 59, 64, 69, 87, 107, 121-22, 189
Dazzling Florescence, 118, 121, 221
Dazzling Simplicity, Lord of, 205
death, 89, 126-27, 133, 158-59, 178
deathbringers: 029, 34, 87; names of, 140
demons: control of, 29, 91-91; dispelling, 11; flavors as, 192; troopers, 6
Dengzhen yinjue, 15-16, 93
Dense Regalia, 176
desires, freedom from, 23, 40-41, 46, 66, 80, 212
destiny: attending to, 169; and body, 199; increase, 136; and inner nature, 206; long, 77; nourishing, 75; *see also* longevity
Devouring Robber, 128
dharmas, 85
Dipper, 16, 49, 56, 59, 75, 102, 151, 174, 197, 201
directions: and organs, 60, 64, 118-20, 161-62, 197, 202; in practice, 16, 91-94, 117-18, 159-61, 175, 212, 214, 218-19; spirits facing, 117-18
Director of Destiny, 47, 54, 138

disease, freedom from, 23, 29, 33-34, 87, 92, 99, 113, 126, 132, 141, 156
Dongfang jing, 167
Dongfang jue, 153, 154, 201-02
Dongfang neijing zhu, 122
Dongfang shangjing, 153
Donghua yupian, 87
Dongshen jing, 19, 112, 151, 164, 165
Dongshen jue, 139
Dongxuan jing, 166
Dongzhen jing, 106
Dragon Brilliance, 119, 221, 133
Dragon Smoke, 118, 221
dragon: and ascension, 177; design, 129; herding of, 10; seal, 136; secluded, 210; shape of, 49, stride on, 205; in *Yijing*, 197
Duren jing jizhu, 185
Duren jing, 185
ears: 030, 35, 67, 70-71, 77, 83, 109, 113, 152; hands on, 128; keen, 208; and kidneys, 129; spirit of, 116, 220
earth bureau, 30
earth door, 154
earth immortal, 77
Eastern Florescence, 85, 87, 91
eating: and drinking, 28, 64, 42, 60, 67, 92; of immortals, 82; of *qi*, 83
eaves, scarlet, 150
ecstatic excursions, 24, 25, 175-76
Edge Point, 116, 220
Efeng, 116, 220
eight arts, 173
Eight Daunters, 24, 110, 205
eight directions, 110, 134, 170
eight extraordinary vessels, 211
eight extremes, 72
eight kinds of jasper, 201, 208-09
eight lights, 166, 167, 219, 221
eight liquids, 209
eight numinous forces, 221
eight regions, 141
eight sages, 170
eight seasonal markers, 218

eight simplicities, 157
eight spirits, 205
eight trigrams, 166
eight winds, 169-70
Elixir Field: father and mother in, 174; and Hall of Light, 68, 148, 161; husband and wife in, 27; inch-size, 40; and Laozi, 3; lower, 22, 30-31, 36, 111, 137-38, 199, 203, 206; middle, 31, 163; One in, 31; perfected in, 43, 50, 136-38; and Purple Palace, 53; *qi* in, 28, 35, 52, 103, 208, 222; refining in, 82; stepping on, 82; upper, 26-27, 35, 68, 104, 109, 116-17, 145, 150, 160; and Yellow Court, 2-3, 115, 131
elixir: 079; flying, 178; ninefold, 201; reversion of, 57, 68, 75; transmission of, 215
embryo respiration, 154
emotions, 40-41, 47, 134, 149, 171, 212
Emptiness Complete, 118, 221
emptiness: 041, 82, 90, 94, 113, 191, 196; and nonbeing, 18, 23, 44-45, 47, 74, 78-79, 86, 120, 142, 164, 169, 176
esophagus, 31, 36, 38-39, 48, 67, 72, 81, 110, 151, 199, 209
essence: accumulation of, 59, 179-80; and blood, 79; chamber of, 41, 163; and clarity, 133; closing in, 36, 50-52; like clouds, 35; combination of, 155; of earth, 192; in Elixir Field, 30-31; firm, 36; flow of, 64; flowery, 65, 71, 196-97; gate of, 40; ingesting of, 84; kidney, 68; jade, 209; leaking of, 59, 64, 79, 100, 105, 108, 142, 155, 157-59; loss of, 175; lunar, 175; maintaining, 66; in men, 37; movements of, 66; nourishing of, 40, 47, 76, 169, 194; palace, 100; preservation of, 34; refinement of, 128; reversion of, 33-36, 47, 82; steadying of, 33,

139, 178; three forms of, 54; in viscera, 37; white, 57; withering of, 155; and womb, 137
eyebrows, 32, 37-38, 67, 68, 72, 103, 112-13, 135, 143, 145, 147, 167, 187
eyes: area between, 32, 37, 134, 147; close, 16, 27, 30, 43, 59, 68, 79, 108, 127, 159, 175-76. 200, 212, 217, 219-20; control of, 44; dragons in, 128; essence of, 196; and gall bladder, 134; as gates, 183; glossy, 52, 71, 79, 98; and heart, 197; inch-size, 40; and kidneys, 28; and liver, 119, 125-26, 200, 202; as pearls, 113; perceptive, 58, 77, 88, 121, 130, 208; pupils of, 29, 134, 150, 203; purple haze in, 102-03; seeing, 62, 67, 88; spirits of, 24, 62, 98, 112-13, 115, 120; as sun and moon, 50, 54, 77, 100, 102, 104, 113, 115;Yellow Court as, 27; as yin and yang, 24, 82;
face, 40, 52, 112, 132, 167; *see also* complexion
fasting, 29, 46, 87, 89, 91, 94
father and mother, 27, 37, 138, 153, 174
feet, 38, 52, 139
Feidu, 128
Feigui shou, 153
Feixing yujing, 170
Filth Expeller, 128
fire, 51, 62, 119, 123
fish trap, 89
five colors: blurred, 54; in body, 83, 159; in celestial building, 39; clear, 67; clouds of, 113, 121, 200; dynamics of, 185; in eyebrows, 32; list of, 76; mingling, 43, 45, 48; in moon, 176; in mouth, 175-77; and organs, 165; pearls of, 162; robes of, 107-08, 170;
five Dippers, 152-53

five directions, 103-49, 95, 4125, 153, 161, 179
five emperors, 125, 159, 161
five flavors, 37, 60, 67, 83, 116, 124, 132, 192, 195, 212
five florescences, 103-04, 124, 203
five grains, 42, 82, 106
five limbs, 141
five numinous forces, 141
five organs, *passim*
five palaces, 63
five peaks, 140, 219
five phases, 5, 8, 48, 57, 61, 76, 118-19,124-25, 131-35, 173-74, 185
five planets, 2, 76, 93, 141, 147, 153-53
five powers, 63
five pungent vegetables, 92, 211
five *qi*, 71, 103, 140
five sovereigns, 177
five spirits, 121
five sprouts, 154, 161-62
Flowery Canopy, 22, 32, 45-46, 65-68, 70, 72, 80, 83, 98, 113, 118, 121, 125, 148, 163, 167, 199
Flowery Pond, 29, 62, 63, 68, 70-71, 82-83, 111, 203
Flowery Root, 80
Flowing Pearls, 104, 145, 150, 161
fluids, 70, 76, 105, 126, 129, 139, 159
Flying Root (elixir), 154, 159, 163
Flying Yellow, 176
food: avoidance of, 211; and stomach, 119, 131, 135, 206, 208; yellow *qi* as, 208; *see also* grain
foot square residence, 40, 158
four directions, 11-12, 25, 29, 37-38, 46, 52, 57, 61, 73, 76, 81, 93, 103, 120, 174, 177, 197,
four limbs, 61, 64, 77
four patriarchs, 85
four *qi*, 103
four seas, 81, 173
four seasons, 57, 61, 78, 102, 125, 173, 189

Fusang, Emperor of, 14, 16, 86-87, 91, 94, 146, 218
Fuya, 128
gall bladder: 088, 111, 133-34, 165, 185-86; and dragon, 210; spirit of, 119, 221
Gan Ji, 5
Gate of Destiny, 22, 27-28, 46, 69, 74, 83, 86, 100, 105, 131, 206
Gate of Life, 23, 100, 130, 148, 206
Gate of Origin, 21
gates and doors, 37, 40-42, 57, 66, 71, 74, 80, 85, 145, 184
Ge Hong, 9, 11
geese, 13, 25
Glowing and Mysterious, 115, 220
goddess, female, 105, 139
golden: *Book*, 87, 91, 215; casket, 37, 72, 79, 80, 146; chamber, 221; flower, 170; lock, 56; golden parlor, 58; pass, 108; pledges, 90; pendants, 134; spring, 139; terrace, 131; towers, 53
Governing Vessel, 21
Graceful Woman, 24, 30, 109, 128
grain, 60, 62, 82, 92, 131-32, 194
Great Abyss, 81
Great Antecedence, 74
Great Chamber, 167
Great Clarity, 48, 81, 113, 149, 160
Great Emperor, 212, 214
Great Emptiness, 173, 205
Great Harmony, 28, 42-43, 46, 58, 60, 83, 105, 149, 165, 188, 193-94
Great Mystery, 80-81, 188
Great One: in center, 65, 166; Chart of, 183; emissaries of, 166; Emperor of, 188-89; and eyes, 145; and gods, 4, 104; as Infant, 53; in Kunlun, 145; names, 137; in Niwan, 52, 145; Palace of, 73, 75, 104, 138; robes of, 170; in Yellow Court, 5, 138
great peace, 41, 61
Great Prime, 115, 220

Great Simplicity, 72, 78, 96, 113, 149, 165
Great Storehouse, 22, 27, 33-34, 39, 42, 73-75, 81, 131, 135, 194-95, 204
Great Tenuity, 46, 86, 127, 173
Great Ultimate, 86, 172
Great Wall, 22, 39
Great Yin, 27, 163
Greater Yang, Lord of, 205
green dragon, 63, 70, 78, 119, 119, 121, 128, 134
Green Emperor, 219
green heaven, 162
Green Lad, 125
Grotto Chamber, 26-27, 37, 43, 45, 50, 83, 86, 97, 103-04, 115, 122, 145, 147, 148, 154-55, 157, 161, 174
Gujin tushu jicheng, 163
hair: black, 35, 66, 88, 203; cutting of, 215; regulate, 40, 57, 64, 71, 203; spirit of, 115, 152, 220; spread, 212; unbind, 63, 84; white, 71, 156, 193
Hall of Light: in abdomen, 34, 64, 199; extension of, 37, 46, 57; in head, 32, 37, 103-04, 145-47, 154, 174, 207; and heaven's gate, 75, 207; Lord Lao in, 88, 92, 135; as lungs, 65; names of, 37; perfected in, 27, 35, 36, 38, 43, 72-74, 76, 97, 136, 174; and Scarlet Palace, 151; in three chambers, 161, 167; in three offices, 86; in three passes, 148; and Yellow Court, 22, 26-27, 86, 167-68
Han dynasty, 2-4, 22
hands, 38, 78-79, 139
Hanging Sphincter, 64-65, 81
Hanming, 118, 221
Hanshu, 19
Hanzhong, 7
Haohua, 118, 221
Haosu jun, 205
harm, freedom from, 33, 99, 122, 132

head: and ears, 30; and feet, 57; and Hall of Light, 37; as heaven, 52, 69, 71; as Kunlun, 38, 53, 150; as lofty terrace, 36; and nine, 62, 184; orifices in, 66; palaces in, 21, 104, 113, 163; *qi* in, 34, 63, 71, 121; spirits of, 34, 103-04, 115-16, 145; and Yellow Court, 26; *see also* Hall of Light, Nine Palaces, Niwan
headdress, 54, 78, 82, 137, 147, 161, 181
healing exercises, 27
health, 1, 23, 29, 35; *see also* diseases, freedom from; youthfulness
heart: chanting in, 175; color of, 5, 33, 57, 72, 111, 113-14, 123; concentrated, 40, 46, 63, 72, 98. 160, 198; and Dao, 102, 146; and emotions, 134, 197; and eyes, 197; Infant in, 31, 33, 61, 72, 113; and kidneys, 5, 58, 129; like lotus, 123; as middle elixir field, 163-64; and mouth, 123; names of, 22; and Nine Springs, 52; as Numinous Terrace, 36, 110, 144; among organs, 120, 123, 156, 181, 202; at peace, 11, 38, 40-41, 63, 66, 71, 83, 87, 91, 93, 97, 123, 136, 140, 163, 178, 190, 207, 213; and red bird, 128; as ruler, 37, 39, 61, 72, 85, 109, 118, 120, 196; as square inch, 144; as Scarlet Palace, 5, 39, 110, 150, 165; spirits in, 73, 118, 120, 123, 150, 154, 167, 200, 203, 221; strumming of, 20, 86, 97; and trigram Li, 123; visualization of, 103, 109, 127, 147, 150; *see also* Cinnabar Prime; desires, freedom from; Red City
heaven and earth, 26, 38, 43-44, 50-52, 56, 71, 88, 101, 141, 154, 172-73, 181 187, 201
heaven's gate, 70, 75, 80, 207
Heavenly Court, 104, 110, 136, 145-46, 154, 167, 187, 207
heavenly halls, 50
Heavenly Hound, 128
Heavenly Sovereign, 101
Heming shan, 6
Hengshan, 14
Heshang gong, 16, 197
Highest Clarity: banquets in, 89; corpus, 13, 15, 17, 170; entering, 24, 160, 169; gods of, 103-04, 145-46; heavens of, 170; Lady of, 104, 145; methods of, 23-24, 154; palace in, 173; Perfected of, 146, 155; *qi* of, 77, 181; school, 1, 19-20; stars in, 153
Highest One, 177
Huainan, Princie of, 20
Huangchangzi, 42
Huangdi jiuding shendan jing, 201
Huangdi Taiyi bamen rushi jue, 163
Huashan, 14
hundred bones, 207
hundred conduits, 69, 129, 203
hundred diseases, 87, 92, 99, 126 130, 136, 194
hundred forms of wayward *qi*, 29, 91, 100
hundred grains, 60, 132, 192, 195
hundred joints, 105, 115
hundred limbs, 198-99
hundred passes, 88
hundred rivers, 158
hundred spirits, 101, 116, 137, 165, 168
hunger and thirst, 34, 42, 62, 63, 127-28, 132, 139, 211
Hunkang, 131
Hunting, 119, 221
Huoluo qiyuan fu, 202
Huoshan, 19
husband and wife, 27, 174
immortal embryo, 5, 88, 94, 97, 179
Immortal Master, 154
immortality, 1, 24, 26, 37, 114, 124, 138, 180
Imperial Lord, 101, 104, 145

incantations, 94, 101, 105-06, 127-28, 147-48, 153, 162, 176, 202, 205, 217, 220, 221-22
incense, 16, 46, 91, 93
inch residence, 33, 132
inch-size field, 40, 144, 158
Infant, 22, 27, 31, 33, 35, 39, 40, 43, 50, 53, 55, 62, 73, 78-80, 111, 113, 130, 210, 221
inherent divinity, 179-80
inner nature, 116
intercourse, dangers of, 138, 155, 157-59
intestines, 39, 79, 91, 101, 111, 135
jade: bolt, 179; chariots, 170; embrace, 49; embryo, 176; halls, 74; maidens, 42-43, 46, 48, 82, 88, 128, 163, 217; nectar, 63, 81, 105, 108, 198, 208; pendants, 125; and rocks, 51; seals, 211; jade spring, 57, 108; stalk, 36; stalk, 42, 80; tower, 121; tree, 35, 144; walls, 53; writing, 87
Jade Balancer, 39, 43
Jade Book, 98, 160, 180, 214
Jade Capital, 206
Jade Chamber, 37, 40-41, 146, 167
Jade Chapters, 87, 92, 166, 212, 214
Jade Clarity, 104-05, 145, 219
Jade Emperor, 104, 112, 145
Jade Florescence, 37, 152, 167
Jade Hut, 140
Jade Morning Light, 1, 95-96, 188
Jade Mound, 115, 220
Jade Pond, 22, 28, 31, 83, 105, 111, 203
Jade Scale, 151
Jade Scripture, 94, 218
jasper chamber, 39, 157
Jasper Sphere, 56, 151, 167
Jiang Shengxiu, 21, 179-95
Jiang, Lady, 15
Jin dynasty, 9
Jinggen, 115, 220
Jinling zhenren, 14
Jinque dijun sanyuan zhenyi jing, 109

Jinque dijun, 20
Jiudan lun, 201
Jiutian shengshen jing, 98
Jiuzhen jing, 111, 124, 130, 177, 181
Jiuzhen zhongjing, 101
Juanzi, 20, 86
kerchief: 181; golden/metal, 58; white, 82
kidneys: color of, 39, 129, 209; and ears, 129; and essence, 22, 62, 209; and Great Harmony, 165; as mysterious homestead, 157; among organs, 5, 57, 77-78, 120; role of, 37; as root, 62; spirit of, 119, 197, 221; stars within, 63; two, 22, 35, 62, 63, 80, 108, 129-30; and water, 143; *see also* Dark Parlor; Dark Towers; Reclining Ox; Secret Doors
King Father, 30, 49, 62, 77-78, 107
Knotted Spangles, 176
Kongxian, 116, 220
Kunlun, 10, 38, 53, 150
Laojun liujia futu, 163
Laojun liujia sanbu fu, 182
Laozi bianhua jing, 3
Laozi ming, 2-3
Laozi zhongjing, 4-5, 23, 95, 113, 137, 150, 163, 166, 168
Laozi: hagiography of, 3-4; and Great Harmony, 58, 83; in heaven, 10; as revealer, 11, 18; as cloud spirit agent of heaven, 168; transformations of, 3, 12, 26
Lesser Lord, 93
Lesser Yang, Lord of, 205
Li Bai, 13
Li Yuan, 12
Li, trigram, 123
Liangqiuzi, 17-18, 85
libationers, 6
Liexian zhuan, 3, 20, 86
Liezi, 191
lights: in body, 21; control of, 89, 221; definition, 86, 93; invocation of,

159; jade, 215; three, 102;; *see also* eight lights
Liji, 99
Lingbao jing, 19, 153, 161
Lingbao wufuxu, 5, 14, 161, 165
Lingfei liujia shangfu, 163
Lingjian, 115, 220
Lingshu ziwen, 175-76
Lingyuan, 135
lingzhi, 82
Liu An, 201
Liu Pu, 14
Liu Xia, 14
Liu Xiang, 3
Liu Yan, 14
liver: cultivation of, 63; and dragon, 210; correspondences, 125-27, 198, 200, 202; like ring, 69; spirit of, 118, 221, and cloud spirit agents, 100; sprout of, 161-62; *see also* green dragon
lock, 30, 32, 56, 108, 125, 179
Longyan, 118, 221
Longyao, 119, 221
lord and minister, 27, 174
Lord Goldtower, 20
Lord Green Lad, 86-87
Lord King, 136
Lord Lao: in center, 10, 86, 92, 135; Central, 84; as Dao, 8; as revealer, 1-3, 6, 18, 25, 26; five, 101; in spleen, 34; triple, 88, 97, 136-37; vision of, 10-11; *see also* Yellow Lord Lao
Lord of the Dao, 16, 58, 83, 94-96, 132, 146, 175
Lü Dongbin, 21
lungs: color of, 111, 118, 122-23; as Hall of Light, 65; among organs, 120-21, 156, 165, 181, 199; spirit of, 118, 122, 182, 221; and Triple Heater, 70, 202-03; and white spirit agents, 100; *see also* Flowery Canopy; white tiger
Luoqian, 116, 220

Luyang, 27
Maintaining Numen, 118, 123, 221
Majestic Brightness, 119, 221, 133-35, 186
male and female: 67, 75-76, 130, 208; know, 44, 63, 174, 197-98, 207; One, 104
mao and *you*, 62, 100, 197
Maoshan zhi, 13
marrow, 79, 88
Mars, 147
Master Meng, 221
Master of Yellow Constancy, 42
men and women, 111, 138, 208
Meng, Master, 15, 93
Merge and Extend, 137
Miaomen youqi, 95
Miaozhen jing, 172
mind, *see* heart
Mingjian jing, 11-12
Mingshang, 115, 220
mirror: eyes like, 104; practice of, 10-12; reflection in, 68
Mistress Cloud Forest, 102
Mistress Jiang, 93
moon: absorption of, 106; cloud spirit agents of, 175-76; essence of, 23, 175-76; like pearl, 45; and yin, 50; *see also* sun and moon; Vast Coldness
Most High, 20, 25, 94-97, 101, 105-05, 132, 145-47, 205, 214
mother and child, 29
Mother of the Dao, 157, 162
mountains: entering in, 171; hiding in, 46; as image 152; and transmission, 215
mouth: as Central Pond, 39; close, 30, 56, 58, 179; among gates, 183; of goddess, 105, 149; and heart, 124; and liver, 162; , and lunar essence, 176-77; as mysterious spring, 108; and pearls, 143, 169; *qi* in, 34, 27, 57, 67, 73, 76, 78 102, 175-76, 199, 212; and speech, 44, 45; spirits in,

112-13, 194; and sun, 159, 177; see also five flavors; Flowery Pond; Jade Pond, saliva; sweet spring; teeth; three passes; tongue
Multi-storied Tower, 22, 38-39, 110, 150, 199, 209
multiplication, of self, 11-12
mushrooms, 82, 111-12, 210-13, 217-18
music, 30, 41
myriad affairs, 49-50, 175
myriad spirits, 206
Mysterious Gloom, 119, 221, 129, 197
mysterious homestead, 157
Mysterious Mother, 36, 56
Mysterious Radiance, 5
Mysterious Sphincter, 22, 32-33, 64-65, 114, 199
Mysterious Towers, Great Lord of, 86
Mystery Dragon Lord, 204
Mystery Gate, 65
Mystery Metropolis, 95
Mystery Prime, 174, 177
Mystery Radiance, 27
Mystery Wonder, 174
Nanhua zhenjing
Nanyue furen zhuan, 13
Nanyue, 14
naturalness, 26, 44-45, 47, 55, 82, 166, 168, 190, 212
navel, 27, 30, 35, 41, 86, 111, 137, 139
Negating Poison, 128
Neiguan jing, 150
Neijing: contents of, 22-24; history, 13-17; text, 1-2, 85; titles, 86-87, 97; transmission, 88-90
Neiwai shenzhi jijue, 111-12
Network of Thousands, 116, 131, 220
nine: storing at, 62-63, 198; yang number, 69, 197
nine administrations, 219
nine auroras, 212
nine bureaus, 97
nine calendar phases, 54
nine chambers, 164

nine chronograms, 148
nine directions, 141, 161
nine emperors, 217
nine fluids, 129
nine heavens, 89, 98, 105, 130, 164, 170, 189
nine mists, 154, 170
nine orifices, 69, 71, 129, 148, 156, 164, 199, 207, 211
Nine Palaces, 104, 117, 145, 149, 164, 166, 173
nine perfected, 117
nine primes, 148
nine *qi*, 97, 162
nine realms of darkness, 113
nine regions, 164
Nine Sovereigns, 101, 117
nine spirits, 138
Nine Springs, 52
nine squares, 184
Nine Tenuities, 148
nine, number, 69
Niwan, 16, 27, 38, 52, 57, 63, 67-68, 86, 101, 104, 115-16, 136, 145, 151, 157, 160, 174, 220
no-death, 8, 23, 33, 38, 50, 60, 63, 68, 88, 117, 143, 156, 194, 216
Noble Capital, 199
nonaction, 23, 44-45, 47, 66, 165, 166, 169, 188
nonbeing, 23, 44-45, 47, 74, 79-82
Nonbeing, Senriority, Mystery, 133
North Culmen, 49, 197
nose: as Central Peak, 121-22; circulation through, 74; as earth door, 154; and gall bladder, 134, 156; as Gate of Destiny, 84; as heavenly center, 114; as human center, 149; as long valley, 159; as Mystery Gate, 66; and nine heavens, 98; among organs, 23, 174, 176; and *qi*, 67, 78; as root of heaven, 69; and smell, 35, 66; ; spirit of, 115, 222; like turtle, 58; visualization of, 130; *see also* breathing, Spirit Hut

Numinous Firmness, 115, 220
numinous forces: attainment of, 103-04; blessings of, 208; clear, 69; and cloud spirit agents, 101-02; doors of, 147; eight, 223; emptiness and, 92; five, 143; green, 83, 163; in name, 120, 125; penetration of, 91; residence of, 113, 145; and spirits, 129, 212-13; summoning of, 93, 144; three, 41, 160 162; and Yellow Court, 27
Numinous Prime, 135
Numinous Root, 22, 28, 31-32, 41, 56, 58, 69, 74, 82, 103-04, 188, 203, 206
Numinous Terrace, 22, 36, 81, 110, 144
One: and creation, 151, 172; in Dao, 79; in Jade Chamber, 37, 41; in Elixir Field, 31, 53: gate of, 67; knowing, 27, 98; maintaining [guarding], 37, 49-53, 61, 83, 110, 142-44, 146, 156, 175, 190; as male, 174; merging with, 177-78; as primordial *qi*, 102; return to, 172, 178; and water, 172
Open Leisure, 116, 220
oratory, 16, 47, 91, 94, 212, 217-18
Orchid Terrace, 165
ordinary people, 60, 81, 85, 171, 187, 192-94
organs, spirits of, 118-19, 221
orifices: in face, 69; two, 78
Ouyang Xiu, 1
Palace of Emptiness and Nonbeing, 74
palaces, in body, 10
Pass Primordial, 21, 23, 26-27, 30, 99-100, 148
passes, closing of, 38
pavilions, twelve, 72
Peach Child, 137
Peach Vigor, 137-38
pearls: eyes as, 98, 113; numinous, 80; red, 111; strings of, 34, 51, 56, 54, 74, 178; studded with, 96

pendants, 143, 177
Penglai, 81
Perfect One, 207
perfected, ranks of, 117-18
petition, 218-19
physical form, five-part, 96, 141
Pingheng, 153
pledges, *see* transmission
potency, 45, 46, 52, 59, 64, 196, 205
power, of text, 91-92
powers, of immortals, 82, 87-88
Primordial Beginning, 95, 161-62
Prince, 37, 138, 146, 153-54
Proper Cord, 116, 220
purification, 16, 29, 46, 178, 211, 217; *see also* chanting, ritual
Purple Chamber, 5, 37, 50, 153, 167
Purple Clarity, 188
purple clouds, 217
Purple Court, 217, 219
purple haze, 98, 102
Purple Palace, 53, 68, 204
Purple Tenuity, 110, 165, 221
Purple Tower, 113, 143, 147
purple, in eyes, 103-04
qi: absorption of, 155, 211; circulation of, 1, 8, 24, 27, 32, 58, 35, 49, 51, 65, 101, 105, 120, 137-38, 155-57, 186, 197-99, 219; eating of, 62, 67; endowment, 81; flow, 45, 105, 61; movements of, 32, 51 052; mysterious. 81; nutritive, 123, 145; primordial, 36, 51, 53, 60, 69, 77-79, 102, 193; six, 88; swallowing of, 65; three, 69; wayward, 29, 46, 58, 73, 77, 87, 101, 106, 121, 128, 160, 185, 186, 205, 208; yellow, 4
Qian and Kun, 23, 56-57, 183, 197
Qingcheng shan, 6
Qingxu zhenren, 14
Qinxin, 20, 86
Queen Mother, 30, 49, 62, 77-78, 107
Queyin, 128
quiet and bland, 23, 40-41, 45-47, 80, 160, 169, 191, 213

Raised Yang, 27
Raising Offspring, 119, 129, 197, 221
Reclining Ox, 174
red bird, 121, 128, 155
Red Child, 27
Red City (Lad of), 22, 39, 113, 136, 146, 151, 156-57, 180, 200, 203
Red Emperor, 152
registers: 006; of the dead, 47; jade, 155; of life, 144, 169
ritual, for *Huangting jing*, 16, 61, 87, 204-06, 214, 217-22; *see also* chanting
River Chart, 184
robes: brocade, 86, 107, 111, 122, 134; cerulean, 108; cinnabar, 33, 108, 111, 113, 125; colored, 170; feathery, 169; flowery, 114; gauze, 107, 117, 123; green, 125, 130, 181; none, 105, 139; pearl-studded, 163; phoenix, 142; purple, 117; red, 31; scarlet, 33, 148; undyed, 122; verdant, 129; vermilion, 29, 31, 33, 46, 124, 137; yellow, 131-32, 136
root: of essence, 115, 220; mysterious, 200; return to, 187; of world, 85
sages: eating of, 60; envisioning, 210; glowing, 89; in heavens, 95; longevity of, 74
saliva, swallowing, 17, 28, 30-31, 34, 56, 63, 71, 74, 81, 83, 92, 94, 103, 106, 116, 147, 159, 194, 203, 217
Sancai tuhui, 163
Sandong qunxian lu, 20
Sanxuan jingbian lun, 18
Saturn, 147
Scarlet Chamber, 37
Scarlet Palace, 5, 22, 33, 35, 38-39, 43, 51, 53, 65, 72, 110, 150-51, 165, 167, 181, 209, 221
seclusion, 12, 96, 170
Secret Doors, 100
sense organs, 44, 174, 183
serenity, 41, 45, 47, 133, 164, 169, 178
seven brilliant ones, 148

seven fluids, 103
seven gates, 58, 183
seven generations, 215
seven leaves, 108
seven mysterious ones, 200
seven orifices, 58, 66, 77, 100, 103, 108, 121-22, 148, 182, 200, 210
seven primes, 121, 152-53, 201, 214
seven spirits, 220
seven stars, 49, 51, 148, 201, 205
seven: and eight, 54; and five, 53; number of return, 189
Shangqing huangqi yangjing sandao shunxing jing, 106-07
Shangqing jin bijue, 98
Shangqing lingshu, 175
Shangqing lliujia qidao bifa, 163
Shangqing wozhong jue, 109
Shangqing zhongjing zhu zhensheng bi, 108
Shangqiu Kai, 190-91
Shaoyang jun, 205
Shengxuan jing, 125
Shenxian shiqi jin'gui miaolu, 29
Shenxian zhuan, 201
Shifang jing, 107
Shigou, 128
Shiji, 18
Shiwen, 19
Shixing biyao jing, 96, 112
Shouling, 118, 221
Shuailing, 127
Siming, *see* Director of Destiny
Six Ding, 42, 46, 82, 137, 162, 178, 213
six domestic animals, 92
six dragons, 157
six harmonies, 40, 83, 101, 153-54, 177, 197
Six Jia, 58, 137, 178, 182
six offices, 63, 75
six perfected, 221
six pitchpipes, 61
six *qi*, 123
six spirits, 178

six virtues, 90
six viscera, 8, 22, 37, 43-44, 62, 76, 87, 120, 129, 133, 157, 178, 198, 206-07, 221
soldiers, 182-86
Song He binke gui Yue, 12
Southern Palace, 49
Southern Perfected, 91
Southern Ultimate, 147
Sovereign Emptiness, 95, 96
Sparrow Yin, 128
Spirit Court, 21
Spirit Florescence, 162
Spirit Hut, 22, 28, 32, 34, 79-80, 103
Spirit Tower, 22
spirits: assembling, 204; in body, 10-11; in their brightness, 21, 41, 56, 61, 67, 73, 77, 80, 193, 199, 205-07, 210; and heart, 39, 120; as infants, 220-21; list of, 220-21; movements of, 66; myriad, 135; nourishing of, 52; in oneness, 71; staying, 43; talking to, 45; wandering, 41; weeping, 158
spleen, 29, 33-34, 36, 73, 75, 78, 86, 92, 103, 119,131-32, 135, 194-95, 204-06, 208, 210, 221
Spring Beginning, 161
square and round, 35, 65, 117, 131, 35, 142, 207
square inch, 35-36, 142
stars, 17, 24, 62, 69, 78, 93, 147, 154, 156
stench, 192-93, 199, 211
stillness, 23, 61, 169, 196, 211, 213
Stinky Lungs, 128
stomach duct, 105, 139
stomach, 42, 74, 91, 94, 101, 131, 135, 194-95, 205, 208
Su Lin zhuan, 20
Subduing Arrow, 128
Suishu, 29
Suling dayou miaojing, 109
Suling jing, 109, 125, 205
Sun Simiao, 29

sun: absorption of, 105-06; incantation for, 159, 175; move with, 22-23; seven, 53; shining with, 221; cloud spirits of, 159, 175; *see also* timing
sun and moon: in abdomen, 28; carried, 78; in chest, 5; dressing in, 84; as eyes, 54, 77, 126, 208; as metaphors, 93; move with, 22-23; orbits of, 53, 153; shining, 38, 45, 75, 101, 130, 198; at sides, 17, 123
sweet spring, 56, 70, 74, 81, 83, 105
taboo, 155-56
Taidan yinshu, 117
Taiguan, 127
Tail Gate, 157
Taiping dao, 7
Taiping guangji, 13
Taiping jing, 5, 19, 23, 133, 209
Taiping yulan, 13, 108
Taiqing jing, 9
Taishang basu benchen yinshu, 173
Taishang jing, 19
Taisu danjing jing, 112
Taiwei balu shu, 173
Taiwei huangshu jiutian balu zhenwen, 173
Taiwei lingshu, 127, 152
Taixu jun, 205
Taiyang jun, 205
Taiyin, 27
Taiyuan, 115, 220
talismans, 58, 111, 121, 142, 153, 177, 182-83, 186
Tang dynasty, 19
Tangshan, 20
Tao Hongjing, 14-15
Taokang, 137-38
teacher, 89
teeth: clicking, 17, 28, 31, 63, 71, 94, 107, 127-28, 147, 159, 175, 203, 217-18, 219-21; firm, 35, 203; as lock, 56; regrowing, 88; rinsing of, 64l and stomach, 131; spirit of, 116, 220; as white stones, 155

ten colors, 185
ten directions, 16
ten heavens, 189
tendons, 76, 79
terrace pass, 103, 145
three bright ones, 174
three bureaus, 164, 215
three chambers, 161
Three Clarities, 95-96, 98, 135, 176
three elixir fields, 97, 102, 109, 138, 142, 144-45, 149-50, 156-58, 163-69, 200
three emperors, 200
three grottoes, 117
three heavens, 125
Three Kingdoms, 2
three leaves, 70
three life senses, 172
three lords, 173
three luminants, 34, 49, 59, 61-63, 71, 75, 109, 141, 172, 174, 198, 217, 218; *see also* sun and moon
three mysteries, 209
three numinous forces, 158, 160
three offices, 83
three officials, 116
Three Palaces, 149-50, 160, 191
three passes: 034, 38, 63, 142, 148, 156, 184; list of, 70, 139, 149
three perfected, 152,
three ponds, 111
three powers, 173, 184
Three Primes, 20, 97, 103, 116, 135-38, 141, 160, 173-74, 215
three *qi*, 51, 156, 210
three simplicities, 102, 170
Three Sovereigns, 3, 11
three spirits, 142, 169
Three Terraces, 3, 150
three treasures, 109, 172
three worms, 29, 139-40; *see also* deathbringers
three yang, 49, 54-55
three yin, 54-55

three: in creation, 209; and five, 45, 49, 167, 172-73, 183, 219
throat, 39, 67, 71; *see also* esophagus
thunder, 58, 65, 107, 119, 133, 186
Tiandiren jing, 20
tiger: register, 177; seal, 211; soldiers, 134; talisman, 211
timing, of practice, 63, 101, 196-97, 201, 219
Tongming, 116, 220
tongue: curling of, 30, 56, 179; above esophagus, 65, 114; and essence, 32; and fluid, 31, 69, 74; and heart, 39, 124; as lock, 56; names of, 111; as red bird, 156; spirit of, 24, 116, 220; *see also* Numinous Root
Tongzhi, 21
transmission: gaps in, 86; pledges in, 214; rules of, 84, 90, 218-19
trigram Li, 186
Triple Heater, 63-64, 70, 120, 133, 198, 202
Tunzei, 128
turtle: as image, 58; and snake, 128
Twelve-storied Tower, 53, 150, 166
twenty-four qi, 166-67
two primes, 117
Upper Mystery, 129
vague and obscure, 26, 44, 48, 66, 70, 79, 209-10
Valley of the Rising Sun, King of, 14, 16, 86, 88, 90, 94, 218
Vast Coldness, 106
Venus, 147
Verdant Florescence, 115, 130, 220, 152
Vibrant Numen, 127, 152, 158
virtues, 90, 119
vision: of Dao, 61; eternal, 23, 36, 48, 144, 153, 201; inner, 30, 43, 68, 80, 88, 168, 210; of self, 44
visualization, 1, 10-11, 17, 30-31, 41, 73, 107, 110, 115, 117-18, 126, 135-38, 142, 150, 157, 158, 161, 165, 168, 217

Waijing: history, 2-13; text, 1-2, 86
Wang Bao, 14
Wang Xizhi, 12-13, 19, 25
Wang Zhiyin, 17
warriors, in body, 11
water and fire, 57
weapons, 72, 134, 183, 184-85, 186, 219
weblines, 88
Wei Huacun, 13-14, 86
Wei Yangyuan, 13
Weiling shenzhou, 182
Weiming, 119, 221
Whirlwind Terrace, 210
White Florescence, 136
White Prime, 37, 104, 145, 122, 146, 153, 201
white spirit agents, 40, 44, 54-55, 64, 87, 100
white stones, 155
white tiger, 63, 78, 121, 128
Womb Radiance, 127, 152, 158
womb, 39, 47, 111, 137, 155
Wuchen xingshi jue, 113, 143, 147
Wuchengzi, 13, 19-20, 25, 86-94
wuji, 75, 204
Wushang biyao, 108, 111
wusi, 131
Wuying, 37, 126; see Blossomless
Xi Mi, 14-15
Xiang'er zhu, 7-8
Xianjing, 19, 102, 121, 137, 159, 203, 210, 212
Xiaojing, 99
Xiaomo jing, 112
Xiuzhen shishu, 25, 85
Xu Huangmin, 15
Xu Hui, 110
Xu Jian, 19
Xu Mai, 14
Xu Mi, 110
Xuanguang, 27
Xuanguang yunü, 5
Xuanmiao neipian, 139, 172
Xuanming, 119, 221

Xucheng, 118, 221
Xujue, 16
Xunzi, 19
Yang Changlu, 17
Yang Renfang, 1
Yang Xi, 14, 110
yang: brightness, 104; great, 51; primordial, 27, 55, 73; pure, 77, 180-81, 197
Yangluo shan, 14
Yangxing yanming lu, 29
Yao, 19
Year Star, 162
Yejun Mizhai, 1
Yellow Court: arts of, 25; in circulation, 35; and earth, 187; as Elixir Field, 115, 131, 204; as eyes, 27; in head, 21-22, 26-27; history of, 2-4; Infant in, 73; and Lord Lao, 97, 136, 168, 195; methods of, 154-55, 194, 201, 217-22; as spleen, 5, 27, 78, 86, 119, 135, 144, 204, 206; Perfected of, 5, 29, 42, 78, 86, 88, 107, 132-33, 167, 180, 213, 222; students of, 154-55; in three locations, 136
Yellow Florescence, Jade Maiden of, 213
Yellow Lad, 180
Yellow Lord Lao, 4-5, 18, 27, 95, 104, 111, 124, 135-36, 145, 152, 167, 173, 177
Yellow Springs, 55, 60
Yellow Tower, 187
Yellow Wilderness, 144
Yellow-Garbed Master, 146
yellow: as color, 25, 65, 93; in lungs, 122; nurturing of, 208; in spleen, 103-04
Yijing, 19, 126, 143, 172, 183, 197
yin and yang: alignment with, 8, 29, 51, 59-60, 65, 67, 69, 83, 114, 120, 154, 156, 173, 196-97; functions of, 12, 18, 24, 123, 130, 155, 209-10; as gates, 37, 137; intermingling of,

42, 52, 64, 129, 152, 181, 208; root of, 115; ruler of, 138; on sides, 208; and stars, 38, 77-78, 100, 208; in *Xiang'er*, 8; in *Yijing*, 172
Yin Xi, 16
yin, great, 78, 209
Yingming, 27
Yingxuan, 115, 220
you and *mao*, 36, 38, 58, 65; *see also* directions
Youjing, 127
youthfulness, 29, 35, 52, 68, 101, 156, 160, 169, 192-93, 202-03
Youtian, 116, 220
Yuanjing jing, 161
Yuanlu jing, 170, 211
Yuanyangzi, 18, 113, 130, 135, 148, 203, 206
Yuchen jun, 1, 188
Yuhua, 152
Yujing zhenjue, 214
Yuli jing, 4, 113, 137, 162-63, 166, 168
Yulong, 115, 220
Yunyi, 152
Yuqing jinshu, 132
Yutai jing, 95, 168
Yuyi and Jielin, 24, 176
Yuying, 119, 221
Zhang Daoling, 6
Zhang Lu, 7-0
Zhen'gao, 14-16, 93, 96, 109, 112, 155-56, 205
Zheng Qiao, 21
Zheng Yin, 9
Zhengji, 153
Zhenglun, 116, 220
Zhengyi fawen tianshi jiao jieke jing, 8
Zhonghuang jing, 9, 120, 135, 174, 204, 206
Zhou Yishan, 122
Zhou Zhixing, 5
Zhouyi, 126
Zhu Huang, 3

Zhu Wuliang, 17
Zhuangzi, 19, 49, 96, 133, 142, 175, 183, 194, 202
Ziwen lingshu, 159